# Inclusive Education

## About the Authors

**Dr. Ashima Das** is consultant to several reputed national and international organisations. Since last ten years she has been working in the field of counselling psychology, disability, mental health, health research and development. She pursued her doctoral degree at Tata Institute of Social Sciences. She is a recipient of National Kusuma Best Young Researcher Award (2010) for her distinguished work in the field of education of children with disabilities. She was an Inlaks Visiting Fellow to the Asia Research Centre, London School of Economics in 2009 for her doctoral work on education of children with disabilities. She has published extensively, one of her well-known book Differential Childhood published in 2010 deals with developmental perspectives and inclusive educational initiatives for children with disabilities.

**Dr. Shankar Das** is a Professor and the Chairperson of the Centre for Health Policy, Planning and Management in the School of Health System Studies at the Tata Institute of Social Sciences (TISS), Mumbai, India. He has been actively involved in teaching, training, research and consultancy work in the field of public health, mental health, disability, human resource management and human development. In the year 2009-10 he had pursued higher studies at London School of Economics (LSE), UK under the TISS-LSE Faculty Fellowship to develop Master in Public Health in Health Policy, Economics and Finance at TISS. In 2012 he was a Visiting Fellow at the LSE to develop cross-cultural Indo-UK policy research in area of elderly health care. Dr. Das has published extensively in reputed peer reviewed journals and written books on diverse subjects. He has extensively contributed to the field of health and development with his writings, direct practice and training/supervision of professionals in many government and civil society organisations.

**Dr. Ruth Kattumuri** is Co-Director of the India Observatory and Asia Research Centre at the London School of Economics (LSE). In over two decades of experience in higher education in UK and India, Dr. Kattumuri has pioneered several innovative knowledge and skills development programmes. Her research interests include growth and inclusion, climate change and environmental sustainability. She has a PhD from LSE. She is a Cambridge Commonwealth Fellow and is also adviser to education and development related organisations in UK and various educational institutions in Asia. Prior to joining the LSE, she was a Professor in Statistics and Computer Science at Madras Christian College, India.

# INCLUSIVE EDUCATION

## A Contextual Working Model

ASHIMA DAS
SHANKAR DAS
RUTH KATTUMURI

CONCEPT PUBLISHING COMPANY PVT. LTD.
NEW DELHI-110059

**ISBN-13: 978-81-8069-932-0 (HB)**
**ISBN-13: 978-81-8069-933-7 (PB)**

First Published 2013

*Published and Printed by*

Concept Since 1974

**Concept Publishing Company Pvt. Ltd.**
A/15-16, Commercial Block, Mohan Garden
New Delhi-110059 (India)
*T*: 25351460, 25351794, *F*: 091-11-25357109
E: publishing@conceptpub.com, W: www.conceptpub.com
**Editorial Office:** H-13, Bali Nagar, New Delhi-110 015, India.

**Cataloging in Publication Data**--*Courtesy:* D.K. Agencies (P) Ltd. <docinfo@dkagencies.com>

**Das, Ashima.**
Inclusive education : a contextual working model / Ashima Das, Shankar Das, Ruth Kattumuri.
p. cm.
Includes bibliographical references (p. ) and index.
ISBN 9788180699320 (HB)
ISBN 9788180699337 (PB)

1. Inclusive education—India—Bombay. 2. Children with disabilities—Education India—Bombay. I. Das, Shankar, joint author. II. Kattumuri, Ruth, joint author. III. Title.

DDC 371.90460954 23

# Preface

There have been efforts internationally to include children with disabilities in the educational mainstream. Inclusive education entails increasing the participation of students in, and reducing their exclusion from, the cultures, curricula and communities of local schools. Inclusive education is complex and there are several interrelated factors which affect the process.

This was a qualitative study of describing and analyzing the process of educating children with disabilities in private inclusive schools in Mumbai. The objectives of the research were to explore the process of inclusive education, identify barriers and facilitators and suggest a contextual working model. Data was collected through in-depth interviews and focus group discussions with stakeholder groups, and observations in classrooms.

All interview transcripts were analysed to identify emerging themes and the data were organised, which was done by coding and breaking it down into more manageable texts. For the observation and FGD data, the recurring themes were matched with the themes emerging from the interviews. Where possible, quotes that represent key points have been provided illustrate meaning. Then the themes were connected to existing theories to evolve a model of inclusive education.

The findings were under the four main themes of Support Systems, Challenges, Process and Outcomes for children with disabilities in inclusive schools. The major support systems were identified as academic, physical, psychological and parental. Within 'academic support' the schools offered remedial teaching to the children, gave them concessions and favoured and practiced supportive classroom strategies. As part of physical support, the school endeavoured to enhance the mobility and accessibility for children with differing physical needs by installing elevators and ensuring accessibility of the toilets. Apart from these provisions and the help the children sought from the non-disabled peers, there were no good practices reported. The psychological support was provided by the counsellors, resource teachers and peers. The mothers were found to play an important role in terms of helping the child cope with the demands of the regular school.

The major challenges which emerged from the findings were the negative attitudes of the teachers and peers, shortage of resources and lack of training for handling diversity within classrooms. The 'process' of inclusive education was analysed by the looking at three dimensions of culture, policy and practices. While the former two were more static components of the process, the practice part was designed to suit individual needs and hence more dynamic. The outcomes of educating children with disabilities in inclusive schools were mixed. The outcomes were dependent of the nature/severity of the disability, the support mechanisms in school and environment and culture of the schools. The most common outcome for the children was fulfilment of aspiration of leading 'normal' lives as their non-disabled peers.

The study recommends that the inclusive school must build comprehensive inclusive cultures and must enable access to equal opportunities to all learners by installing support mechanisms, overcoming challenges and building competencies of regular teachers. An emergent model of inclusive education is also presented and discussed.

# Acknowledgements

This book is a product of many years of commitment towards the education of children with disabilities. Our initial thanks are always reserved for our revered deity who has provided us the strength and bestowed us with providence to carry this out to the best of our ability.

We are thankful to the Director of the Tata Institute of Social Sciences, Prof. S. Parasuraman who has always inspired us with his expansive knowledge and progressive thoughts. He has not only strengthened the academic environment at TISS by his far reaching vision and study programmes but also initiated and nurtured the TISS-LSE collaboration.

The journey has been lengthy but extremely enriching while we had the opportunity of working on this less researched arena in Indian context. Our respondents—school principals, teachers, children with disabilities, their mothers and peers in the field deserve a special mention as they were soul of this research. Each one shared their experiences with sincerity and took keen interest in the process. We cannot help but mention again the contribution of the children with disabilities who inspired us and motivated us with their inner strength and enthusiasm.

The faculty at TISS has been very cooperative and never failed to provide their valuable suggestions and directions. For our research, we would like to put on record the support provided by Porf. Vrinda Datta, Prof. Yesudian, Prof. N. Jayaram, Dr. Rajshri Mahtani and Dr. Srilatha Juvva. At LSE, Prof. Peter Townsend and Dr. Taniya Budchardt took keen interest in our work and helped us conceptualise the analytical framework. We also like to thank the staff at the Asia Research Centre who has facilitated the administrative processes.

We would like to thank the TISS and LSE Library staff especially Ms. Shayamala, Kiran, Devyani, Shilpa, Mr. Harish and Mr. Singh for procuring all the required books and journal articles. We feel proud to thank our family and friends for their support, love and blessings.

**Ashima Das**
**Shankar Das**
**Ruth Kattumuri**

# Contents

# 1

# Conceptualising Inclusive Education

*Children with disabilities are not excluded from free and compulsory primary education, or from secondary education, on the basis of disability and can access an inclusive, quality and free education on an equal basis with others in the communities in which they live (UN Convention on Persons with Disabilities 2006: Article 24).*

There have been efforts internationally to include children with disabilities in the educational mainstream. Disability has been proved to be the greater disadvantage in education than gender, household economic status or rural/urban divide (Filmer, 2005). With around 40 million children with disabilities (World Bank, 2003), who remain out of school worldwide, the millennium development goal of achieving 'universal primary education' appears an enormous challenge. Nonetheless, the initiatives in the international arena have brought about significant positive developments in the member countries. Inclusive education is a part of this developmental agenda. It entails 'increasing the participation of students in, and reducing their exclusion from, the cultures, curricula and communities of local schools' (Booth and Ainscow, 1998:2). Globally it is estimated that 70 per cent of children with disabilities, including those with mild mental retardation, can attend regular schools provided the environment is designed to be accessible and the institution has the facility to accommodate them (UNICEF, 2003).

Inclusive education is complex and there are several interrelated factors which affect the process. The development of a child with a disability is influenced by the nested contexts of family, school, community and society at large. In relation to child development, Lerner (1993) proposed the "goodness of fit" which indicated that there has to be a match between developmental needs of the child and the resources and capacities of the environment. The demands, expectations, attitudes, stereotypes and values imposed on the child by home, school and community mould his/her behaviour and actions. These systems are interdependent and are in constant interaction which suggests that a study on any factor related to these systems must take into account the influence of other interacting systems as well. Thus, while proposing this study on inclusive education, it is pertinent to look at the macro picture as well. At the school level the study focuses on changes in classroom organization, resource utilization, and curriculum modification and at the systems level it takes into consideration parental and community support and the legislations and societal views on inclusion. This viewpoint is supported by Singal (2006a) where she asserted that inclusive education could be better understood by identifying the different factors operative within and between these systems. Before spelling out the philosophy of inclusion and meaning of inclusive education, the chapter would discuss the how 'disability' is constructed within Indian society and what are the prevailing ideologies on disability construction.

## Understanding 'Disability'

There are a number of models of disability elucidating the perspectives on disability construction. "Most of the definitions of disability frequently found in scholarly research are actually models made up of several concepts that have either directed or reciprocal relationships with one another" (Altman, 2001:100). Oliver (1983) proposed dual model system based on the distinction made by the Union of the Physically Impaired against Segregation (UPIAS) in 1976 between impairment and disability. UPIAS pioneered the cause of disability and believed in empowering the people with disabilities so that they could engage in changing the society by eliminating the barriers that were seen disabling. Oliver (1990) tried to place all other disability models within the expansive framework of two models; individual and social. The individual model located the 'problem' of disability within the individual and considered these problems stemming from the functional limitations or psychological losses which were assumed to arise from disability. There was a newer understanding of disability as with the introduction of social model of disability in the 1990s. The social model envisioned 'disability' as an outcome of social processes. It contended that 'disability' results from barriers imposed on 'people with impairment' by the society and suggests that elimination of these societal barriers, or education to remove prejudice leading to inclusion (Shakespeare, 1996).

The social model provided a different perspective on disability to the non-disabled population as it voiced the concerns of the people with disabilities. Barton (2003) contended that social model is useful in providing a framework and language to people with disabilities to express themselves and understanding disability within the larger context of socio-economic conditions and relations. Thus, it provides an "alternative and positive view of disability" and has an "educative function". Inclusive education is in consonance with the social model and enables the children with disabilities to lead "normal" lives. Barton (1998) clarified that inclusive education is not just closing down unacceptable system of segregated schooling and sending children with disabilities to the mainstream school. It is about transforming the regular school systems in terms of physical factors, curriculum aspects, teaching and learning styles and goals signifying end of all forms of exclusionary practices within schools.

Table 1.1 summarizes the three key classification systems and related models and their interpretations and definitions of disability. The models related to the first two perspectives shown in the table define disability primarily as a fixed medical condition or impairment with no or limited consideration for the socio-economic or cultural context. By emphasizing the limitations of abilities as a result of an impairment or disability, these models follow an exclusionary approach. Models related to the ecological perspective shift towards a more integrative approach that prioritizes situational and contextual aspects in their definition of disability.

In order to understand the various meanings of these models ascribe to terms, it must be studied from the root. For most models 'pathology' is the starting point but not for all (Altman, 2001). The definitions

**Table 1.1:** Key Classification Systems and Related Models

| | *Impairment Perspective* | *Functional Limitation Perspective* | *Ecological Perspective* |
|---|---|---|---|
| *Definition or inter-pretation of disability* | Disability is considered a health problem or abnormality that is situated in an individual's body or mind. | Disability is directly caused by impairment and defined primarily by medical criteria. In contrast to medical model, consideration is given to the social and physical environment. | Disability is the result of an interaction of impairment, activity limitations, and participation restrictions in a specific social or physical environment. |
| *Relevant Models* | Medical model—Disability is classified or interpreted by disease, illness, abnormality. | Nagi Model—Disability is defined by characteristics of impairment and the situational context. | Quebec disability production process model—Disability is the result of the interaction of personal factors (e.g., age, gender), environmental factors or social context, and life habits (e.g., person's daily activities). |
| | International Classification of Diseases (ICD)—Coding system focusing on diseases and health conditions revised and updated by the World Health Organization (WHO). | International Classification of Impairments, Disabilities and Handicaps (ICIDH)—First classification system focusing solely on disability. Developed by the WHO. Disability is defined by the reduction or lack of ability, caused by impairment, to perform an activity in a way considered normal for a human being. | The social model—Disability is primarily interpreted as society's failure to acknowledge and accommodate the needs of persons with disabilities rather than a medical condition. |
| | | | Human rights model—Disability is defined as a social construct focusing on individuals' human rights and dignity. International Classification of Functioning, Disability and Health—Revision of ICIDH. Disability is defined as the interaction between impairment and externally imposed activity limitations or participation restrictions. |

*Source*: Groschl (2005).

however differ for each model. For instance, Nagi Model (1965) defined pathology as an interruption in normal body processes while the body attempts to restore that normal state. The original WHO model used the concept of 'disease' to represent the medical model that is depicted as etiology, pathology and manifestation. In the second model, ICIDH-2 (WHO 1999) the concept of disease and disorder is subsumed under the context of health. The social model identifies 'impairment' as the first component and 'pathology'/'disease' do not feature in this model. The Disabled People's International defines impairments as "functional limitation within the individual caused by the physical, mental or sensory impairment" (Oliver, 1996:41).

The *impairment perspective* considers disability a health problem or abnormality that is situated in an individual's body or mind. The medical model, which views disability in terms of disease, illness, abnormality and personal tragedy, best expresses this perspective. It focuses on impairment and considers disability a health problem or abnormality that is situated in an individual's body or mind. The medical model assumes that disability as an intrinsic characteristic of individuals with disabilities. This has serious practice implications as it attempts to cure the individuals' abnormalities and defects, which are seen as strictly personal conditions. The medical model was an offshoot of the development in the modern medicine in the 19th century, which enhanced the role of the physician in the society. The rationale that goes behind it is that disabilities are believed to have medical origins, the disabled individuals were supposed to benefit under the directions of the medical professionals. The individual was considered the originator and bearer of the problem. In short, the medical specialists could provide the solution to the problem of disability. The society has no obligation towards the disabled population in terms of adapting to their diverse needs.

The individual with a disability assumes a sick role under the medical model. Just like the societal obligations are relaxed for sick individuals, even the people with disabilities are not expected to fulfil those normal roles like attending school, taking up a job, having a family of their own etc. They are expected to yield authority to the medical professionals whom they require to get better. The medical model as is evident is very narrow in focus. It locates the problem within the individual and proposed only a medicinal cure.

Until recently, the effect of the medical model was seen in most of the policy issues and programmes which concentrate mainly on health thus, placing the authority in the medical professionals. What fits well within this impairment paradigm is the International Classification of Diseases (ICD), which is a system of coding diseases and health conditions that is used by most health services around the world. The World Health Organization (WHO), the body responsible for periodically revising the ICD, released the tenth revision (ICD-10) in 1999. The ICD was developed exclusively in consultation with international medical and rehabilitation professionals, including associations of hospitals and medical doctors; it did not involve persons with disabilities or their organizations. The ICD remained silent on the social and environmental aspects of impairment and disability.

The *functional limitations perspective* arose from attempts to expand the medical model to include non-medical criteria of disability, especially the social and physical environment. Nevertheless, the notion that impairments were the direct causes of disability remained central to this perspective. Also, like the impairment perspective, the functional limitations perspective considered disability in quantitative terms, measuring functional restrictions against a standard. Under the Nagi model (Nagi, 1965: 100-13) *functional limitations* are a distinct concept. The limitations are tied more to activities associated with social roles than to accredited, doctor-tested limitations. Disability was seen as influenced not only by the characteristics of impairments, such as type and severity, but also by how the individual defines a given situation and responds to it, and how others define that situation through their responses and expectations.

Another model which fits in the functional limitation paradigm is the original WHO (1980:27) ICIDH model which had three main components; impairment, disability and handicap. Impairment is defined as "any loss or abnormality of psychological, physiological or anatomical structure or function". There are a couple of points to be noted in relation to this definition; first the term impairment was interpreted to be more inclusive than disorder and, second, to resolve boundary distinctions that lacked clarity in earlier versions, functional limitations were included with impairments (Altman, 2001). Though functional limitation was not a defined concept but it was inherent in the model. 'Disability' was defined as any restriction or lack (resulting from any impairment) of ability to perform an activity in the manner or within the range considered normal for a human being. 'Handicap', in the context of health experiences, is a disadvantage for a given individual, resulting from impairment or a disability that limits or prevents the fulfilment of a role that is normal for that individual (WHO, 1980:14). While this definition acknowledged that handicap is a social phenomenon and is moderated by the expectations of the particular group of which the individual is a member, the focus is more on the disadvantage resulting from impairment or disability. This classification became the most commonly used definition of disability among medical practitioners and other professionals, including medical sociologists, thus popularizing the medical model which emphasizes on impairment as cause of disability and handicap. The environment here is seen as neutral and the onus of preventing impairment from turning into a disability or handicap lies with the individual.

Problems with the existing definitions of disability led the WHO to begin the process of developing a new definitional framework for understanding disability, based on a revised ICIDH. A revision process of the 1980 ICIDH, across all three dimensions—Impairment, Disability and Handicap was initiated in 1993. The aim of this work was to provide a more coherent and widely applicable set of classifications, which would be conceptually valid and useful. The new classification system fell within the ecological perspective. The *ecological perspective* developed in the 1970s as a response to the impairment and functional limitation perspective; however it gained popularity only in the mid-1990s. Like the latter perspective, the ecological perspective rests on three distinct disability concepts: pathology (or abnormality), impairment and disability. However, it sees disability as resulting from the interaction of impairment, activity limitations and participation restrictions in a specific social or physical environment such as work, home or school.

According to the ICIDH-2 (WHO, 1999:16), in the context of health condition, impairment is defined as "problems in body function or structure as a significant deviation or loss". Limitations in certain functions such as the inability to carry out a basic function of the body or body part, a concept that was included in 1980 within impairments, is still included in the new version. The new term that was introduced to replace 'disability' is 'activity'. It was defined as the performance of a task or action by an individual (*ibid*: 18). Specifically, the activity dimension is seen to represent the integrated use of body functions in a purposeful way to perform the individual's life tasks (Altman, 2001). In order to give specific recognition to the environmental influence on handicap, the term was reconceptualised as participation. It was defined as "an individual's involvement in life situations in relation to health conditions, body functions and structures, activities and contextual factors" (WHO, 1999:19). The contextual factors are defined as the features, aspects and attributes of, or objects, structures, human-made organizations, service provision, and agencies in the physical, social and attitudinal environment in which people live and conduct their lives. The objective of these contextual factors is to present a list of potential objects, structures and organizations, or features, aspects or attributes of things, which might help a person with impairments or activity limitations to increase their level of participation in some domain, or alternatively which might be responsible for decreasing the level of participation.

This ecological perspective on disability was also reflected in the International Classification of Functioning, Disability and Health (ICF), adopted by the World Health Assembly in 2001. The final document was the International Classification of Functioning (ICF), which took a very strong approach to the social model of disability as against the medical model previously used (DPI, 2005). It however did not mean that the medical aspects are ignored by the ICF; in fact, it was based on an integration of these two opposing models. In order to capture the integration of the various perspectives of functioning, a "bio-psycho-social" approach was used. Thus, ICF attempted to achieve a synthesis, in order to provide a coherent view of different perspectives of health from a biological, individual and social perspective.

ICF belonged to the family of international classifications developed by the World Health Organization (WHO) for application to various aspects of health. The WHO family of international classifications provides a framework to code a wide range of information about health (e.g. diagnosis, functioning and disability, reasons for contact with health services) and uses a standardized common language permitting communication about health and health care across the world in various disciplines and sciences. In WHO's international classifications, health conditions (diseases, disorders, injuries, etc.) are classified primarily in ICD-10, which provides an etiological framework. Functioning and disability associated with health conditions are classified in ICF. ICD-10 and ICF are therefore complementary. Functioning is an umbrella term encompassing all body functions, activities and participation; similarly, disability serves as an umbrella term for impairments, activity limitations or participation restrictions. The ICF further recognized that disability is a universal human experience and not a concern to a minority of humanity: every human being can suffer from a decrement in health and, thereby, experience some disability.

Another model which refers to the larger social context as being very important in the development of disability is the Quebec disability production process model (Figure 1.1) which was developed by a team at University Laval, Quebec, Canada led by social scientist Patrick Fougeyrollas (1999) is an archetype of the ecological perspective. The Quebec model contributed greatly to the review and

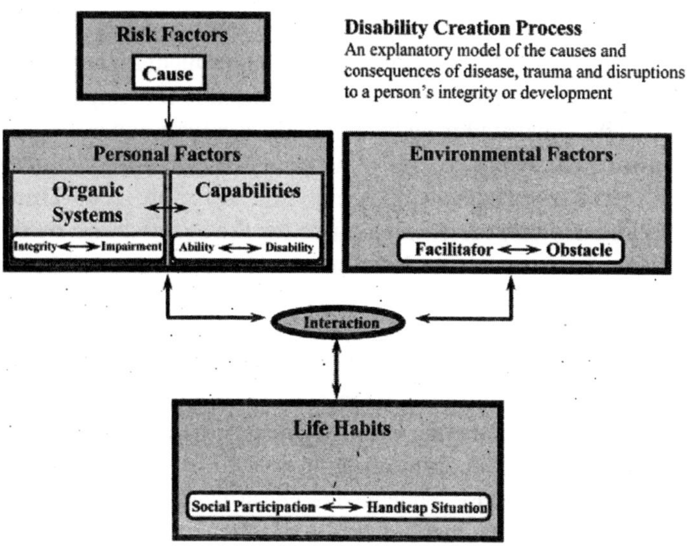


**Fig. 1.1:** Quebec Disability Production Process Model.

eventual improvement of the ICIDH, rejected the linear cause-and-effect explanation of disability. It presented disability as the interaction of three kinds of factors: personal factors (age, sex and cultural identity), environmental factors (the social context in which the person lives) and life habits (the person's daily activities). The Quebec model shifted the focus from a fixed impairment that is part of a person's organic system to other, more changeable factors that affect that person's participation in society. In the Quebec model, disability depended on the environment in which a person lives and carries out daily activities. If the environment is adapted to the person, the disability can change or even disappear. The Quebec model urges for; environmental changes so as to accommodate the entire populace, adopting a proactive approach for prevention of handicaps and creating equal opportunities for all.

**Contextualising the Models**

All societies differ in the way they respond to disability, depending on their attitudes and available resources. In Indian and Asian Societies, disability is associated with bad deeds of previous births (Ghai, 2001; Karna, 2001 cited in Ghosh, 2005). In fact, all kinds of sufferings are explained by the '*Karma*' (meaning 'deeds') theory. 'Disability' is regarded as a form of divine punishment for any unjust or bad *karma* that the person may have committed (Paranjpe 1986). This belief has emanated from the religious scriptures and is invoked to explain all life events. To quite an extent this has fortified charity driven interventions for the needy and marginalised. These interventions are considered favourable for the beneficiaries by the providers which could be State sponsored charities, NGOs or benevolent individuals.

In the past, children with disabilities were seen as contaminants of human race. They were either eliminated or served as objects of entertainment. Philanthropists were concerned about the inhuman treatment rendered to them and therefore, advocated for their institutionalisation. The children with disabilities were placed in asylums where the staff responded to their basic needs. These asylums, however, were not meant to be educational institutions (Bender 1970). Special schools were established in the 19th century for children with sensory impairments. The special schools were concentrating more on the vocational skills. The curriculum of a special school also varied to a great extent in comparison to regular schools. In India, first special school was established by Anne Sharpe in 1887 in Amritsar for the visually challenged children. During the post-independence period, the government established many special schools. By 1966, there were 115 schools for the visually challenged, 70 schools for the hearing and speech impaired, 25 schools for orthopaedically challenged and 27 schools for the mentally challenged (Goel & Rao 2008).

There has been a dramatic change in the way 'disability' is constructed and educational services are designed and delivered to children with disabilities around the world. This positive change came by after the concept was 'normalisation' was developed in the Scandinavian countries particularly in Denmark and Sweden in 1960s. Wolfensberger (1972:28) defined normalisation as, "Utilisation of means which are as culturally normative as possible, in order to establish and/or maintain personal behaviours and characteristics which are as culturally normative as possible". Another development which affected the ideology change was the designation of the year 1981 as the International Year of Disabled Persons and when the United Nations General Assembly adopted the World Programme of Action Concerning Disabled Persons. It strongly encouraged the inclusive practices in education. When the programme was reviewed in 1987, human rights of people with disabilities was given utmost importance and incorporated as the guiding philosophy of the World Programme.

The 1980s saw the advent of disability rights perspective which had become popular amongst the leaders of disability. The rights-based approach to disability essentially means viewing persons with disabilities as subjects of law. The ultimate aim of the approach was empowerment of people with disabilities and to ensure their full participation in political, social and cultural life.

Chib (2002) notes that in India, a number of social welfare policies and traditional charities could be seen clinging to the medical model where the people with disabilities are designated a passive role of recipients. There are a number of special schools, sheltered workshops and protection homes for people with disabilities which have been established by religious and philanthropic agencies signifying existence of charitable and medical approaches to service provision.

This book appreciates and aligns with the social model of disability and would subscribe to all related philosophy and practice. The human rights model is a distinct subgroup of the social model. It understands disability as a social construct. The human rights model positions disability as an important dimension of human culture, and it affirms that all human beings irrespective of their disabilities have certain rights which are inalienable. Inclusive education is a matter of children's 'right' rather than an opportunity. The rights of the children have been laid out in the Convention on the Rights of the Children (CRC) of 1989 and reiterated through the recent UN Convention on the Rights of Persons with Disabilities (2006). The CRC encompasses the civil and political, social, economic and cultural rights of children. The rights defined in the convention could be classified under four clusters of survival, development, protection and participation. There is a clear indication of educating children with disabilities in mainstream schools for safeguarding their right to be part of the society. The UN Convention on the Rights of Persons with Disabilities has explicitly spelt (Article 24) that the children with disabilities must be included in the general education system. Though the conventions have been widely ratified by the member nations, there are reported good practices and violations all over the world. 'Disability' in children renders them even more vulnerable to violation of their rights. Children with disabilities have universally suffered discrimination, violence and abuse, poverty, exclusion and institutionalization (International Save the Children Alliance, 2001:2). Jones (2000), while screening the 'country reports' of the member nations to the UN Committee on the Rights of the Child, observed that majority of the children were mostly referred under Article 23 which pertains to rehabilitation and special care and rarely under the other articles. This indicates 'welfare' rather than 'rights' approach of nations towards their children with disabilities.

It would be pertinent to elucidate the understanding about inclusive education and its national interpretation.

## Defining Inclusive Education

The concept of inclusive education could only be operationalised once the philosophy behind it is understood. It is known that a reluctant society would not be able to provide equal rights to all its learners. Inclusion calls for a transformation of the ideology. Inclusive education is part of the strategic intervention. The aim of inclusive education is not only to cater to all learners but also to resist exclusionary pressures. Inclusion means much more than integration, it signifies that the child with disability is provided a similar environment and experiences as his/her non-disabled peers. A better understanding of the inclusion philosophy would help us gain clarity on the subject matter and facilitate accreditation of the inclusion processes.

Inclusion requires restructuring of cultures, policies and practices in schools in order to respond to the diversity in learners. If certain prevalent understandings of inclusive education are examined, it could be deduced that most definitions mention inclusive school as one which provides education to 'all' learners. Table 1.1 lists some popular definitions of inclusive education which aids the understanding and illuminates the concept.

**Box 1.1: Some definitions of inclusive education**

"Teaching that takes into account the increasing range of differences between pupils is often called inclusive education" (Leeman and Volman, 2001: 367).

Inclusion in education has been defined as 'increasing the participation of students in, and reducing their exclusion from, the cultures, curricula and communities of local schools' (Booth and Ainscow, 2000:7).

Inclusive education does not simply refer to the placement of children with special needs into normal schools, but it is also concerned with the conditions under which we can educate effectively all children (Barton, 1997).

Inclusive education is the practice that provides school experiences to children with special needs, in the same school and classrooms they would have attended anyway had they not had special needs. It is a process during which all children, regardless of their abilities and need, participate in the same school (see Thomas, 1997).

Inclusive education as the process with which schools try to respond to all pupils as individuals, reviewing the organization and provision of their curriculum (Sebba and Ainscow, 1996).

There are some ground values of inclusion in schools. Firstly, the child with disability does not have to always try to achieve normal standards. There also has to be no minimum criteria of ability for seeking admission to an inclusive school. An inclusive school accepts all learners and provides equal opportunities to all students. Secondly, it also celebrates diversity in a pluralistic society. The non-disabled children have much to learn from children with disabilities and *vice versa*. Thirdly, all actors in inclusive education must collaborate to give best results of inclusion. In addition, 'inclusion' values each individual and respects his/her uniqueness. Inclusion in schools, places the teaching/learning responsibility on the school rather than on the child with disability.

For this volume, the wider understanding of inclusive education is borrowed from Loreman, Deppler and Harvey (2006). They define inclusion of children with different abilities in all aspects of schooling that other children are able to access and enjoy. For achieving this goal, the regular schools have to adapt themselves to the needs and demands of all children and must prepare to celebrate diversity. They further note that their definition of inclusion does not imply that children with diverse abilities would not receive specialized assistance or teaching outside of the classroom when required, but rather than this is just one of many options that are available to, and in fact required of all children.

## Distinguishing Inclusive Education from Integration

The education of children with disabilities has been characterized by changing terminology which has philosophical underpinnings. The idea is to identify most neutral terms and definitions in the process, remove pejorative connotations for people with disabilities. With reference to children, there has been a remarkable change in the way they are addressed; from an earlier denomination of 'abnormal children' to the most recent 'children with special needs'. Since the latter encompasses a wider range of children, it appeared appropriate to use 'children with disabilities' to maintain clarity and distinction. As regards, educational model, history is full of terminology ranging from mainstreaming, integrated education to inclusive education.

The two terms had been revolutionary in the field of education of children with disabilities. Inclusive Education is a more recent concept and in a way a replacement of an old ideology. Integration demanded that "additional arrangements will be made to accommodate" children with disabilities "within a system of schooling that remains largely unchanged"; inclusive education, on the other hand, aims to restructure schools in order to respond to the learning needs of all children (Ainscow, 1995:1). Hence, integration meant placing the child in a regular school and placing the burden of coping on the child with disability and his/her family. Inclusive school on the other hand, means the restructuring of the school's policy and structures to accommodate a child with disability. Walker (1995 in Thomas *et al.,* 1997) attempted to summarize the difference between integration and inclusion and laid out a comparative table (Table 1.2). The main point of difference is the 'rights' approach in inclusion which underlay that the school must accommodate all children and must address all their educational needs. In context of India, Julka (2005) diagrammatically differentiated between integrated and inclusive education (Figure 1.2) where she touched upon a range of factors from curriculum, economics, teacher effectiveness, rights etc. The diagrams are self-explanatory and clearly bring out the differences in the two ideologies.

**Table 1.2:** Differences between Integration and Inclusion

| *Integration Emphasises* | *Inclusion Emphasises* |
|---|---|
| Needs of 'Special Students' | Rights of all students |
| Changing or remedying the subject | Changing the School |
| Benefits to the student with special needs of being integrated | Benefits to all students of including all |
| Professionals, specialist expertise and formal support | Informal support and the expertise of mainstream teachers |
| Technical interventions (special teaching, therapy) | Good teaching for all |

*Source*: Walker, 1995 cited in Thomas *et al.,* 1997:14.

Thus, the older concept of integration brings with it an inherent notion of 'coping' which rests with the child rather than the school. Inclusion is a child-friendly approach which stresses on educational outcomes for all children and not just allowing the child with disability to be in the regular setting.

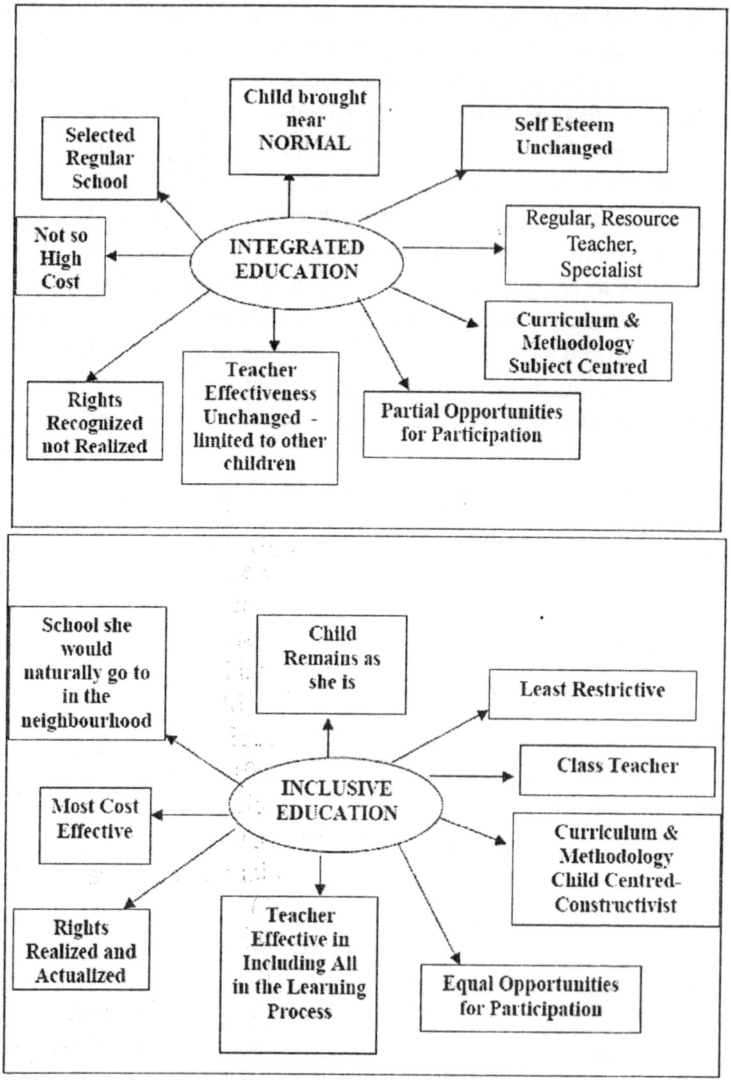


*Source*: Julka (2005).

**Fig. 1.4:** Differentiating Integrated Education from Inclusive Education

Inclusive practice relies on knowledge, skills and understanding, resources and attitudes. Positive attitudes are a necessary starting point but by themselves they are rarely sufficient without the other elements. Schools may need to develop skills and knowledge by working with specialist professionals brought into the school. This can enhance the capacity of the school to act in inclusive ways in relation to children with a range of special needs. Thus, it is indicated that inclusion is distinctly different from the notion of integration, in which students with disabilities are educated together. There are several critical elements of inclusive education which would be elaborated in the next segment.

## Characteristics of Inclusive Schools

Inclusive schools command an educational change. In order to make conventional schools inclusive, Hegarty (1993) suggested following changes to be brought in regular schools:

*Curriculum*: What is taught, with particular reference to establishing a balance between offerings a mainstream curriculum framework and taking account of individual needs.

*Pedagogy*: How it is taught, again with reference to providing specialist support without isolating people from peers.

*Academic organization*: How the school organizes itself to deliver curriculum effectively to the widest possible range of pupils by means of appropriate pupil grouping, arrangements for supplementary teaching and time-table construction.

*Staffing*: Teachers, classroom assistants and support staff, all to be deployed flexibly, but with a shared dynamic focus on achieving 'school for all'.

*Professional Development*: Essential underpinning of any school reform, to encompass attitude change, increased understanding and skill development.

*Parental Involvement*: Collaboration to include sharing of information, involvement in curriculum delivery, parent support and liaison with professional agencies.

*External Support*: Special schools and support agencies to provide essential input—training, assessment, curriculum planning, therapy—but without usurping the school's principal responsibility.

Here the common features of inclusive school (Inos and Quigley 1995) shall be discussed in order to bring some uniformity to the concept. The schools may have some of these features, as the concept of inclusive schools is developing these features are not universal.

*A Sense of Community*: All children are respected irrespective of their abilities and a feeling of belongingness in inculcated in the children.

*Common Vision*: All stakeholders share a common vision of fostering inclusive culture and enhancing outcomes for all children which produces strong sense of community.

*Problem Solving Teams*: Multidisciplinary teams comprising professionals and parents for making decisions on important areas concerning children's needs. The team members give specific perspective to the needs of the child.

*Parent Partnerships*: Parents must be included as full members of the inclusive team. It is vital to recognize the parents' perspectives, address their needs and concerns regarding the child.

*Teacher Partnerships*: Partnering of regular and special education teachers to achieve educational outcomes is an important characteristic of inclusive education. In such situations, teachers learn from each other, gaining inspiration and finding solutions to problems they had difficulty solving alone.

*Paraprofessionals as Partners:* Insightful perspective in planning and consistent service delivery are two vital roles which paraprofessionals play on the problem-solving team.

*Students as Problem Solvers:* Successful inclusive schools involve students as partners in the school community. As students are allowed a greater participation in the community, they become more responsible and effective in the inclusive process. Common among inclusive schools is the use of students as:

- *Peer mediators*—students trained to help resolve disputes among other students.
- *Peer tutoring*—students help other students learn and review material.
- *Cross-age tutoring*—older students helping younger students.
- *Cooperative learning*—teams of students problem solving and working together.
- *Buddy systems*—two children who agree to help each other; may be made up of any two children, regardless of educational status, who want to help each other.

*Community Partnership:* The involvement of the community could be enhanced through awareness and seeking support in form of volunteers, tutoring and looking for newer ways of increasing their participation as macro agents.

*Using a common and neutral language*: Usage of common and neutral language by all stakeholders brings about greater cohesion and a sense of community.

*Requires extensive planning*: All activities and practices in inclusive set-ups require extensive planning and scheduling for collaboration.

*Providing services in the classrooms*: If the services for children with special needs are provided in the classroom it leads to considerable success. The regular teachers should be provided with training for implementing specialized techniques which the resource teacher employs in order to bring cohesiveness and offer general instruction to all children.

*Flexibility*: The most vital challenge facing inclusive school is efficient management of instructional time, teach curriculum and above all, build a sense of community. This demands flexibility of the school administration and spontaneity of the teachers.

*Co-Teaching*: All teaching partnerships require collaboration, adjustment, and extensive communication. General education and special education teachers bring knowledge and skills to teaching. When paired together, these teachers pool their expertise. Generally, regular teachers have in-depth knowledge concerning specific curriculum or subject area, whereas special education teachers know how to modify and breakdown curriculum and how to adapt methodologies to meet the needs of individual children. When general education and special education teachers are placed in a situation where they can work together, they have more to offer the students and each other.

The above features represent an 'ideal inclusive school', which is not universal. Singal (2007) contends that in India inclusive education is understood and practiced differently from the western world. In fact there is "a tendency to be 'politically correct' by taking on current trends in the west without a real or common understanding of their meaning, resulting in dilution of service quality" (Kalyanpur, 2007:5 quoted in Singal, 2007). This book considered an 'inclusive school' as one where the children with disabilities studied alongside their non-disabled peers with some support mechanisms for continuing their education in that school. However, in the future some positive changes could be expected as inclusive education has become a global agenda and nations are taking up the cause of inclusive education seriously.

**Inclusive Education: A Global Agenda**

There are a number of international developments which have impacted inclusive education in member nations. They are UN Convention on the Rights of the Child (1989), the UN Standard Rules on the Equalisation of Opportunities for Persons with Disabilities (1993) and the UNESCO Salamanca Statement (1994), The Biwako Millennium Framework (2003), UN Convention on the Persons with Disabilities, 2006. All of these documents recognise the human right perspective and stand for equal opportunity for education to all children. A glimpse of the main provisions pertaining to inclusive education would provide an insight into international perspectives.

The Convention on the Rights of the Child first time spelled out the right of children with disabilities to be in mainstream schools. The Article 23 affirms that the States Parties should recognize that children with disabilities "enjoy a full and decent life", in societal conditions which promote dignity and self-reliance and enhance active participation in community activities. It further states that the child with disability should be educated in a way that will allow him or her to achieve the 'fullest possible social integration and individual development'. The UN Committee on the Rights of the Child has since interpreted this as a goal for inclusion for all children. Article 2 says that all rights in the Convention shall apply to all children without discrimination—and it specifically mentions disability. Articles 3, 6, 12, 28 and 29 in the Convention give further support to inclusive education for all children with disabilities.

Amongst the major international developments was the proclamation of 1983-1992 time frame as the United Nations Decade of Disabled Persons. A key outcome of this decade was the adoption of Standard Rules on the Equalization of Opportunities for Persons with Disabilities in 1993 by the General Assembly. Though the rules do not have a legal binding, they have moral implications and incite political commitment in the Governments to take action for providing equal opportunities to all its citizens with disabilities. The Rule 6 of the Rules pertains to Education. It asserts that States should recognize the principle of equal primary, secondary and tertiary educational opportunities for children, youth and adults with disabilities, in integrated settings. It ensures that the education of persons with disabilities is an integral part of the educational system.

What paved way for inclusive education was the Salamanca Statement and Framework for Action on Special Needs Education (1994) adopted by the World Conference on Special Needs Education. The responsibility of educating the children with disabilities rests with the nation's government. It upheld the aim of 'education for all' by suggesting some foundational changes in programmes and policies. The Statement solicits governments to give the highest priority to making education systems inclusive and adopt the principle of inclusive education as a matter of law or policy. It emphasizes that every child has a basic right to education and every child has unique characteristics, interests, abilities and learning needs. Therefore, the educational institutions must prepare to cater to the diverse learning needs. It recommends the nation's government to undertake demonstration projects and encourage exchange programmes with countries that have had success with inclusion.

A more recent advancement which supplements the Salamanca Statement is the Biwako Millennium Framework (2003). It confirms that in the Asian and Pacific region education for children with disabilities is largely provided in special schools in urban areas and is currently available to limited number of children. It asserts that the education of all children with disabilities must take place in local or community schools. This development would help in breaking down barriers and negative attitudes and bring about social integration and cohesion within communities.

The most topical initiative which supports inclusive education is the UN Convention on Rights of Persons with Disabilities (2006). It clearly acknowledges that children with disabilities should not be excluded from the general education system on the basis of their disability. The general educational system must facilitate their effective inclusion. The educational providers must arrange for individualized support measures to maximize their academic and social development.

These global initiatives have caused the member nations to promulgate policies and programmes for children with disabilities in their countries. This places an obligation on the member nations to comply with the international ideology and standards for safeguarding the rights of the children with disabilities towards accessing mainstream education. The chapter would cover major developments in inclusive education in various countries of the world. This would help in understanding the extent to which the inclusion has been implemented in schools around the world. Some nations like USA, UK, Nordic countries, Australia have achieved a great deal in this field and other nations could learn about policies and good practices from their accomplishments.

### *(A) United States of America*

The development of special education in USA dates back to 1960s and was a federal government initiative under the leadership of President Kennedy. He had been the main force in spreading awareness about disability and shaping it into policy (Osgood, 2005). In the 1960s and early 1970s services to children with disabilities became available through Head Start and other federal early childhood programmes. Head Start was a comprehensive programme designed to foster the healthy development of young children from low-income families. The programme has grown from eight-week summer programme for preschoolers in 1965 to a year-round programme serving children aged 0-5 years and pregnant women. The unique characteristic of the programme was that it admitted children with disabilities as well.

Despite the early efforts, around one million children with disabilities were excluded from schools and hundreds of thousands remained in state run institutions (American Youth Policy Forum and Centre on Education Policy 2001). The passage of *Education for All Handicapped Children Act* in 1975 brought about significant changes in the education of children with disabilities. By the late 1970s and early 1980s integration of children with mild and moderate disabilities in regular settings began on at least part-time basis. In 1986, the 'Regular Education Initiative' that stood for amalgamation of the special and general education services. The inherent viewpoint was that the children with disabilities should be the shared responsibility of all educators rather than sole responsibility of special educators (Will, 1986). It was not until the early 1990s with the international developments (discussed above) that the policy and practice began to reflect the commitment towards inclusive education. The first significant step towards this was the reauthorization of the Education for All Handicapped Children Act as Individuals with Disabilities Education Act (IDEA) in 1990. The IDEA provided funds to states for the education of children with disabilities. It contained detailed requirements for the receipt of these funds, including the core requirement of the provision of a free appropriate public education (FAPE).

Currently, there are three federal laws which provide equal educational opportunities to children with disabilities on par with their non-disabled peers (Inos and Quigley, 1995). The first one is Section 504 of the Rehabilitation Act of 1973. The law required that each school educate the students with disabilities in their jurisdiction unless the school can prove that the child's needs cannot be met in the general classroom. The second federal law is the Individuals with Disabilities Education Act, 1990 (IDEA). It introduced the legal concepts of the "Individualized Education Plan" (IEP) and least restrictive environment. This law guaranteed that students with disabilities needs will be identified and met in the classroom, or if this is not possible, provided as near to the student's home and in the least restrictive environment possible. The third federal law, the Americans with Disabilities Act of 1990 (ADA), provides a clear and comprehensive national mandate for the elimination of discrimination against individuals with disabilities. It guarantees equal opportunity for individuals with disabilities in employment, public accommodations (including most private schools, child care centres, etc.), transportation, State and Local Government Services (including public schools), and telecommunications.

### *(B) United Kingdom*

In UK the most prominent historical development was the Warnock Committee Report of 1978 which placed the education of children with disabilities in its top priorities. It emphasized that the early years

(0-5 years) are crucial in terms of child development and these are especially important for children with disabilities. This period could help them develop their abilities to their fullest potential and could prevent secondary disabilities. The Education Act of 1981 was developed in line with the Warnock Committee Report and underscored the importance of integrated education for children with disabilities.

Though United Kingdom has a rich history of special education, Wall (2003) contends that for most part in the educational history, children with disabilities had remained unacceptable to the society. Much of the recent legislation for special needs education in England has been enabling, participatory and progressive. Since 1997, the government had embraced the concept of inclusion in many aspects of social policy. In education, the Office for Standards in Education (OFSTED) which inspects and judges schools on the extent to which they are inclusive of pupils with Special Educational Needs (SEN) and the recent anti-discrimination legislation the Special Educational Needs and Disability Act (SENDA, 2001) has strengthened the right to a mainstream school place for children with disabilities. In addition, other initiatives such as the Department for Education and Skills (DfES) guidance Inclusive Schooling: Children with Special Educational Needs (DfES, 2001a), the revised Special Educational Needs Code of Practice (DfES, 2001b), Removing Barriers to Achievement (DfES, 2004) and Every Child Matters (DfES, 2003), together provide a firm legislative context for further developments in inclusive education nationally. It would seem, therefore, that the government's strategy for SEN, demonstrates a commitment to inclusive education as a model for meeting special needs (cited in Rouse & Florian 2006).

### *(C) Nordic Countries (Norway, Sweden, Finland, Denmark and Iceland)*

Nordic countries have led the movement of inclusion. The idea of 'normalisation' originated there and ever since the early 1970s Nordic countries have promoted the idea of "society for all". These efforts have resulted in policy shift from charitable approaches to individual centred rehabilitation and over the last two decades the shift had been towards equalization of opportunities, empowerment and inclusion of all people with disabilities (Nordic Disabled Person Organisations 2001).

Sweden, Iceland and Norway offer a "one track approach" that is, they have developed policies and practices which ensure inclusion of almost all children within the regular educational system. However, in Finland and Denmark, a "multi-track approach" is followed where a variety of services are provided between the mainstream and special needs systems. There are supportive legislations which have brought about effective inclusion in the Nordic countries such as Folkeskole, 1994 (Denmark), Comprehensive Instruction Law, 1999 (Finland), Swedish Education Act (Sweden), Education Acts (Iceland), The Act on Primary and Lower Secondary Education, 1975 (Norway) (Meijer 2003).

A majority of the schools in the Nordic countries at primary and secondary schools are public and the percentage of children in private schools is much lesser in OECD countries except for Denmark. At the upper secondary level, Nordic countries (Denmark, Norway, Sweden and Finland) are among countries with lowest social segregation. The reasons for this are greater comprehensiveness, an even standard of education, less private schools and lesser opportunities for school to select their pupils (Arnesen and Lundahl 2006). Due to the efforts of the nations' government Norway and Iceland have less than 1 per cent, Denmark and Sweden have 1-2 per cent children and Finland has 2-4 per cent of children with special needs in segregated settings (Meijer, 2003:129).

### *(D) Australia*

In Australia, the children with disabilities lacked equal opportunities till the first half of the 20th century. For children with disabilities, this period was significant only in terms of establishment of special schools for sensory, intellectual or physical disabilities which were run by private charities with support from the state government. The public policy on disability underwent a dramatic change during the 1960s and 1970s. There is no specific legislation which promotes inclusive education; the national educational policies do stand for social justice and provision of equal opportunities for all students in

Australian schools. The rights of those at-risk of under-participation and under-achievement in Australia are protected by the Education Act 1989, Anti-Discrimination Act, 1991, Disability Services Act, 1992 and the Disability Discrimination Act, 1992 (DDA). The aim of the DDA was to protect people with disabilities against discrimination and it also extends to discrimination in education.

There has been a strong movement in the last 20 years in Australia towards educating students with disabilities in mainstream schools and in mainstream classes. In 2002, the majority of children with disabilities attended mainstream rather than special schools; 81 per cent of children with disabilities attending government schools and 91 per cent of children with disabilities attending non-government schools were in mainstream settings (AIHW, 2004).

### *(E) Inclusive Education in Developing Countries*

The estimates reveal that majority of the world population of people with disabilities are residing in developing countries of Asia, Africa, the Caribbean, Latin America and the Middle East. This population consists of some 150 million children and only 2 per cent of them receive any kind of rehabilitative services (cited in Eleweke & Rodda 2002). It is predicted that by the year 2025, the number of people with disabilities will have risen from the current 600 million to 900 million worldwide, of which 650 million will be in developing countries (disability.dk, 2003, p. 1). The UNESCO Reports (1996/7, 1999) suggest that the implementation of inclusion in some developing countries, e.g. Benin Republic, Burkina Faso, China, Chile, Ghana, Guinea, India, Ivory Coast, Jordan, Lesotho, Loa People's Democratic Republic, Malawi, Morocco, Mongolia, Palestine, Peru, South Africa and Uganda, most of these programmes remain 'pilot projects' and factors such as the absence of support services, relevant materials and support personnel are the major problems of effective implementation in these countries (*ibid*). For example, in Asia the resources and facilities were not up to the mark and the countries were catering to less than 1 per cent of the population with special needs (Kohli, 1993). Ozoji (1995) observed that most schools in developing countries lacked the basic material helpful for children with disabilities. The chapter would look at the initiatives on inclusive education in a couple of countries as examples, before illuminating the Indian context on policy and education system. This would help us in understanding the current situational contexts of inclusive education in developing nations.

### *(F) Pakistan*

The international revolutionary decade in the field of disability (1983-92) generated increased awareness about disabilities in Pakistan. The first step towards inclusive education was the National Policy for the Rehabilitation of the Disabled (1986). It resulted in preparation of children with disabilities for integration in regular schools situated in the vicinity of special schools (UNICEF 2003). The National Policy for Persons with Disabilities 2002 recognised the need for affording the education facilities to a maximum number of children with disabilities, their integration shall be ensured by adopting the following measures:

- provision of special aids and equipment,
- alignment of policies between the Federal Government, the provincial governments and the district governments at the level of relevant Ministries and Departments,
- changes in curriculum in collaboration with relevant departments, agencies, and
- provision of specialized aids and equipment.

In addition, the new National Curriculum has made efforts to include principles of human rights, upholding diversity and difference along with universal rights (National Report of Pakistan 2008). However, UNICEF (2003) reported that the philosophy of inclusive education is not articulated. It is because the Ministry of Women Development, Social Welfare and Special Education do not play any role in the policy formulation of regular schools. Neither does it have any administrative control to implement an inclusive education policy. As far as the role of the Ministry of Education is concerned, the National Education Policy for 1998 does not include any mention of special or inclusive education. Any government-level initiative for inclusive education must start with a special education section in the

Ministry of Education. This will shift the responsibility for providing appropriate education as a right to all children, including children with disabilities, to the Ministry of Education; this would be the most appropriate place for design and implementation of a policy on inclusive education. Special schools run by the Ministry of Women Development, Social Welfare and Special Education can continue providing support to children with severe disability for the time being.

### *(G) Bangladesh*

Ahsan and Burnip (2007) have given a detailed summary of developments in inclusive education in Bangladesh. According to their review, about 10 per cent of the 140 million people in Bangladesh suffer from disabilities and around 89 per cent are out of education. They have clearly outlined the efforts and gaps in the policies and programmes. An encouraging step towards universalizing primary education was enactment of EFA and Compulsory Primary Education Act (1990). Here, it was specified that child could be kept out of the primary education system only if there was a "valid ground". This 'valid ground' was a physical or unavoidable condition of child's appearance that can cause difficulty in participating in school's activity and child's limited intellectual ability as assessed by the Education Officer. The authors however inform that these 'Education Officers' are not trained in this capacity. There are no dearth of legislations and policies which deal with aspects of inclusive education. A chronological trail of the current country initiatives reveals that National Child Policy (1994), National Disability Policy (1997), a new educational policy was implemented (2000) where mainstreaming of children with special needs received official recognition, followed by enactment of Bangladesh Persons with Disability Act (2001) where Part D has been dedicated to Education. The authors have pointed out that despite the inclusive education policies and practices are in place, there are lacunae in their implementation.

In Bangladesh, special education, integrated education, inclusive education and placement in mainstream schools are available for children with disabilities (DPE & CSID, 2002). However, it is important to note that special schools are still considered by parents and educators the best option for all children with disabilities, though constitutionally Bangladesh supports a uniform system of education. DPE and CSID (2002) research found that most children with disabilities in Bangladesh who are in education attend mainstream regular schools as there is an absence of special education opportunities due to a lack of resources.

### *(H) India*

There is insufficient information on education of children with disabilities in the nineteenth century in India because of lack of documentation (Alur, 2002). The first attempt to integrate was initiated by the Royal Commonwealth Society for the blind and the Christopher Blind Mission. The visually challenged children were integrated in regular classrooms where they were expected to devise self-learning mechanisms during sessions where oral repetition was dominant pedagogy (Chaddha, 2003). During the pre-independence period, the provincial governments took sporadic interest in educating children with disabilities by dispensing *ad hoc* grants to schools and institutions run by the voluntary sector (Gupta, 1984 as cited in Alur, 2002).

During the post-independence period, it was the Kothari Commission (1966) which highlighted the importance of educating children with disabilities. It expressed that the education of children with disabilities must be a part of the general educational system suggesting that educational facilities must be extended to the blind, deaf, orthopaedically challenged and mentally challenged (Pandey 2006). In 1974, the centrally sponsored scheme for Integrated Education for Disabled Children (IEDC) was launched which is presently being implemented in over 90,000 schools in the country. The scheme was introduced to provide equal opportunities to children with disabilities in general schools and facilitate their retention. It provides facilities like expenses related to books, stationery and uniforms, allowance for transport, reader, escort etc. to students with disabilities. It also supports appointment of special teachers, provision of resource rooms and removal of architectural barriers (MHRD, 2009).

The first pilot project on integrated education in India came in the form of Project Integrated Education for the Disabled (PIED).

PIED launched in 1987, was a joint venture of MHRD and UNICEF. This project was implemented in one administrative block each in Madhya Pradesh, Maharashtra, Nagaland, Orissa, Rajasthan, Tamil Nadu, Haryana, Mizoram, Delhi Municipal Corporation and Baroda Municipal Corporation. In these ten blocks, 6000 children with special needs were integrated in regular schools. The success of PIED led to the inclusion of the component of Integrated Education of the Disabled (IED) in DPEP, a scheme launched by the Government of India for the development of elementary education. At present, IED in DPEP is going on in 242 districts of 18 states. In these states, approximately 6.21 lakh children with special needs have been enrolled in regular schools with adequate support services (GOI, 2003).

The National Policy on Education (1986) and its subsequent actions in pursuit of the goal to attain 'education for all' have had considerable impact. The World Declaration on Education for All acted as a catalyst and further promoted the processes already initiated in the country. The Rehabilitation Council of India (RCI), a statutory body of the Ministry of Social Welfare was established in 1986, followed by an Act to implement its objects in 1992. In essence, the Council and its Act, aims to regulate the quality of training of Rehabilitation Professionals. In 1999, the government passed the National Trust for Welfare of Persons with Autism, Cerebral Palsy, Mental Retardation and Multiple Disabilities Act for the economic rehabilitation of people with disabilities. These legislations have been instrumental in bringing about perceptive change in the attitudes of government, NGOs and people with disabilities.

The most important legislation which comprehensively covers issues related to people with disabilities is the Persons with Disabilities (Equal Opportunities, Protection of Rights and Full Participation) Act, enacted in 1995. The chapter V of the Act concerns education. This act makes it mandatory to provide free education to children with disabilities in an appropriate environment until the age of 18 years. Even though the new legislation made access to regular schools easier, it is still not guaranteed as an equal right for all students. Segregation into separate special schools breaches the underlying principles of the United Nations Convention on the Rights of the Child (1989) yet the Government still sanctions the exclusion of significant numbers of children. This contradictory situation is a barrier to the assumption by regular schools of full responsibility for all students in their areas [Figure 1.3(i)].

The Indian Government recently promulgated the National Policy for Persons with Disability, 2006, which clarifies the framework under which the state, civil society and private sector must operate in order to ensure a dignified life for persons with disability and support for their caregivers. It includes: extending rehabilitation services to rural areas, increasing trained personnel to meet needs, emphasising education and training, increasing employment opportunities, focusing on gender equality, improving access to public services, encouraging state governments to develop a comprehensive social security policy, ensuring equal opportunities in sports, recreation and cultural activities, increasing the role of civil society organisations as service providers to persons with disability and their families.

Most recent advancement is the Right of Children for Free and Compulsory Education (2009) which guarantees right to free and compulsory to all children of the age six to fourteen years. For education for a child with disability, the act has to be read in conjunction with the Chapter V of the Persons with Disability Act, 1995. Chapter V of the PWD Act ensures that every child with disability is entitled to a free education up to the age of 18 years. The government and local authorities must endeavour to promote integration of students with disabilities in regular schools, promote setting up of special schools in order to make them accessible to children living in any part of the country.

Sarva Shiksha Abhiyan is an effort to universalize elementary education by community-ownership of the school system. It is in response to the demand for quality basic education all over the country. The SSA programme is also an attempt to provide an opportunity for improving human capabilities to all children, through provision of community-owned quality education in a Mission mode. The SSA had been launched as the shared responsibility of the Central and State Governments in partnership with the local governments and the community. The Sarva Shiksha Abhiyan will not disturb existing structures in States and districts but would only try to bring convergence in all these efforts. Efforts will be made to ensure that there is functional decentralization down to the school level in order to improve community participation. There will be a focus on the

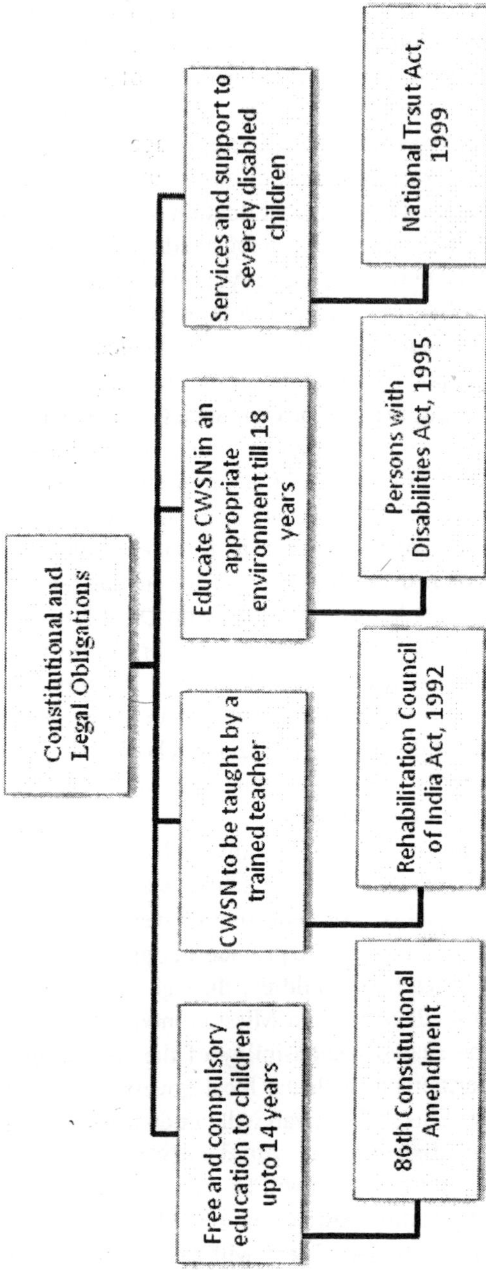


*Source*: GoI (2003).

**Fig. 1.3(i): SSA Plan Manual.**

educational participation of children from SC/ST, religious and linguistic minorities disadvantaged groups and the children with disabilities [Figure 1.3(ii)].

The National Council of Educational Research and Training (NCERT) with the objective of addressing issues of equal opportunities had formulated the national curriculum framework (2005). The states have been, subsequently, adopting or adapting these curricular guidelines to develop their own detailed curricula, syllabi and curricular materials.

The highlights of the curriculum are—

- The curriculum should provide enabling opportunities to all learners. The teaching-learning processes must respond to the diverse needs of the learners. Teachers must explore strategies to aid learning of all learners including children with disabilities. This could be achieved effectively if there is collaboration amongst teachers and even with outside organizations.
- The teachers must give individualized attention to learners and should be flexible with activities and tasks. The curriculum suggests that children and older learners must be involved in classroom planning to enrich the class proceedings. This would allow teachers to respond to special needs of some learners without making it in obvious exception.
- Schools need to upgrade their status as centres which prepare

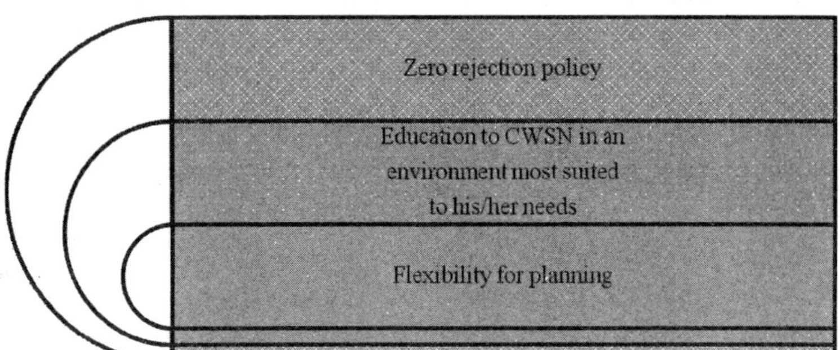


*Source*: GoI (2003).

**Fig. 1.3 (ii):** Three Aspects of Inclusive Education in SSA.

children for their adult life as well especially children with disabilities.

- Some simple adaptations in playground, equipment and school rules could make it accessible to all children.
- Providing a multisensory learning experience to all children as their learning styles are different.
- The children with different learning abilities have to be provided with varied options like sign language, Braille etc. depending on the child's needs.
- The schools must uphold quality within the lansdscape of cultural and socio-economic diversity.
- Curriculum design must reflect the commitment to UEE (Universal Elementary Education) not only in representing cultural diversity, but also by ensuring that children from different social and economic backgrounds with variations in physical, psychological and intellectual characteristics.

The section delved in detail on the policy and programmatic provisions for education of children with disabilities. However, policy commitments of governments in a number of areas remain in large part unfulfilled (World Bank, 2007) and have failed to bring the children with disabilities into mainstream education (Julka, 2005). Alur (2003) observed that in India there is a dichotomy between policy and practice; the government promotes the 'inclusionist' philosophy through its schemes and extends a parallel support to the 'segregationist' policy by promoting the idea of special schools through their assistance to voluntary organisation schemes. Thus, it is important to elucidate the mainstream educational context and endeavour to locate the 'inclusive schools' within that.

## Educational System

India has the second largest education system (World Bank, 2003) and largest number of children out of school (Huebler, 2007). The estimates reveal that almost 21 million children, or close to 17 per cent of children in the 6-10 years age group, are out of school and the chances of attaining the target of universalisation of primary education by 2015 seems impossible unless the nation addresses the issue of school attendance among the poor (*ibid*). Primary education encompasses the first 5 years (6 to 11 years old) of school education (Grades I–V), while the next three grades (11 to 14 years old) are those of upper primary education (Grades VI–VIII). Together these 8 years of education are now a fundamental right of all children according to the 86th Amendment of the Constitution enacted in December 2002 (Department of Education, 2004) and the Education Act (2009). Education at the pre-primary level is not compulsory and provisions vary significantly between rural and urban areas (Kaul, 2002). In parallel to the formal school system, India has also built alternative systems of education, namely Non-Formal Education (NFE) and the National Institute of Open Schooling (NIOS) (formerly the National Open School).

The Government actively supports special schools, but it is not directly involved in establishing or running them. Rather, the Ministry of Social Justice and Empowerment, formerly known as the Ministry of Welfare, provides grants-in-aid to various Non-Governmental Organisations (NGOs) that run these schools. Out of the children with disabilities enrolled in schools, majority are being educated in special schools (UNICEF, 2003). The special schools are concentrated more in the urban areas, with Mumbai having the highest number of special schools (Mukhopadhyay and Mani, 2002). It was estimated that there were about 2,500 special schools in the country (Rehabilitation Council of India, 2000). Government records suggest that approximately 450 of these special schools receive government grants towards their operational costs, while the majority are managed by autonomous voluntary organisations and receive no government support (Government of India, 1995).

In order to gauge the national response towards education of children with disabilities, it is vital to know the magnitude of childhood disability. It is difficult to estimate the number of children with disabilities in India. The Census of India 2001 reports 7.73 million children and young adults in the age group of 0-19 years. Singal (2006) has cited office of the Chief Commissioner for Persons with Disabilities (2003), which notes that the figures available are highly unreliable and range between 6 million and 30 million children with disabilities in India. It further notes that the Rehabilitation Council of India takes the figure of 30 million children with disabilities as the best estimate. There are noted discrepancies related to education of children with disabilities. Singh (2003) reported 3 to 4 per cent of children with special needs have access to education with or without support services. However, Mukhopadhyay & Mani (2002) have deduced that only 1 per cent of children with disabilities in the 5-15 age group have access to education. A recent World Bank Report (2007) has highlighted that 38 per cent of the children with disabilities in the age group of 6-13 years are out of school. Irrespective of the estimate, in India the fact remains that a majority of children with disabilities are denied the basic right to education.

In Maharashtra (whose capital is Mumbai), there are 600 special schools which are exclusively for children with various types of disabilities (UNICEF, 2003). This study however targets private schools, thus it would be imperative to understand the types of private schools in India and their numbers in Maharashtra. The main types are: 'private unaided' schools which means that the schools are privately owned and funded and rely on user finance to quite an extent and 'private aided schools' which means that the schools which are largely funded by the government (90-95%) but their management is private (De *et al.*, 2002). In Maharashtra, the private aided (primary and secondary) schools are about 5218 and private unaided are approximately 4220 (MHRD, 2009).

The Non-Governmental Organisations also (NGOs) play an active role in the provision of services for people with disabilities. They have been involved in the field of educating children with disabilities since the early 1950s, particularly in urban areas. The NGOs are supported by the government through various grants. In the 1970s and 1980s, there was an increase in the number of NGOs in India (UNICEF, 2003). Some of these NGOs are making consistent efforts towards including children with disabilities into regular educational settings. In Mumbai, some NGOs partner with regular schools to enable them to become inclusive.

This study was conducted in private inclusive schools of Mumbai, which is India's financial capital. It covers an area of 437.71 sq. km. (MCGM, 2009) and houses about 11.9 million people (Census, 2001). There are approximately 2110 primary schools and around 1224 secondary schools in Mumbai (Government of Maharashtra website). The Municipal Corporation of Greater Mumbai (MCGM) has recognised 974 private primary schools out of which 574 are unaided and 401 are aided. The MCGM has 49 secondary schools under its management (MCGM, 2009). The children in this study represent the very select group of children with disabilities who have attempted to transit from segregation to inclusion. These children with disabilities are among a minority who have secured admission to 'private inclusive school' and are being educated alongside their non-disabled peers. Mukhopadhyay (2003) reported that the private schools which are voluntarily providing inclusive education are mostly located in urban areas. There has been an expansive growth of private schools in the country due to the fact that government schooling has not been able to provide quality education (Nambissan 2003; Singal & Rouse, 2003; Balasundran, 2005).

This writing assumes importance because the field of inclusive education is new in India and the literature on inclusive education is scant (Singal, 2005:345). The review the literature on inclusive education in India has concluded that the terminology has found usage in the Indian literature but the empirical research in this area has been weak, as researchers have been vague about their key concepts, they have failed to draw insights available from others studies, and have remained oblivious to the need for gathering empirical data. The review suggests that current propositions and arguments about inclusive education have remained at the level of theory and no concrete steps or processes have been undertaken or systematically developed (*ibid*).

We explore the process of inclusive education in Mumbai and proposes a theoretical model. As one progresses from the first to the last chapter, there is a sequential flow of information describing the process and outcomes of research. The initial chapter tries to capture the wide inclusion reality along with specifics of inclusive education. It attempts to provide an overview of developments in inclusive education around the world.

The subsequent chapter on 'theory and research' examined relevant theories and research in a systematic manner; clarifying the concepts related to inclusive education to gradually elucidating theories. It also presented the research review on various aspects of the subject and also the stakeholders. This extensive review provided a base for the conceptualization of research. The next chapter details out the process of investigation; the field study which was carried out in seven inclusive schools of Mumbai. It also contains details on demographics of the research participants. This is to facilitate the understanding of the audience and make further inferences.

The study outcomes constitute the next chapter and are presented within four themes of support systems, challenges, process and outcomes. Finally, the last chapter models the theory and substitutes the findings into the proposed model of inclusive education and recommends some essential steps for strengthening the process in the current context.

# 2

# Theory and Research

The theoretical and research review on inclusive education has provided a greater insight into the understanding and delivery for children with disabilities. The chapter would sequentially delve on the interwoven concepts of 'inclusive education'. It was a complicated task to bring together the related concepts as their application varies across countries and the literature on inclusive education is largely from Western countries. There would be a constant endeavour to contextualize the information to the Indian context.

This segment would in general review literature on inclusive schools and specifically with reference to children with disabilities. This would encompass discussions on inclusive schools, effective inclusion practices, effective teaching and teacher characteristics, role of parents, peer support and perceptions and outcomes for children with disabilities. The outcomes for children within inclusive setting are dependent on a variety of factors, namely school's environment, policies, culture and ethos, teacher's training, attitudes and skills, peer support and familial support. The chapter would elucidate the concepts which have been theorised and researched.

## Constructing an Inclusive School

Schooling is vital to child's development. It is, therefore, important that a child must attend school where his/her abilities are respected, educational needs are met and potential is realized. The concept of inclusion is premised on the principle that all people with disabilities have the right to be included in 'naturally occurring settings and activities' with their non-disabled counterparts (Erwin, 1993: 1). For children with disabilities for whom a dual system of education exists and a number of associated factors which determine the choice of school, an inclusive school in its real sense of term would be the uncontested choice. There are a number of definitions for an 'inclusive school' and it would be useful to look at some prevailing definitions in the field and define it for this study.

Many definitions of inclusive education have evolved throughout the world. The most common definition of inclusive education is the practice of educating students with moderate to severe disabilities alongside children without disabilities in general classrooms within their home neighbourhood schools (Brown *et al.*, 1983, 1989a, 1989b; Gartner & Lipsky, 1987; Stainback & Stainback, 1989; Giangreco & Putnam, 1991; Wheeler, 1991; Lipsky and Gartner, 1992). "Inclusion includes physical integration, social integration, and access to normalized educational, recreational, and social activities that occur in school" (Ryndack & Alper, 2003:15). The presentation of the definitions would be according to content and philosophy. Firstly, the definitions which focus on restructuring schools for serving all learners would be portrayed. These definitions adopt an institutional perspective and focus on organizational arrangements for bringing about effective inclusion.

> *Inclusive education is the process with which schools try to respond to all students as individuals, reviewing the organisation and provision of their curriculum (Sebba & Ainscow, 1996).*

> *Inclusive education is virtually the practice that provides school experiences to children with special needs in the same school and classrooms they would attend if they did not have special needs. It is the process during which all children, regardless of their abilities and needs, participate into the same school (Thomas, 1997).*

> *Inclusive education as the process of increasing the participation of students in, and reducing their exclusion from, the cultures, curricula and communities of local schools.*

> *Inclusion gears towards restructuring of the cultures, policies and practices in schools so that they respond to the diversity of students in their communities. Inclusion is concerned with the learning and participation of all students, not only those with impairments or those who are categorised as having 'special educational needs'* (*Booth* et al., *(2000:12)*.

> *Inclusive education acknowledges that all children can learn, respects differences in children e.g. age, gender, ethnicity, language, disability etc., enables education structures, systems and methodologies to meet the needs of all children, is part of a wider strategy to promote an inclusive society, and is a dynamic process that is constantly evolving (Save the Children, 2008).*

Some definitions lay stress on the human rights aspect of inclusion. All children have the right to education and it is important to provide equal opportunities to them. Inclusion within the educational system is a right for all learners and that neither parents nor professionals have the right to choose segregation for their children. Inclusion proponents argue that our schools must mirror this inclusive and diverse society (Gartner and Lipsky, 1987; Giangreco and Putnam, 1991).

> *Inclusive schooling propels a critique of contemporary school culture and thus, encourages practitioners to reinvent what can be and should be to realize more humane, just and democratic learning communities. Inequities in treatment and educational opportunity are brought to the forefront, thereby fostering attention to human rights, respect for difference and value of diversity (Udvari-Solner, 1997: 142).*

> *Every child has unique characteristics, interests, abilities and learning needs and therefore, if the right to education is to mean anything, education systems should be designed and educational programmes implemented, to take into account the wide diversity of these characteristics and needs (UNESCO, 1994: viii).*

Few definitions focus on stakeholder's role and responsibilities in dealing with diversity amongst learners.

> *...Everyone belongs, is accepted and is supported by his or her peers and other members of the school community in the course of having his or her educational needs met (Stainback & Stainback, 1990: 3).*

Though the meaning of inclusive education clearly communicates that it encompasses all 'differences' in children, for this book there is a need to spell out that the concept only pertains to 'children with disabilities'. Rogers (1993) gave a general yet extremely useful definition of inclusive education. It communicates the idea that the child must be eligible to attend neighbourhood school and the school must transform itself in terms of arranging resources for fully benefiting the child.

> *The term inclusion is used to refer to "the commitment to educate each child, to the maximum extent appropriate, in the school and classroom he/she would otherwise attend" (Rogers, 1993: 1). It involves bringing the support services to the child, rather than moving the child to the services, and requires only that the child will benefit from being in the class, rather than having to keep up with the other students (Rogers, 1993).*

The concept of inclusive education was introduced in India by Jangira in 1997 when he made reference to the Warnock Report. The credit of expanding the notion of special education was endowed on the Warnock Committee Report which revolutionized the earlier thought systems focusing on categorization and labelling. This, he argued, had further 'evolved into a broader and natural concept of inclusive schooling in recent years' (Jangira, 1997: 496). As the developed world is moving towards providing an inclusive system of education, the developing countries like India are left with little choice but to follow trail. Thus, he contended that inclusive education is not an alternative but is inevitable. On the other hand, Mani (2000: 9) notes that he is the first proponent of inclusive education in India, as it is he who had suggested such an approach in the 1980s, when referring to the concepts of 'dual teaching model' and the 'multi-skilled teacher plan'. 'Dual teaching model' he elaborates as involving: regular classroom teachers with support instructional material and limited competency oriented training can usually look after disabled children in addition to their regular classroom responsibility (Mani, 2000: 10). He also noted that a 'token incentive' may be provided for the teachers for their additional work with children with disabilities (p. 7) (cited in Singal 2005).

The way inclusive education is defined and understood has tremendous effect in the way it is conceived amongst schools and the idea is propagated to the teachers, administrators, peers, families and communities. In Indian context, however, Singal (2005:9) perceived inclusive education as "a concept that has been adopted from the international discourse, but has not been engaged within the Indian scenario". In India the concept of 'inclusive' and 'integrated' education are used interchangeably (Julka 2005, Singal 2005a), and has been applied to placement of children with disabilities in the regular schools where there is a provision of aids and appliances and teachers are trained to manage children with disabilities. There is little emphasis on connotations of school, curriculum and teachers flexibility for all children (*ibid*). Thus, Singal (2007) contends that in India inclusive education is understood and practiced differently from the Western world. In fact, there is "a tendency to be 'politically correct' by taking on current trends in the West without a real or common understanding of their meaning, resulting in dilution of service quality" (Kalyanpur, 2007:5 quoted in Singal, 2007). Ideally, "inclusive education means attending the age appropriate class of the child's local school, with individually tailored support" (UNICEF, 2007). Hence, it is difficult to find a suitable definition for the Indian context where the concept is new and developing. Nonetheless, for this study we may consider an 'inclusive school' as one where the children with disabilities studied alongside their non-disabled peers with some support mechanisms for continuing their education in that school.

Balasundran (2005) had identified some problems in the implementation of inclusive education in India. Currently, the education for children is mild disabilities is provided under the Integrated Education Programme and the special schools for more children with severe disabilities under the Ministry of Social Justice and Empowerment implemented through state governments and NGOs. A major deterrant has been lack of statistics on the prevalence of disability. Surveys conducted by the NSSO (National Sample Survey Organisation) in 2002 and the Census in 2001 show varying figures with the NSSO quoting 1.8 per cent (1.85 crore of the country's population) and the census quoting 2.19 per cent of the population. (2.19 crore). Another reason she quotes as a hurdle is the disparity in educational services in the government and private sector. There is question of 'quality' in education provision in both systems and the private institutions fare much better when it comes to teacher-student ratio and educational resources.

## Characteristics of Inclusive School

There are certain 'school factors' which influence students achievements like professional leadership, learning environment, high expectation, positive reinforcement, monitoring student's progress and parent-school cooperation (Ayres, Sawyer, and Dinham, 2004; Bentley, 2000; Steve Dinham, Cairney, Craigie, and Wilson, 1995; Alma Harris, 1999; Owens, 1998).

Kuth (2005) identified some common characteristics of inclusive schools; committed leadership, democratic classrooms, reflective teachers, a supportive culture, engaging and relevant curriculum, and responsive instruction.

1. *Committed Leadership*: People in the leadership positions like principal, administrators, board members have a key role in inclusion. They provide encouragement and support to teachers, educate families and communities about the school's philosophy and commitments, celebrate success and solve problems.
2. *Democratic Classrooms*: Democratic classroom is an approach where everyone (students, teachers, staff, and family of students) is responsible, contribute and participate in the teaching-learning process. Everyone is treated with respect and dignity, their opinion is respected and the individuals work in close cooperation.

3. *Supportive School Culture*: The inclusive school culture is 'open, accepting and caring'. The leaders and educators take interest in creating cultures which is enabling and welcoming for instance, invite and implement suggestions from students, parents and community, and give equal opportunities to all students.
4. *Engaging and Relevant Curricula*: The curriculum and instruction in inclusive school must be appropriate to suit individual needs and learning styles to nurture each child's abilities and talents. The teachers must inform children about the diversity amongst learners and must promote cooperative learning.
5. *Responsive Instruction*: Teachers have to be flexible and must be skilled to adapt materials, lesson structures and instructional arrangements.

There are five components of inclusive education as proposed by Halvorsen and Neary (2001). Firstly, for schools to be inclusive the classrooms must accommodate same aged children, with no special classes except for enrichment activities for all students. Secondly, the core curriculum must be adapted well in planning and curriculum development and participation of all learners must be solicited and encouraged. Thirdly, the teachers must employ best instructional strategies and best practices in education to enhance learning of all learners. Fourthly, student responsibility for learning must be promoted. Lastly, the staff should be provided necessary training on inclusive practices.

Anderson (2003) extended the key characteristics of Halvorsen and Neary (2001) and suggested that the critical component strategies needed to support inclusive practice are: (a) principals who provide leadership in restructuring, (b) collaborative teaming for building community, and (c) instructional strategies that support the learning of all students. Depeller and Harvey (2004) suggested that for successful inclusion favourable attitudes have to be corroborated by structures that support cooperation and problem solving amongst teachers, parents and students.

## Critical Dimensions of Inclusive Classrooms

With the generic understanding of the characteristics of the schools, it would be vital to delve on the critical dimensions of the inclusive classrooms. The development of clear procedures for the classroom helps in optimising the learning.

### *Physical Layout of the Classroom*

The primary consideration in an inclusive classroom is whether or not all children will be able to access it. Ramps are important for enhancing access not only for the children using wheelchairs but also using walking frames or those with general mobility difficulties. The doors must be wide enough to let the wheelchairs in. For children with visual impairments the doors should either be fully opened or fully closed to ensure that they do not walk in and out of half-opened doors. Other considerations may include arranging the class in such a way to facilitate the children with disabilities to move around easily (Loreman, Deppler & Harvey, 2006:178-179).

There are variety of ways in which the classroom seating could be planned; traditional expository teaching seating plan, ability groups and heterogenous groups seating plan. The traditional expository teaching seating plan could be described as one where the students are seated in rows of desks facing the teacher and where the teacher provided instruction from the front of the classroom. However, this arrangement poses significant disadvantages for the children with disabilities who may be restricted to the front row under the gaze of the teacher (*ibid*:181-182). Woolfolk (2001) discussed that though this arrangement has academic advantages the social barriers it presents are problematic. They are only able to interact with peers seated next to them. McInerney & McInerney (2002) suggested that all children must be given the opportunity to interact with one another in order for effective learning to occur at all.

The teacher may choose to group the student according to their abilities, knowledge, skills in a range of areas. Woolfolk (2001) found it advantageous in terms of learning for groups. However, there are perceived disadvantages in such arrangements where there is social stigma attached to the weaker groups in the class as suggested by

McNamara & Waugh (1993). In sharp contrast to the ability groups is the heterogenous groups seating plan where children with mixed abilities are placed in the same group. This arrangement facilitates peer tutoring and cooperative group work (McInerney & McInerney, 2002).

### *Facilitating Friendships*

Inclusive school communities focus on social as well as academic outcomes for children. Friendships matter to children, their parents, and teachers because they provide children with the opportunity to develop important skills and attitudes and, perhaps most important, they enhance quality of life for children and their families (Meyer, Park, Grenot-Scheyer, Schwartz, & Harry, 1998).

Based on what we know to be the benefits of having friends, and conversely the negative effects of being socially isolated, many schools actively strive to foster friendships among children. Some of the strategies used to promote friendships include (Soodak 2003): (a) selecting activities that involve cooperation and collaboration rather than competition, (b) creating rituals that involve all members of the class, such as class meetings and friendship circles, (c) using children's literature to promote discussions about friendship and belonging, and (d) setting up classroom rules to encourage respect, such as requiring turn-taking or not permitting any child to be left out.

### *Individualized Education Plan*

Bailey (1994) defined as "a document describing children's skills and stating goals for services as well as strategies for achieving those goals" (p. 29). Wolery (1994) described the essential information that is required on an IEP—

- A statement of the child's present levels of educational performance, including academic achievement, social adaptation, prevocational and vocational skills, psychomotor skills, and self-help skills.
- A statement of annual goals which describes the educational

performance to be achieved by the end of the school year under the child's Individualized Education Programme.

- A statement of short-term instructional objectives, which must be measurable intermediate steps between the present level of educational performance and the annual goals.
- A statement of specific educational services needed by the child (determined without regard to the availability of services) including a description of.
- All special education and related services which are needed to meet the unique needs of the child, including the type of physical education programme in which the child will participate.
- Special instructional media and materials which are needed.
- The date when those services will begin and length of time the services will be given.
- A description of the extent to which the child will participate in regular education programmes.
- A justification of the type of educational placement that the child will have.
- A list of the individuals who are responsible for implementation of the Individualized Education Programme.
- Objective criteria, evaluation procedures, and schedules of determining, on at least an annual basis, whether the short-term instructional objectives are being achieved.

Bruder (1994) emphasized that planning and implemention of IEP requires collaborative effort, thus the team must also comprise family members. There are various advantages of individual programme plan; ensures accountability of the person responsible for providing instruction (Goodman & Bond, 1993), helps to compensate for lack of attention on relevant areas for children with diverse abilities (Clough, 1998), provide opportunities for parents to voice their concerns on what the child should learn (Strickland and Turnbull, 1990), outline how certain aspects of curriculum will be taught and the additional resources required (Ryndack & Alper, 1996), provide framework for assessment (Goodman & Bond, 1993) and are useful records at times of transition (Deppler, 1998).

Some of disadvantages of IEP could be that they are not linked to the regular curriculum and hence may isolate the child (Ryndack & Alper, 1996), represent additional paperwork for teachers (Gerardi *et al.*, 1984), not used by many teachers to guide instruction, often focus on training rather than education and are prescriptive in nature (Goodman & Bond, 1993).

While there may be many disadvantages, most of these could be overcome if the plan is viewed as fluid document that operates within the context of regular class curriculum (Loreman, Deppler & Harvey, 2006).

## Outcomes of Inclusion

The researchers suggest that while not all of the benefits listed necessarily exist in all cases, they represent a range of benefits that have been experienced when inclusion of reasonable quality has been provided based on observations and research conducted in the United States (Giangreco, Dennis, Cloninger, Edelman, & Schattman, 1993; Giangreco, Edelman, Cloninger, & Dennis, 1993; Helmstetter, Peck, & Giangreco, 1994; Hunt, Staub, Alwell, & Goetz, 1994; Janney & Snell, 1996; Kozleski & Jackson, 1993; Peck, Donaldson, & Pezzoli, 1990; Rankin *et al.*, 1994; Salisbury, Palombaro, & Hollowood, 1993; Sharpe, York, & Knight, 1994; York, Vandercook, Macdonald, Heise-Neff, & Caughey, 1992).

### *Impact on Students with Disabilities*

- Educational programmes are more relevant and focused.
- Increased access to typical environments (e.g., school, community, work).
- Access to new experiences/opportunities in school and beyond school.
- Access to peer models.
- New relationships and friendships.
- Raised expectations.
- Increased awareness and responsiveness to people environment activity.
- Increased skill acquisition.
- Greater enjoyment of school.

Stainback and Stainback (1984) suggested the following reasons for supporting inclusion

- the dual system of education assumes two different kinds of learners; regular and special. It is, however, difficult to place children in strict categories as the learning characteristics fall along a continuum.
- Individualized educational planning benefits all children.
- Instructional methods could prove useful to all children with or without disabilities.
- The dual system classification sometimes results in wrong diagnosis for children.
- The dual system results in competition and duplication of effort from regular and special educational stream.
- The most negative results of the existing dual system is the 'deviant' label on children with disabilities.

However, the outcomes are not just positive, Smith *et al.* (1998:27) have spelt out disadvantages of inclusion which might lead to negative outcomes for children with disabilities.

- General educators are not involved sufficiently and therefore, they are not interested in the inclusive model.
- The general and special education teachers do not have adequate collaborative skills in order to make inclusion successful.
- Lack of empirical data for support to the model.
- Full inclusion might result in poorer quality of education for children without disabilities.
- Current funding, training and certification of teachers are based on dual system of educational service.
- Some children with disabilities perform better in special educational services.

A consideration of the possible outcomes of inclusion is a vital step towards its implementation and gauging its importance. Though it is pertinent to highlight both positive and negative aspects, it may be wiser for the implementers to focus on the positive side rather than the potential obstacles of inclusion.

Sasso, Simpson & Novak (1985) contended that when the children with disabilities spend the entire school day with their non-disabled classmates, they are bestowed upon numerous opportunities for social interactions which are unavailable in segregated settings. These opportunities help them develop better communication skills and form friendship with their non-disabled peers. Brown *et al.* (1983, 1989a) underscored that inclusion also helps in inculcating appropriate models of behaviour in students with disabilities. The children learn socially acceptable behaviours through observation and imitation. Another advantage of inclusion is that the educators often develop higher standards of performance for children with disabilities (Brown *et al.*, 1989a; Snell, 1987). It is thus, an opportunity to live a normal life like other children and acquire functional, academic, social, vocational and recreational skills which would prepare the students for living and working in the community even after leaving school.

It is often believed that inclusion only has benefits for children with disabilities and has no advantages for children without disabilities. Some critics have also voiced concerns about negative impact on education of children without disabilities due to loss of instructional time and lopsided teacher attention. Nonetheless, if properly implemented there could be several advantages for children without disabilities as well. The greatest advantage is learning to live and participate in a pluralistic society by knowing and responding to individual differences and human exceptionality. Secondly, the children without disabilities learn that their peers with disabilities are in more ways similar to them than they are different. They know them as equal beings and learn to appreciate their positive characteristics and abilities. Thirdly, they get an opportunity to know about many human service professions like special education, speech therapy, physical therapy, recreation therapy and vocational rehabilitation (Ryndack & Alper, 2003).

It is pertinent to know the research outcomes for educating children with disabilities in inclusive classrooms. In a study conducted by Blackorby *et al.* (2005) in United States involving 11,000 students had confirmed that children with disabilities who spend more time in general classrooms are absent less, perform closer to grade level than their peers in special schools and have higher achievement scores. The study also pointed out children with disabilities in regular educational setting perform poorly than their non-disabled peers. Nonetheless, it has established that despite outcome differences between students of various kinds of disabilities, overall the students with disabilities outperformed their peers in the segregated settings when standards-based assessments were used (cited in Artiles *et al.*, 2005).

Another study which points towards positive effects of inclusion was a collaborative action research project in an inclusive setting in Greece (Argyropoulos & Stamouli, 2006) for assisting a blind child has reported many positive effects of inclusion on the child as well as her classmates. The aim of this research was to achieve better inclusion in terms of the blind student's participation in the school subject matters. The impetus for this research was the problems that the teachers of a public rural primary school were facing with respect to the education of an integrated sixth grader blind student (12 years of age and having average intelligence) with particular reference to subjects which require more visual assimilation like Geometry and Geography. It was a six month project, where collaborative teaching model was followed. The results of this research indicated that the interactions between the classroom and support teachers had a great influence on the child's psychology. It also reported change in attitude of her sighted peers. The sighted peers were reportedly interested in the way the child with disability used her specially designed instruments and explored tactile representations. The class responded favourably to team teaching.

Some other studies have shown that including young children with disabilities in integrated settings has produced positive social outcomes for children with and without disabilities. Children with disabilities have increased levels of social contact with children without disabilities, give and receive higher levels of social support, and have larger friendship networks than disabled peers in segregated settings (Fryxell and Kennedy, 1995; Hunt *et al.*, 1994; Salisbury *et al.*, 1993).

McGregor and Vogelsberg (1998) suggest that firstly, children with disabilities demonstrate high levels of social interaction with their non-disabled peers in an inclusive school setting when compared to a segregated setting. This socialization was greater if there was adult support and if the children with disabilities were represented in the school in their normal proportion. Secondly, in inclusive settings social competence and communication skills in children with disabilities are highly improved. This is attributed to the interactions with their non-disabled peers, who assist the children in developing age appropriate behaviours. Thirdly, some research work points towards better academic gains as the inclusive schools follow a more rigorous programme than the special schools. Fourthly, inclusive education results in social acceptance of children with disabilities due to frequent and close interaction amongst all pupils. Lastly, there are enhanced friendship networks of children with disabilities with their non-disabled peers as compared to segregated settings. Teachers also play a facilitative role in developing these friendships.

Gouveia (1997) also reported that children with disabilities in the inclusive settings are subjected to a more varied curriculum and thus, benefit more academically. Most often the special education classes "focus more on functional skills and less on subjects such as science, fine arts, literature and social studies"(*ibid*: 1).

There is a tendency among children to compare themselves with others, as a result they find solace and comfort in those who like them and exhibit similar behaviours (Rothlisberg, Hill, & D'Amato 1994), thus putting the children with disabilities at a disadvantage. When they endeavour to socialize with the non-disabled peers they receive negative responses which results in isolation. This may decrease the chances of the child's ability to develop and practice social skills, which can be a contributing factor to social isolation in adulthood. The children who are denied social experiences have to deal with loneliness (Helper, 1997).

Heiman and Margalit (1998) found that "social skills reflect the individual's ability to exhibit appropriate behavior by using skill such as cooperation, self-control, and understanding the needs of others, as well as the ability to initiate social interaction" (p. 155). Pearl, Farmer, Van Acker, Rodkin, Bost, Coe, and Henley, 1998, found that "the poor social acceptance of students with disabilities often has been viewed as being the result of social skills deficits" (p. 168).

'Loneliness' is another key factor which affects the formation of relationships with other children. It reflects a conflict between reality and the individual's expectations of interpersonal relations. The roots of loneliness can be traced back to early childhood and the modes of mother-child attachment, in non-effective social interactions, which are manifested from individual inadequacies in using social skills, or both. When individuals feel lonely, they are less likely to involve themselves in social relationships, they generally talk infrequently, ask fewer questions, don't attend to social interactions with other individuals, and don't try to form social relationships (Heiman & Margalit, 1998).

Factors such as lack of social skills and loneliness can manifest themselves in the child with disability as maladaptive behaviour (Helper, 1997). For instance, Heiman & Margalit (1998) found that "Studies that examined the social skills of non-disabled students with deficient social skills revealed they have a greater tendency to develop behavioural problems in school and are more likely to drop out of school or to develop emotional disturbances" (p. 155). Evidence suggests that many students with disabilities exhibit problematic behaviour, which results in them being socially rejected by their peers. Non-disabled children often view peers with disabilities as having problematic social behaviours and as being more disruptive than students who are low achievers (Pearl, Farmer, Van Acker, Rodkin, Bost, Coe, & Henley, 1998).

Different social environments would therefore be expected to influence an individual's self-concept in different ways. Rohner's theory (1980, reviewed in Mrug, Wallander, 2002) postulates that feeling accepted or rejected by one's significant others will affect the way a person views and evaluates oneself and the world. Feeling rejected by others will lead to greater hostility, low self-respect, emotional instability and unresponsiveness, and a negative view of the world, whereas feeling accepted by others will lead to a lower feelings of hostility, higher self-concept, emotional stability and responsiveness, and a positive view of the world. Recognizing the mechanisms of mutual functioning of the teacher on students' self-concept and achievements is extremely important for the success of integrated students with special needs (Fulgosi-Masnjak, 2003 cited in Schmidt & Cagran). Enhancing the self-concept of students with special needs that are included in regular primary school classes has a positive impact on their academic achievements as well as on their personal and social development. Factors that appear to influence the self-concept of students with special needs include the following: severity or degree of disability, age of onset of disability, acceptance of the disability by parents, type of schooling (education in regular school or special school) and special support, labelling, and identification group adherence (Cambra, 2002; Jambor, Elliott, 2005; Montgomery, 1994; Mrug, Wallender, 2002; van Gurp, 2001; Westling Allodi, 2000).

Earlier research conducted on the self-concept of deaf students and their hearing peers in regular settings has shown inconsistent results. On the one hand, research (Leigh, Stinson, 1991; Leob, Sarigiani, 1986; Maxon, Brackett, van den Berg, 1991) has reported finding lower self-concept in students with hearing impairments in comparison to their hearing peers, whereas others have found no significant differences between the groups (Cates, 1991; Koelle, Convey, 1982). The study of Appleton, Minchom, Ellis, Elliott, Boll and Jones (1994) compared 79 young people with physical disabilities, in terms of global self-worth and their perceived self-competence in 9 fields, to their peers without disabilities. They discovered that young people with a disability reported a lower degree of perceived competence in academic and athletic domains and in social acceptance, but there were no differences in the perception of their control of perceived self-competence in connection with behaviour conduct, or in their global self-worth.

A study on the self-concept of children with learning disabilities (Montgomery, 1994) and receiving support in regular classes shows that those children have a lower academic self-concept than their peers without disabilities, but the two groups do not differ in global self-concept or in other dimensions of self-concept, like social competence, affective, physical, or family.

The results of more recent studies (Cambra, Silvestre, 2003) indicate significant differences between integrated students (students with hearing impairments, physical disabilities and learning disabilities) and their counterparts in the social and academic dimensions, which is lower in children with special needs, but the differences in physical self-concept dimension are not statistically significant.

## Research on Stakeholders

### *Research on Parents*

Quite a number of research documents emphasized that the special child care demands faced by the parents of children with disabilities can cause significant stress for the parents (e.g., Farber, 1960; Gath, 1973; Tumbull, Brotherson, & Summers, 1986). These demands persist throughout childhood and into the adult years, and require continuous adaptation by the parents to both ongoing stressors and frequent crises (Wikler, 1986). Amongst the parents, greater amount of burden falls on the mother. A number of studies have examined the daily challenges and increased levels of maternal stress of mothers caring for children who have disabilities (Feinberg 1985, Holroyd & Guthrie 1986, Bouma & Schweitzer 1990, Alexander *et al.* 2002). The extraordinary work required by children with disabilities is often physically, mentally and emotionally taxing, and requires considerable skill, knowledge and responsibility on the behalf of mothers (Spalding & McKeever, 1998, McKeever & Miller, 2004). May (1997) described mothering a child with disabilities as mothering 'plus extras'.

In India research on families having members with disabilities has been reviewed with reference to the following aspects (Kashyap, 1991:273-281):

- The effect on the family of the presence of a individual with disability: She has cited seven studies where the researchers have focused on the effect of presence of children with disabilities. She noted that very little and very limited research has been done on children with disabilities and their families.
- The influencing factors within the family: Of the fourteen research studies she had referred dealing with this aspect; twelve studied only the attitudes of the parents towards their children with disabilities as the influencing factors.
- The family's coping strategies: Only one research has been reported in her review in the important area of coping by families. Gandotra (1985) studied the ways and means used by twenty-five home makers to cope with the problems arising from the presence of individual with disability in the family (cited in Kashyap, 1991).

- Professional intervention for helping the family to cope. In this category seven studies were reviewed that reflected that professionals had emphasized on families of the mentally challenged children and that too on educational programmes for training parents in behaviour modification techniques.

The research review of families with individuals with disabilities by Kashyap suggests that families of the mentally challenged children have received more attention by the researchers as compared to the other disabilities. Also, some very important areas like coping and adaptation by the families, interventions other than education and training, influencing factors within the families apart the parental attitudes towards their disabled children, sibling relationships need consideration by the researchers. "Research in understanding of families and working with the families in the true sense is still eluding Indian scene" (Peshawaria *et al.*, 1995:12). More often than not the emphasis is on the epidemiological aspects. Major focus of the studies has been studying the attitudes of parents towards their children with disabilities and the disability, which has received the maximum attention of the researchers, is mental retardation.

For this study, we were more interested in writings concerning parental perceptions of inclusion (e.g. Giangreco, Edelman, Cloninger, & Dennis, 1993; Kasari, Freeman, Bauminger, & Alkin, 1999; Lamorey & Bricker, 1993; Reichart, Lynch, Anderson, & Svobodny, 1989; Stoiber, Gettinger, & Goetz, 1998). The idea that self-esteem and personal competence are a result of being a part of mainstream society has been the basis for including children with disabilities in classrooms with children without disabilities (Bennett, Lee, & Lueke, 1998). The importance of parents' involvement in their children's education and the value of family school collaboration (Comer & Haynes, 1991; Comer, Haynes, Joyner, & Ben-Avie, 1996; Swick, 1993; White, 1988), support the need to understand the experiences and beliefs of parents of children with disabilities concerning their children's educational placement. A study by Swick and Hooks (2005), provides an in-depth description of the parents of children with disabilities and their experiences and beliefs that influenced them to choose an inclusive educational placement for their children with disabilities. This study gathered data from the parents of five children with disabilities, teachers and administrators involved with those five children and where possible, peers and siblings of the children. Each of the parents involved in this study perceived inclusive educational placements as the best placement for their children with disabilities. This common belief was attributed to four reasons—First, each parent expressed a desire for his or her child to live as normal a life as possible. Second, they believed that as parents they should be valued and involved in their children's education. Third, each expressed a belief that segregated settings were limiting for their children academically. And fourth, they all believed that segregated settings did not provide situations that supported social development.

Most research studies have examined the impact of including children with disabilities in regular classrooms on children with disabilities but a study by Peck *et al.* (2004) has established the positive effects of including children with severe disabilities on their non-disabled peers as perceived by their parents. They studied parents' perceptions of the effects of their non-disabled child's participation in a classroom in which a child with severe disabilities was enrolled full time. They distributed questionnaries to parents of non-disabled children ($n = 659$) in grades kindergarten through 6 who were enrolled in 1 of 25 elementary classrooms in which at least one peer with moderate to severe disabilities was included on a full-time basis. Children with disabilities enrolled in these classrooms had all been categorized as "severely handicapped" and had a wide variety of diagnostic labels, including mental retardation (moderate through severe), autism, cerebral palsy, and Down syndrome. The chronological ages of the children ranged from 5 to 12 years. Survey responses from 389 parents indicated that they generally perceived their non-disabled child to have benefited from this experience. A minority of parents held negative views of inclusion. Analysis of narrative comments on surveys returned by some of these parents indicated that concerns about behavioural disruption and loss of teacher time allocated to their child were the major source of their dissatisfaction. Survey comments suggested in some cases that parents did not view academic and social learning experiences to be highly related.

Parents perceive positive outcomes for children with disabilities placed in integrated settings, including more appropriate social interactions, more interactions with children without disabilities, higher levels of social play and more advanced play (Demchak and Drinkwater, 1992).

**Teachers**

Teacher's attitude is one of the most important variables in the education of children with disabilities (Smith, 2000). Teacher's beliefs underlying the philosophy of inclusion are important predictors of the outcomes of inclusion (Ringlaken & Price, 1981). Teachers' judgments about children with disabilities could have a significant influence on children's emotional, social and intellectual development. Since general educators' willingness to include students with disabilities in their classrooms is critical to the success of inclusion, a number of researchers have stressed the importance of understanding teachers' attitudes and beliefs towards inclusion (Bain & Dolbel, 1991; Roberts & Zubrick, 1992; Forlin & Cole, 1993; Hasazi *et al.*, 1994; Forlin *et al.*, 1996; Smith, 2000).

There is an abundance of studies examining teachers' beliefs, attitudes, and perceptions about students with disabilities and inclusive education (e.g. Gerber, 1992; Fulk & Hirth, 1994; Minke *et al.*, 1996; Villa *et al.*, 1996; Cornoldi *et al.*, 1998; Chiang, 1999; Balboni and Pedrabissi, 2000; Opdal & Wormnaes, 2001; Wall, 2002), including qualitative studies that use interview data (e.g. Giangreco *et al.*, 1993; Brantlinger, 1996). Agbenyega (2007) has concluded through his study in Ghana that attitudes and concerns of teachers affect their acceptance and commitment to implementing inclusion. It is worth noting that inclusive education was not leading to equal and appropriate educational outcomes, particularly for students with disabilities because of inappropriate school practices, such as rejection of students with disabilities by regular teachers, inappropriate resources, and lack of provision of generic support and training services.

It has been established that the inclusion of children with disabilities is most efficient when teachers' attitudes are positive towards the integration of children who are disabled in their classrooms and children's attitudes and behaviours are influenced by experiences that they have at school (Florin & Cole, 1994).

Singal (2007) had concluded that the teachers in inclusive classrooms were engaged in adapting the classroom organisational framework, rather than differentiating the learning experience for the child with disabilities. This is evident from the teachers' efforts to seat the child with more 'able' peers, giving her/him extra time, a reduced syllabus and making small adjustments within the dominant chalk and talk pedagogy adopted in the classroom. In addition, teachers also showed high dependency on 'others', namely parents and special educators, for the child's learning.

## Teacher Training for Inclusive Education

Teacher development has to be the heart of initiatives for developing inclusive practices in schools (Aniscow, 2003). There is an increasing international concern about teacher preparation in inclusive education and whether or not the training that they receive is adequate (Edelen-Smith, Prater & Siloe, 1993; Reed & Monda-Amaya, 1995; Lombard, Miller & Hazelkorn, 1998). In a study, Richards and Clough (2004) investigated if school experiences had affected original understandings and views on inclusion of 120 preservice teachers. The results indicated that few of the preservice teachers had any prior experience of people with disabilities, and found the greatest benefits in terms of teacher preparation were obtained in their practical school experiences. Forlin, Tait, Carroll, and Jobling (1999) surveyed 2,375 preservice teachers about their attitudes towards people with disabilities by assessing levels of discomfort in social interactions. They found that more frequent contact with people with disabilities resulted in less discomfort in interactions. Hopper and Stogre (2004) compared attitudes of preservice teachers who participated in site-based programmes for students who have special needs with those who did not. The comparison between those in site-based classes and those in non-site-based classes yielded statistical significant differences between the groups, with site based programmes yielding more positive findings for attitudes, social influence, and perceptions of control.

It is important to note that there are also exceptions to this trend.

For example, Marshall, Stojanovik, and Ralph (2002) conducted a study involving the attitudes of preservice teachers toward students who had specific speech and language difficulties. Unlike the results of the studies described above, these researchers found no significant relationship between preservice teachers' previous experience with students who have difficulties and their attitudes. They did note differences in attitude based on availability of resources (both workload and knowledge based) and the types of disability that the students might have.

Lancaster and Bain (2007) conducted a study in which they investigated the effect of an inclusive education course on the self-efficacy of preservice elementary educators and also sought to establish whether changes in self-efficacy co-varied with the type of field-based experience included in the course. The results indicated that an improvement in student self-efficacy co-varied with participation in the inclusive education course, although the field-based placement did not differentially affect self-efficacy at a statistically significant level.

The professional preparation of teachers has been recognized to be crucial for the qualitative improvement of education since the 1960s (Kothari Commission, 1964-66). In India, Jangira (1995) suggested ali teachers should be provided with the requisite knowledge and skills to enable them to respond to special needs in the classroom. The National Policy on Education recommended that all preservice teacher-education programmes should include a component on special needs.

Panda (2005) had suggested that for successful inclusion, the attempt must be a shift from 'theory to practice' to 'practice to theorization'. This calls for integrating cognate disciplines for arriving at composite understanding of educational components. This would help in understanding each learner not only from psychological perspectives but also from educational and social perspectives. There is greater need for pedagogical shift in transacting and organizing activities.

### *Research on Peers*

Considerable research on social relationships between young children has been conducted over the last several years. Only recently have researchers begun to examine the relationships among children with disabilities and revealed that relationships between children with and without disabilities do exist, have similar characteristics and attributes of those between typically developing children, and develop in a similar manner (Buysse, 1993; Hall, 1994; Staub, 1998; Staub *et al.*, 1994).

The effectiveness of peer tutoring is supported by substantial research evidence, and provides teacher with another instructional alternative to cater for the diverse range of students. Peer tutoring has been found to have a positive influence on student's academic performance (Hedin, 1986; Gartner, 1990; Topping & Lindsay, 1993), social acceptance of students with disabilities and increasing interactions amongst students with disabilities and their non-disabled peers (Garcia-Vasquez & Ehly, 1992; Fulton *et al.* 1994), affective and social skills development for both the tutor and tutee (Mastropieri & Scruggs, 1987; Foreman, 2000), self-efficacy and attitudes to learning (Cohen *et al.*, 1990), higher-order cognitive skills development (Vaughn *et al.*, 2001; Gersten *et al.*, 2001), and organizational skills and completion of academic class work (Coenen, 2002) (cited in Loreman, Deppeler & Harvey 2006:169).

Attitudes of the non-disabled peers are important in the inclusion of individuals with disabilities in the classroom. The success of integration is determined through contact that children who are disabled and non-disabled children have with one another (Roberts & Lindsell, 1987).

## Towards Effective Inclusion

The existing system of segregated education of disabled children has augmented the gap between regular and special schools. Research supports the fact that educating disabled children in pull-out programmes is not a viable approach to education. There is also enough research evidence to prove that the children with disabilities could be educated effectively in regular schools if appropriate practices and methods are used (Banerjee and Daily, 1995; Bishop, 1995).

In this segment the paper would highlight some effective practices in inclusionary settings particularly, classroom management and school reform. Education system is strictly examination oriented, high pressured and fiercely competitive. The proposal of educating all children in one classroom is often considered impossible under such circumstances. The regular teachers are trained in a way that they remain indifferent to the needs of children with special needs in class.

Some students in school cannot meet the curriculum's requirement due to their differential abilities. This non-performance in school work also results in development of social and/or emotional problems. To cope with uniqueness, diversity and range of educational problems of these students; a resource room arrangement has been initialized in many schools and found effective.

**Process of Inclusion**

In response to the call for full inclusion, several alternative service delivery models have been developed and implemented. Each model has its own unique quality, yet there are several common elements among them. One key element, and what proponents believe is paramount to the success of full inclusion, is the collaboration between general and special education teachers. By sharing responsibilities through team teaching, the two sectors are able to develop a more comprehensive programme that could adapt to the needs of all students (Reynolds, Wang, & Walberg, 1987). The implementation of different teaching strategies and the modification of assignments to accommodate individual students is another element found among these models. Methods of teaching provided in these programmes ranged from highly structured to opened-ended exploratory learning activities (Wang, Rubenstein, & Reynolds, 1985; Affleck, Madge, Adams, & Lowenbraun, 1988). Adaptations and accommodations made within the class are provided for individual students, and in some circumstances, for the entire class. Direct instruction provides small groups and individual students with remedial instruction, while independent study time is provided to those students who need less support (Zigmond & Baker, 1996). The use of peer tutors and cooperative learning is another strategy employed, as stronger students can help provide additional support to those having difficulties mastering concepts (Affleck, Madge, Adams, & Lowenbraun, 1988).

Gartner and Lipsky (1997) had reported three working models for effective inclusion. Where the number of children with special needs is less in a regular classroom, the *Consultant Model* could be opted. The consultant model requires the help of the special teacher to teach difficult skills to the children with special needs. The other model is named the *Teaming Model* that requires the special and regular teachers to function as a team. The special educator provides student information, possible instructional strategies, modification ideas for assignments/tests, and behaviour strategies. The team meets on a regular basis, establishing consistent communication among the team members. Another model is called *Collaborative or Co-teaching Model* which entails perfect synchronization between special and regular educators as they are co-teachers. Both are responsible for instruction planning and delivery, student achievement, assessment, and discipline. Co-teaching is defined as two or more professionals delivering substantive instruction to a group of students with diverse learning needs. This approach increases instructional options, improves educational programmes, reduces stigmatization for students, and provides support to the professionals involved. Co-teaching is an appropriate service delivery approach for students with disabilities who can benefit from general education curriculum if given appropriate supports. Teachers and related service professionals who are flexible and have good judgment are likely to be successful in this role. Co-teachers need preparation, administrative support, and opportunities to nurture their collaborative relationships. Co-teaching programmes should be planned and implemented systematically. Deliberate and ongoing communication among everyone involved is essential (Cook & Friend, 1995).

Though the implementation of models could prove beneficial for inclusive classrooms, the educators must remember that the effectiveness of the model lies in its translation in classroom contexts; the main agents for which are teachers. Thus, it is extremely important to prepare these teachers to handle diversity in their classrooms from the time they commit themselves to the teaching profession. Pre-service preparation of the teachers is of paramount importance in inclusive education. The model suggested by Whitworth (1999) for inclusive teacher training takes into account the differences in abilities of learners in the classroom. In order to address this diversity within the classrooms the Whitworth's model focuses on two dimensions; outcomes of the model and specific programme components.

The specifics of the teacher training programme components have been illustrated in Fig. 2.1. A very essential part is the Collaborative Teaching Component. The educators collaborate for teaching, planning and evaluation. The approaches as collaborative learning arrangements and activities requiring students to develop and practice group process skills could prove beneficial for the classroom. Another component is the instructional techniques and strategies that the teachers must possess for teaching in diverse settings. Pre-service preparation must address appropriate accommodations in curriculum, instructional activities and evaluation procedures, effective identification, development and utilization of resources and various instructional arrangements such as multi-level teaching, cooperative learning and peer tutoring. The last component is related to the field based experiences of the prospective teacher. The teachers must get the opportunity to work in collaborative inclusive settings. The next segment of the model deals with the possible outcomes of the teacher's training. Reportedly, there is a narrow range of diversity with which the teacher is comfortable. It, therefore, makes it difficult to address the diverse needs within the inclusive classroom. It is important that the teachers are aware and trained to handle diversity in the classroom. Adaptability to change is another vital consequence of the programme.

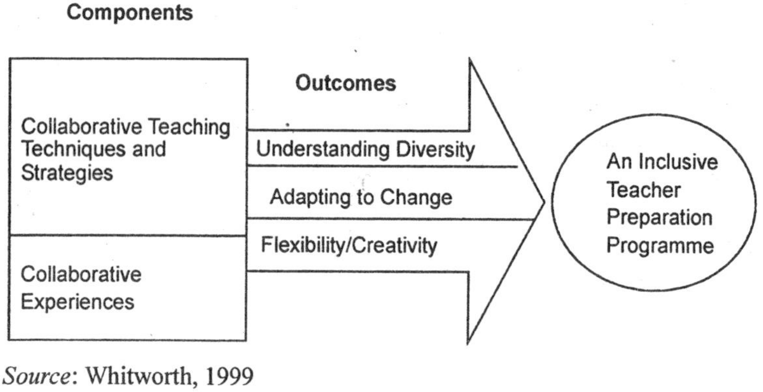


*Source*: Whitworth, 1999

**Fig. 2.1:** An Inclusive Teacher Preparation Model

There is little doubt that the classrooms of the future would be governed by inclusivity rather that exclusivity. This positive change also demands flexibility and creativity on part of the teachers which could be enhanced/developed by providing experiential pre-service training to the teachers.

## Types of Resource Models

There are at least five different types of resource programmes that operate in schools (Wiederholt, Hammil and Brown, 1983:6-11); Categorical Resource Programme, Cross-categorical Resource Programme, Non-categorical Resource Programme, Specific Skill Resource Programme and Itinerant Resource Programme. In the *categorical resource programme*, the services are reserved for students who are officially diagnosed as disabled. Each resource room caters to different categories of disability. The *cross-categorical resource programme* differs slightly from the categorical resource programme in serving two or more disability categories at a given instance. Here, the students are grouped according to instructional level rather than diagnostic labels. The *non-categorical resource programme* was designed to meet the educational needs of students with mild or moderate learning and/behaviour problems, including both disabled and non-disabled students. *Specific skill resource programmes* are organized around the training of skill areas primarily in reading, mathematics or speech. The special skill programmes serve the non-disabled children and hence, are useful in school settings which make use of the categorical and cross-categorical resource programmes. The *itinerant resource programme* could use the organizational format of any of the above mentioned resource programmes is literally a resource programme on wheels. It is useful in school settings which either do not have resources to support a full-time resource programme or does not house enough students who qualify to warrant a full-time teacher.

Inclusion is practically not so simple. The paper has shown how every aspect of the inclusive education has to be looked into for effective inclusion. Be it the preservice preparation or the implementation of the models within the classroom, all requires sustained efforts of the educators. Though educating the pupil is largely a responsibility of the educator, one cannot undermine the importance of the family in the educational process. Thus, Transdisciplinary teams assume great importance in inclusive settings.

Transdisciplinary functioning means professionals from different streams work together alongside the family members of the child. The transdisciplinary approach is recommended because it: (1) prevents the fragmentation of services along disciplinary lines, (2) avoids duplication of services, (3) views the whole child's development as integrated, and (4) emphasizes the importance of the family as equal, contributing members of the team (Losardo & Notari-Sylverson, 2001; McWilliam, 2000). The focus of the team is integrated development of the child and hence effective communication between team members becomes an indispensable component. The assessment, planning, intervention and monitoring require the team members to come together. This certainly means that team members must be willing to share their knowledge with each other and be open to acquiring new skills (McWilliam, 2000).

The main thrust of preparation for inclusion has been to prepare the general education teacher as well as the student with exceptionalities for this educational initiative. Students without disabilities are often not the prevailing focus in these efforts. The typically developing peers have a great role to play in inclusion. They must be aware and prepared for this prospect. As far as possible they must be involved in the classroom processes.

There is no perfect recipe for inclusion. There are however some requisites for inclusion. Each classroom has to be a community, which satisfies every child's need to belong. The child needs a response as an individual from the educators and his/her peers. The educator must focus on child's strengths. Cooperative learning should be a goal for all; there must be sincere attempts in classrooms, families and society to minimize competition and promote cooperation.

## Evaluative Practices

The last decade has seen development of a number of evaluative instruments which has resulted in improved understanding of inclusive practices. In 1995, Rossman and Salzman (1995) concluded most evaluative measures were not comprehensive. The evaluations had focused either on student outcomes or on support for parents, staff and students. Since then, a number of approaches and evaluative instruments have been developed.

The most popular is the Index of Inclusion developed by Booth, Ainscow, Vaughan and Shaw (2000) in order to enable the schools to carry out a self-evaluation of problems in developing inclusive practice. The Index for Inclusion is a set of materials to guide schools through a process of inclusive school development. It is about building supportive communities and fostering high achievement for all staff and students.

The school could use the Index to:

- adopt a self-review approach to analyse their cultures, policies and practices and to identify the barriers to learning and participation that may occur within each of these areas.
- decide their own priorities for change and to evaluate their progress.
- use it as an integral part of existing development policies, encouraging a wide and deep scrutiny of everything that makes up a school's activities.

Inclusion is a holistic approach that has to permeate the whole school experience of staff, students, parents and the community. The three dimensions of culture, policies and practice has been elucidated below—

*Dimension A—Cultures*: The creation of inclusive school cultures entails the promotion of those beliefs and value systems that create a secure, accepting, collaborating, and stimulating community for all students.

*Dimension B—Policies*: The development of inclusive school policies entails the introduction of explicit aims for promoting inclusion in School Development Plans and other guidelines for practice in the management, teaching and learning in our schools.

*Dimension C—Practices*: The organisation of inclusive school practices calls for practices that reflect inclusive school cultures and policies by ensuring that classroom and extra-curricular activities encourage the participation of all students and draw on their knowledge and experience outside school.

Another evaluative model called the Disability Rights in Education Model (DREM) developed by Peters, Johnstone & Fergusan (2005) is considered for its international application. This model was developed with the help of "input of disabled people that attempts to provide a cross-cultural framework for evaluating inclusive education programmes"(p. 141). This model supports McDonnells's (2003:261) contention of educational systems as having two different structural levels: "deep structures of theories, values, assumptions and beliefs, and surface structures of day-to-day practices in the organizations and operation of schools". The model thus attempts to understand both these structures for proposing educational reform. Inclusive education is seen as a dynamic process of interrelationships between these structures that is driven by a fundamental philosophy. The DREM provides a multi level framework at local/school, nation-state, and international levels. The DREM illustrates the dynamic interrelationship of outcome, resources, contexts and inputs. For each level, the outcomes at the top of the model and the intermediary enabling outcomes are specified according to the content area. These outcomes are decisive of whether or not a programme is responsive to disability rights and social justice. The influencing factors for these outcomes are the resources, contexts and inputs.

For the purpose of this study, we shall be concentrating on the local/school level of the model. This segment of the model has helped the authors to put the findings against a framework for evaluation and analysis (Figure 2.2).

## Researching 'Inclusive Education'

It is pertinent to discuss some of the methodological issues in carrying out a research on inclusive education. Farrel (2000) had cited a number of such concerns provided by Madden and Slavin (1983), Danby and Cullen (1988) and Hegarty (1993). Some of the main ones are discussed below:

- When evaluating the effectiveness of inclusive education it is virtually impossible to use matched control group designs where one group of pupils is placed in integrated provision and another is placed in a special school. This is because of

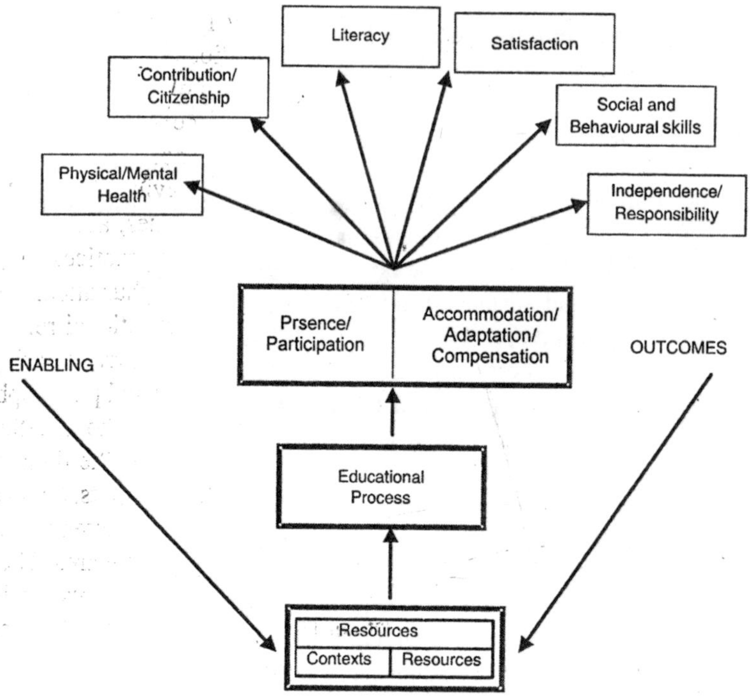


*Source*: Peters, Johnstone & Fergusan (2005).

**Fig. 2.2:** Disability Rights in Education Model: Level 1—School.

the ethical problems involved in allocating different provision to similar pupils for research purposes only and to problems in matching accurately pupils with SEN so as to be certain that the two groups have the same characteristics.

- The range of problems evident in pupils with special needs is so great that it is difficult to generalize from one study to another unless one can be absolutely sure that the studies that are being compared were conducted on similar pupils.
- Similarly, the variety of inclusive provision which pupils can experience is so great that it is difficult to compare the findings from different studies as it is not always easy to judge whether the groups experienced similar of entirely different forms of inclusion.

Despite the considerable methodological problems in inclusion, a great deal of research has been carried out and extensive review material has published (e.g. Farrell, 1997b; Hornby *et al.*, 1997; Jenkinson, 1997; Lindsay, 1997; Sebba and Sachdev 1997, Thomas *et al.* 1998).

This qualitative study acknowledges the methodological limitation the area poses. The literature has greatly helped in conceptualising the present study and preparing a generalised framework for the model. The theoretical and the research review helped in analysing the findings and helping to suggest future directions for research.

# 3

# The Study

This chapter would spell out the ontological and epistemological underpinnings of the research and also explicate the research design and methodological plan of the undertaken research exercise. The research methods have been carefully sorted by analysing the research questions. There is an array of approaches for conducting research which delve on understanding social phenomenon (Dick, 1995; Graziano and Raulin, 1993; Patton, 1990; Morgan, 1983; Burrell and Morgan, 1979). Guba and Lincoln (1989) and Burrell and Morgan (1979) both provide frameworks for decision-making for the choice of a methodology. Both concur that explicating ontological and epistemological assumptions are the primary steps in determining the choices available from which to select a methodology for use in inquiry.

Ontology signifies a particular view about social reality which is under study. There could be two possibilities while considering the nature of social reality—objective and subjective. The objective nature of social reality contends that 'reality' remains unaffected by the actors, while the subjective nature of social reality signifies that the individual's mental constructions and their critical engagements with the objects under study impacts the situation being studied. This research considers 'social reality' as subjective and getting impacted by the constructions of the social actors thus aligning to the worldview that individuals perceive and construct what the practices and experiences mean for them which accounts for actions and behaviours.

Epistemology relates to how this 'reality' can be known. The epistemology is the relationship between the knower and what is sought to be known. Burrell and Morgan (1979) suggested that this relationship depends on acknowledging whether the knowledge is objectively knowable or subjectively knowable. Guba and Linclon (1989) asserted that it is "impossible to separate the inquirer from the inquired into" (p. 88). Identifying epistemology becomes a vital step towards design of research because of its influence on outcomes of the research (see Kersten & Ison, 1994).

On the basis of our assumptions about ontology, epistemology and human nature, we were able to identify the features of a methodology that suited our inquiry. It had to allow us to deal with a social situation in which we as individuals interpret for ourselves the meaning of the experiences that we are having. It would need to allow for participation so that shared interpretations could be developed. The methodology had also to take into account the fact that these interpretations would be emerging as more experience accumulated and that experience would in turn determine the type of experience that followed. It would also need to provide ways of understanding how participants interpret and respond to their experiences. And finally, the methodology would need to provide ways of modifying the world or taking action in it.

In terms of the specifics of our researching the inclusive educational system, the chosen methodology would need to accommodate the fact that the children with disabilities and other stakeholders would be making their own interpretation of their inclusive educational experience and the emergence of new issues as experiences accumulated with these new issues contributing to what would happen as the research progressed.

Table 3.1 illustrates the methodology which would be the bedding rock of the research namely; ontology, epistemology, methods and the logic of inquiry. It would be interesting to first look at the logic of enquiry, which is abductive, "it is sometimes described as involving induction, but this grossly underestimates the complexity of the task involved" (Blaikie, 2000:25). The idea of abduction refers to the process used to generate social scientific accounts from social actors' accounts; for deriving technical concepts and theories from lay concepts and interpretations of social life (*ibid*: 114). It has vividly surfaced from the literature that "inclusive education" in India is an emerging concept and is understood and practiced differently. In order

**Table 3.1:** Methodology

| *Ontology* | *Epistemology* | *Methods* | *Logic of reasoning* |
|---|---|---|---|
| Viewing the social reality as the social construction of the participants. | Assumes that people employ interpretive schemes which must be understood, and that the character of the local context must be articulated. | In-depth interviewing was used to gather information from the child as well as the significant others (parents, teachers, peers). Observation in classrooms was also employed as a method. | Abductive; describing and understanding the concept of inclusive education as understood by the research participants thereby producing a technical account from lay accounts. |

to study the phenomenon of inclusion of children with disabilities in the regular classrooms in the Indian context, this appeared to be the most promising approach.

This was a qualitative study of describing and analyzing the process of educating children with disabilities in inclusive classrooms. A qualitative research design was adopted to assist in providing rich 'context bound' information (Creswell, 1994), with an underlying belief that situations are complex and hence must be portrayed from many dimensions rather than focusing on a narrow field (Bogdan & Bilklen, 1992). The intent would be to focus on the participants perceptions and experiences, and the way they make sense of their lives (Merriam, 1988), with an attempt to understand not one but multiple realities (Lincoln & Guba, 1985). The researcher is "bound within a net of epistemological and ontological premises which regardless of ultimate truth or falsity become partially self-validating" (Bateson, 1972 cited in Denzin & Lincoln, 2000:19). The Fig. 3.1 illustrates the process of research. The starting point was drawing up the proposal; formulating the research questions, setting objectives and preparation for entering the field. Thereafter, the process involving participation, deliberation and analysis was concurrent which culminated into a book.

## Conceptual Framework

The conceptual framework guiding this study has been illustrated in Fig. 3.2. The framework has been derived from the literature review

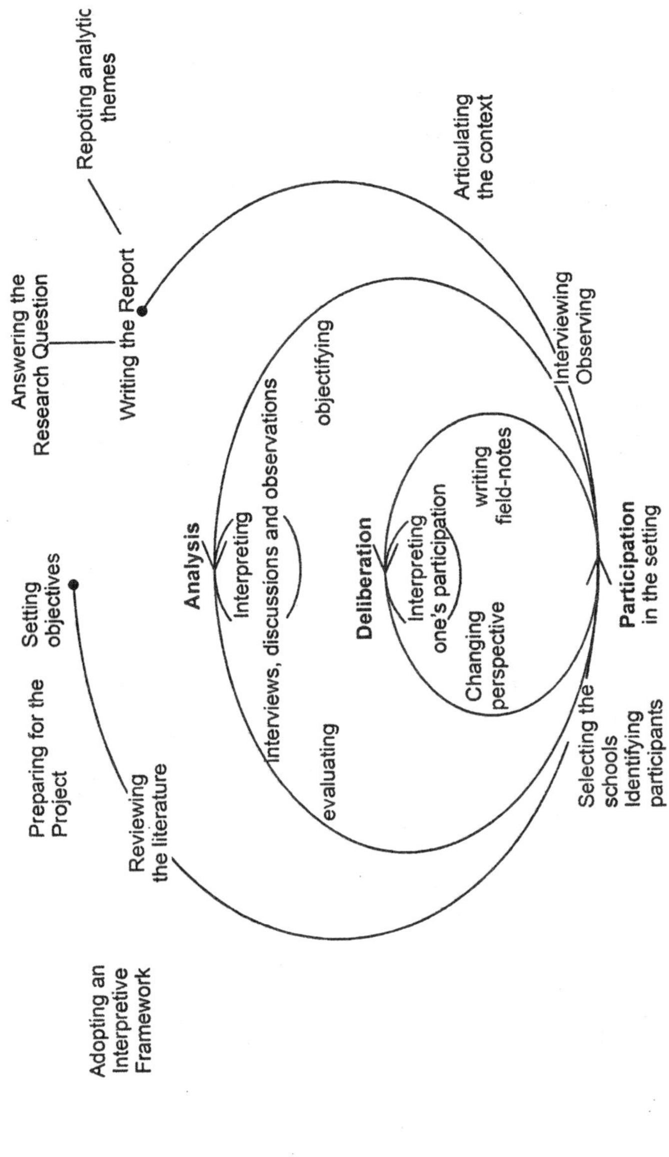


**Fig. 3.1:** The Process of Research

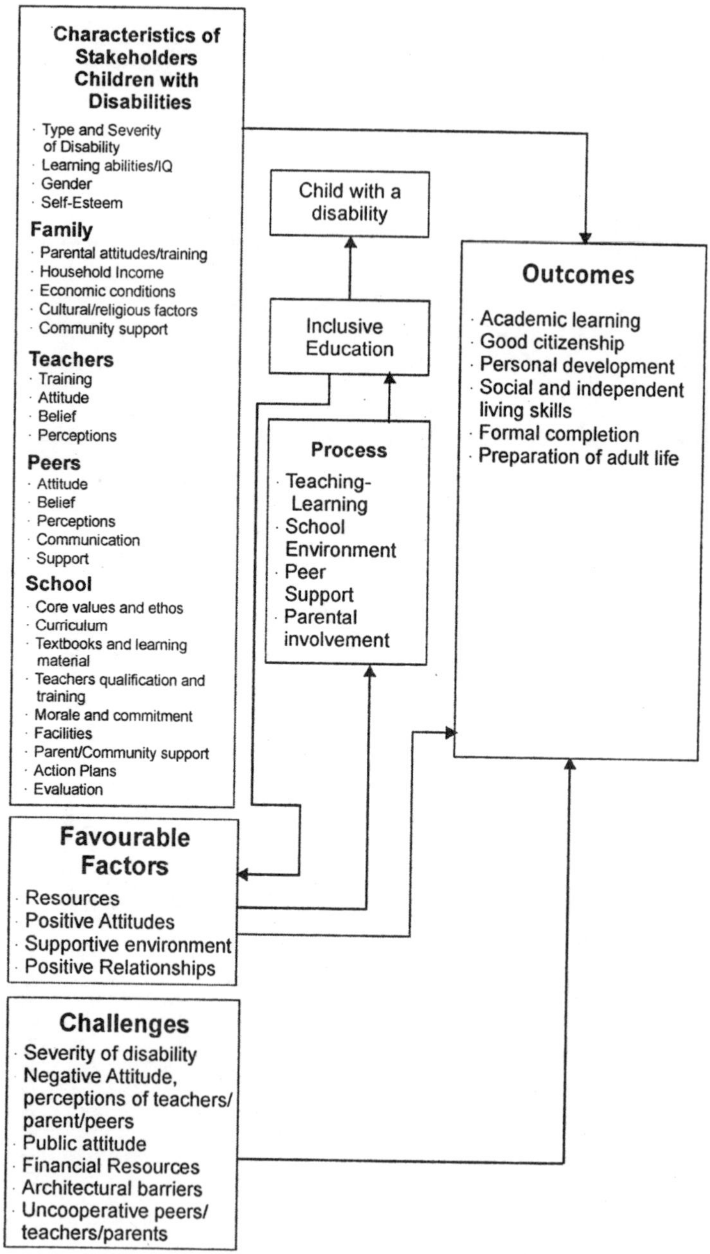


**Fig. 3.2:** Conceptual Framework

and depicts the lines of enquiry for this research. It centres the child with disability in an inclusive school. As the concept of inclusive education is still evolving in India, there are no set standards for schools. Thus, the schools have both characteristics which may benefit and encourage students with disabilities and ones which may deter their full participation in school proceedings. In an inclusive setting, the child with disability is in constant interaction with his/her typically developing peers without evident disabilities. The framework helps us to understand the promoting factors and barriers as perceived by the child and how inclusive environment as a whole impacts the outcomes of inclusive education.

The research study was conducted in inclusive schools which provide education to children with disabilities. The focus of the study was to elucidate the process of the delivering inclusive education, ascertain the factors promoting inclusive education, determine the challenges and examine the outcomes of inclusive education for children with disabilities. The main stakeholders of educating children with disabilities in inclusive classrooms are the children with disabilities, their families, their typically developing peers in the classrooms, the teachers and the school. The characteristics of these stakeholders would affect the process of inclusive education and the final outcomes. A few of these characteristics might promote inclusive education while others may act as a challenge, for instance positive attitude of the teachers towards children with disabilities might promote inclusion and would have positive outcomes for children with disabilities as well and *vice versa.* Student characteristics are of critical importance to the process of inclusion. A study by Singal (2006) highlighted that the Principals of inclusive schools in Delhi garnered a perception that there were "socially accepted" categories of disabilities like, "blindness", "physical problems" and "mild learning disabilities" are more likely to be included than others. The access and retention in inclusive educational system is affected by factors at all levels of inputs: student, school, family/community and national.

At the school level, there are three major intertwined dimensions of the educational experience, namely school cultures, policies and practices (see Booth & Ainscow, 2002). In the family, the most influential are socio-economic and cultural factors: family economic survival needs, traditional societal attitudes towards disability that may involve shame, guilt, under-expectations, and sheltering/ patronization. These factors often combine with distance to school, mobility, school-building accessibility, discrimination, shortage of trained teachers and resource supports to address teachers' working conditions, and shortage of school resources. A UNESCO report (2001) stated that many parents believe that the irrelevance of the curriculum was one of the reasons for not sending the children to school. "They feel the curriculum is not geared to real life, and fruitful years of income generation will be lost even if the child receives only a primary education." Thus, curriculum development was seen as an important input to the inclusive education.

The teacher characteristics also impact an inclusive set-up to a large extent. There have been many studies which have focused on attitudes of teachers towards inclusive education. Another area of research in inclusive education is the teacher training programmes and their efficacy in dealing with diversity within classrooms. The Teacher Development Initiative in India noted that the gravest concern towards execution of the project was the "attitude of the administrators who have insufficient time and patience to learn and understand its [the programme's] objective (Jangira and Ahuja, 1994:38).

The educational outcomes for children with disabilities in India have remained poor. The illiteracy rates for children with disabilities have remained much higher than general population and school attendance is much lower in comparison to non-disabled children (World Bank, 2007). The outcomes of the process of inclusive education are difficult to measure. The student achievement and academic performance are one indicator may or may not been linked to success in adult life. Thus, the outcomes will be looked at cumulatively for looking at the success of inclusion. Stubbs (1993) suggested that IE programmes look for improvements at all levels: individual, family, community, organization, and government. Specific indicators include: presence, participation, choice, respect, knowledge and skills. Lynch (2001:22) advocated for evaluation of IE programmes at all levels (institutional and teacher performance as well as student performance) and against the goals of inclusion within a democratic, human-rights-based environment.

**Research Questions**

The specification of research questions (i.e., what is to be studied) and research strategy (i.e., how to conduct the study) is an extremely important part of any research project (Yin, 1989:19). Developing the research questions based on our interest and the focus of our research was extremely interesting. The review of literature helped us to formulate our research questions which were relevant to the context and would help in larger goal of knowledge building in the field.

1. What are the components of inclusive education?
2. What are the factors which promote education of children with disabilities in regular educational system?
3. How are the characteristics of the main stakeholders affecting the process of inclusive education?
4. What is the process of inclusive education delivery system?
5. What are the outcomes of educating children with disabilities in regular schools?
6. What are the challenges facing the inclusive educational systems?
7. How these inclusion processes in school could be strengthened?
8. What are the barriers to participation and learning experienced by students?
9. What practices can help to overcome these barriers?
10. To what extent do such practices facilitate improved learning outcomes?
11. How can such practices be encouraged and sustained within schools?

**Objectives**

The research objectives pursued in order to answer the research questions were:

- To study the profile and characteristics of the main stakeholders in education of children with disabilities in regular schools.

- To explore the process of inclusive education.
- To identify the factors which promote education of children with disabilities in regular schools.
- To ascertain the challenges of educating children with disabilities in regular schools.
- To understand the impact of educating children with disabilities in regular schools.
- To suggest ways to strengthen process of inclusion.
- To document an emerging model for educating children with disabilities in regular classrooms.

**Data Sources and Methods**

Qualitative research is inherently multimethod in focus (Brewer & Hunter, 1989). However, the use of multiple methods, or triangulation, reflects an attempt to secure an in-depth understanding of the phenomenon in question. Triangulation is not a tool or a strategy of validation, but an alternative to validation (Denzin, 1989a, 1989b: 244; Fielding & Fielding, 1986: 33; Flick, 1992: 194). The combination of multiple methods, empirical materials, perspectives and observers in a single study is best understood, then, as a strategy that adds rigour, breadth, and depth to any investigation (see Flick, 1992: 194).

Table 3.2 illustrates configured data sources and methods for the major research questions. This was prepared by analyzing each research question against the myriad of available research methods. The ontological and epistemological position of the researchers has guided the choice of the research methods. This qualitative study is based on data from children with disabilities in private inclusive schools in Mumbai, India. We employed the case study method as it allows an intensive study (Shepard, 2003) within its real-life context of children with disabilities. It provides an in-depth and systematic way of looking at events and helps in gaining a sharpened understanding of causality and provides a sound base for extensive exploration in future research (Bent, 2006). A total of ten in-depth interviews were conducted from seven inclusive schools in Mumbai. The interviews related to children's perceptions and experiences regarding themselves and their placement in regular educational

**Table 3.2:** Data Sources and Methods

| *Research Questions* | *Data Sources and Methods* | *Justification* |
|---|---|---|
| What are the components of inclusive education? | In-depth Interviews with *Regular Teachers, Resource Teachers, Principal/Head of the School*<br>Secondary data analysis like literature on curriculum, pedagogy of schools. | Assuming that it is important to gather information from people who have the responsibility to implement inclusion. The researcher contends that their experience and insight is vital in shaping future educational trends for all students.<br><br>Interviews with teachers who are the main agents of inclusion would provide their accounts of how they had been handling inclusion/ integration of children with disabilities in classrooms.<br><br>Interviews with children with disabilities and their typically developing peers would reveal their experiences and learning in inclusive/integrated settings and how they negotiate these inclusion experiences.<br><br>Interviews of families of children with disabilities would help the researchers to know about their accounts, reported experiences about the inclusion process. |
| What are the factors which promote education of children with disabilities in regular educational system? | In-depth Interviews with *Regular Teachers, Resource Teachers, Children with disabilities, Typically developing children, Parents* | |
| What is the process of inclusive education delivery system? | In-depth Interviews with the *Principal, Regular Teachers, Resource Teachers* | |
| What are the outcomes of educating children with disabilities in regular schools? | In-depth Interviews with the *Regular Teachers, Resource Teachers, Children with disabilities, their peers, Parents*<br>Observation in Classrooms | |
| What are the challenges facing the inclusive educational systems? | In-depth Interviews with the *Regular Teachers, Resource Teachers, Children with disabilities, their peers, Parents*<br>Observation in Classrooms | |
| How these inclusion processes in school could be strengthened? | In-depth Interviews with the *Regular Teachers, Resource Teachers, Children with disabilities, their peers, Parents, teacher trainees*<br>Focus group Discussions with the Regular teachers, teacher trainees and resource teachers | |

settings were noted down. The interviews were audio-taped and later transcribed for analysis. Many researchers have subscribed to audio-taping of interviews in order to avoid bias (Borg & Gall, 1989; Silverman, 1995). Borg and Gall (1989) suggested that it could prevent unconscious selection of text favouring the bias of the researcher. In this research it particularly helped as the interview span with children lasted more than an hour in most cases and the questions related to the research were interspersed with lot of other information sharing. Children often got distracted if the researcher resorted to note-taking.

The indepth-interviews were also conducted with the Principals, Regular and Resource teachers and the Parents of the children with disabilities. The interview guides for each of the group helped in intensive probing of the related issues. The concerns raised with the Principals included—What are the basic requirements for an inclusive school, how do the admissions criteria reflect the needs, attributes and diversity of potential students? In what way the school is different from other schools, what were the support systems available for children with disabilities etc.? The principals provided information on logistics and administrative issues in an inclusive school. The process related information was mainly sought from the regular and resource teachers. The questions mainly pertained to the process of teaching, collaboration between resource and regular teachers, challenges the teachers face in dealing with children with disabilities and the advantages of having 'all' children in the classroom. The parents essentially highlighted their role and participation in inclusive schools, the challenges they face in education their children in inclusive schools and the advantages they perceive in such schools.

The other methods which were employed were Focus Groups Discussions (FGDs) with the regular and teacher trainees. The FGDs conducted with the teacher trainees of a special three-year BA in Integrated Education programme for understanding their perceptions on inclusive education and their anticipatory feelings about support and challenges in the field. The other themes which were explored were motivation to join the course, their role as integrated teachers, curriculum and reflections about the course. The focus group discussions with the regular teachers encompassed the components of inclusive education, perceived barriers and supports within the school setting, suggestions for overcoming the barriers and what practices could strengthen the process of inclusion.

The FGDs normally lasted for about an hour and there were around 8-10 participants. The FGDs were utilised for exploring the depth and nuances of opinions regarding the issue of inclusive education and understanding differences in perspectives. Apart from this Observation in classrooms where we assumed the role of complete observer; we were detached and passively recorded behaviour from a distance. Certain observations which were recorded were pedagogy, meeting of physical needs, seating arrangement and place allotted to the child, child's participation and teacher's efforts to involve the child.

**Sampling Strategy**

The interviews were conducted in seven inclusive schools using theoretical sampling. All these seven schools were private where there was a requirement of monthly fees along with subsidiary expenses on uniforms, books, school activities and transport. They were all mainstream schools with a Resource unit with at least one Resource teacher within campus to assist the children with disabilities. The schools were implementing the "Resource Room Model". Smith *et al.* (1993) define 'resource room model' as one where the children with disabilities attend resource room for special assistance in deficit areas and spend the rest of the day in general classrooms with their non-disabled peers.

"As no definition of inclusive education exists in India"(Singal, 2006), thus the seven schools were chosen based on information from key informants and practitioners/NGOs. Those inclusive schools which had at least five children with disabilities on roll were selected for this study. The idea behind this inclusion criterion was to have children with different disabilities being catered to by the school. For instance, a school with one child with a locomotor disability would only be dealing with the mobility issues and may/may not have other resources like a resource room or therapy room etc. Another assumption which guided this was that the number of children with disabilities would be scattered in different grades bringing to light issues related to particular classrooms like variation in curriculum, teaching strategies etc. A number larger than five was being too optimistic as the concept is still new and in its earlier stages of implementation. This also helped in further selection of the students taking into account refusal and non-response. A preliminary enquiry with the schools on the list suggested that none of the state administered inclusive schools in Mumbai had at least 5 children with disabilities hence all seven schools in our study were private schools.

This study was conducted among private schools offering inclusive education, hence the children belonged to high-income families who were able to pay (on an average Rs. 12000 per annum) for the education of their children. These private schools have monthly fees which makes it inaccessible to few sections of the society, only sometimes a few 'bright' children are admitted to these schools as a charitable gesture (Singal and Rouse, 2003). For purposes of confidentiality, since the number of children with disabilities in each of the selected schools is very small, the names of the schools have not been disclosed.

Additional information pertaining to the child's participation was secured from interviews with principals of the seven schools, twenty regular teachers, twelve resource teachers and fifteen of their non-disabled peers. The principal of the school had communicated to the teachers the purpose of our visits to schools and seeking information from them through an internal circular. The researcher had to resort to convenient sampling for the regular teachers. The researcher used to spend time in the 'staff room' and those teachers who visited the place during that time and showed willingness to share their experiences were included. Most of the regular teachers agreed for the interview except a couple of teachers who did not wish to compromise on their free time. Out of the seven schools, six had only one resource teacher and they were all included in the study. One school had nine resource teachers and six out of those shared their concerns. The fifteen non-disabled peers were identified by the children themselves as their 'good friends' so the researcher explored their attitudes towards their peers with disability.

As teacher training emerged to be an important concept, a perspective from the teacher trainees on the developing field of inclusive education appeared imperative to the research. We, therefore, purposefully organised FGDs with the teacher trainees of the B.A. in Integrated Education, a three-year course. As it is one of few integrated courses run for teacher trainees, it was included in the sample to analyse the inputs given to teachers for handling diversity in classrooms.

## Data Collection and Analysis

Data was gathered through in-depth interviewing, observation in classrooms and focus group discussions guided by the research objectives. While observation and interviews were conducted hand-in-hand; the observations were carried out in the classrooms and the interviews with teachers were conducted in the staff room based on teacher's availability. FGDs were conducted at a time and place suggested by the participants. Considerable time was spent on rapport building to make the children feel less pressured. A tape recorder was used with consent and only if the child and other interviewees felt comfortable. The data was collected from July to December 2008 where we spent approximately fifteen working days with each school. The interviews were conducted with the help of an interview guide that contained the list of issues and probes were included wherever considered essential. The questions intended to gain an understanding of how these students viewed their physical, social and psychological self, their abilities, class placement, the legitimacy of inclusive education, and the extent to which they regarded themselves as part of the wide school and community culture and felt accepted by their classmates, friends and teachers. There were two children who had problems with communication (Sania and Tanmay) and therefore, the interviews were conducted using mothers as proxies. However, the children were present when the interview was conducted. The mothers sporadically made efforts to explain and seek information from the children. There was indeed a concern whether the proxy responses had adequately reflected the views of the children. Though it may be considered as a limitation to the study but there were no better alternatives. As Stancliffe (1999) also stated that a well-informed guess is desirable in cases where the person is unable to communicate his/her own views.

Before each interview, the purpose of the study was explained to the prospective participants. It was also made clear to all participants that there would be no consequences to their schooling or in any other way by not participating, that there was no compulsion to participate and accordingly consent was obtained from both the children and their parents before conducting the interviews. The interviews were conducted in English and Hindi depending on the understanding of the respondents. The interviews conducted in Hindi were later translated by the researchers.

The permissions from the Principals of the schools were obtained with relative ease. However, identifying the children and procuring informed consent from their parents was time consuming and cumbersome. The parents were apprehensive about the interviews, anticipating the resultant reiteration of the fact that the child had a disability and any negative impact of the questions related to child's disability. We had sent request letters to thirty parents through their children, twelve of them returned the consent forms with regret note. Ten parents sought clarifications through phone and personal meetings. Eight of them did not respond at all. Thus, the sample comprised children and parents who showed interest in the research and provided written consent to be interviewed in the school.

This study focuses on two key areas: (i) the child's understanding of self and (ii) children's comprehensive experience of inclusive environment. Both areas govern their participation in inclusive schools and the development of their individuality, and the process of inclusive education delivery system. The perspectives of the teacher trainees and practitioners in the field were also incorporated to enrich the data. The data obtained from multiple sources was combined to prepare case studies. Cross-case comparisons resulted in common themes. Atlas-ti (qualitative data analysis software) was used for analysis.

All interview transcripts were analysed to identify emerging themes and on what Miller (2000) (quoted in Welsh, 2002) terms as 'organising' the data, which was done by coding the text and breaking it down into more manageable texts. A code-book which included a detailed description of each code, inclusion and exclusion criteria (MacQueen *et al.*, 1998) was maintained and used actively. In a few cases examplers of real text for each theme have been shared for better understanding. For the observation data, the field notes were scrutinized for recurring themes and were matched with those themes emerging from the interviews. The data generated from FGDs was analysed to identify key themes that emerged from the discussion. Where possible, quotes that represent key points have been provided to illustrate meaning. Then the themes were connected to existing theories to evolve a model of inclusive education in India.

During the process of analysis, the main themes which emerged coincided with the earlier conceptualisation. The findings are discussed within the theme of support systems within inclusive schools, the challenges faced by the children with disabilities, the process of inclusive education and the outcomes of educating children with disabilities in inclusive schools. The themes are not exclusive of each other and there are areas of overlap. However, each segment has brought out significant findings which were integrated in the final chapter.

**Research Context**

The Mumbai Metropolitan Region as defined by the Mumbai Metropolitan Region Development Authority Act, 1974, covers full Districts of Mumbai City and Mumbai Suburbs and part of the Districts of Thane and Raigad. It is a highly urbanised area with 13 Municipal Councils, 7 Municipal Corporations and a few non-municipal towns. In addition, there are more than 900 villages in this region. Considerable changes in the growth and distribution of population and employment are observed in the region over the last couple of decades. The literacy rate for both male and female is increasing in Greater Mumbai since 1981. The proportion of the literate population in the total population, which was 68.16 per cent in 1981 has increased to 77.45 per cent in 2001.

In Mumbai the education system has different levels managed by different institutions. While secondary and higher education are under the purview of the institution supported by State Government, Central Government as well as private institutions, provision of primary education is largely under the Municipal Corporation of Greater Mumbai (MCGM). However, this responsibility is shared by private institutions as well.

The primary education system of Mumbai Municipal Corporation is the largest urban primary education system in Asia. There are more than 4.85 lakhs children who receive education in 8 mediums of instruction: English, Marathi, Hindi, Gujrati, Kannada, Tamil, Telugu and Urdu. The MCGM has recognised 1069 private schools for imparting primary and secondary education to the students. Out of these 438 schools are given aid by the MCGM and 631 schools are unaided (see Table 3.3).

The share of children with disabilities in enrolment ratio is 1 per cent of the total enrolment in India. There are about 1.62 million children with disabilities enrolled in elementary classes (Std I-VIII) across the country of which 1.24 million are in Primary and 0.38 million are in Upper primary classes (Mehta, 2007). As regards nature of disability about 21 per cent are visually challenged, 10 per cent have hearing impairments, 12 per cent have speech impairments, 17 per cent are mentally challenged and 12 per cent have other disabilities (*ibid*).

In Maharashtra (whose capital is Mumbai), there are 600 special schools which are exclusively for children with various types of disabilities (UNICEF, 2003). This study however targeted private schools, thus it would be imperative to understand the types of private schools in India and their numbers in Maharashtra. The main types are: 'private unaided' schools which means that the schools are privately owned and funded and rely on user finance to quite an extent and 'private aided schools' which means that the schools which are largely funded by the government (90-95%) but their management is

**Table 3.3:** Number and Types of Schools in Mumbai

| *No.* | *Type of School* | *No. of Schools* |
|---|---|---|
| 1. | Municipal Primary School | 1092 |
| 2. | Municipal Secondary School | 49 |
| 3. | Municipal Unaided Secondary School | 120 |
| 4. | Mumbai Public School | 65 |
| 5. | Mentally Challenged School (M.R.) | 09 |
| 6. | Total Municipal Schools | 1335 |
| 7. | Private Aided Schools | 438 |
| 8. | Private unaided Schools | 631 |

*Source*: Office of Education Officer (2009).

private (De *et al.* 2002). In Maharashtra, the private aided (primary and secondary) schools are about 5218 and private unaided are approximately 4220 (MHRD, 2009).

The Non-Governmental Organisations also (NGOs) play an active role in the provision of services for people with disabilities. They have been involved in the field of educating children with disabilities since early 1950s, particularly in urban areas. The NGOs are supported by the government through various grants. In the 1970s and 1980s, there was an increase in the number of NGOs in India (UNICEF, 2003). Some of these NGOs are making consistent efforts towards including children with disabilities into regular educational settings. In Mumbai, some NGOs partner with regular schools to enable them to become inclusive.

This study was conducted in private inclusive schools of Mumbai, which is India's financial capital. It covers an area of 437.71 sq. km. (MCGM, 2009) and houses about 11.9 million people (Census, 2001). There are approximately 2110 primary schools and around 1224 secondary schools in Mumbai (Government of Maharashtra website). According to the Office of Education Officer, Mumbai (2009) there are 1096 schools out of which 631 are unaided and 4384 are aided. Out of children with disabilities enrolled in schools, majority are being educated in special schools (UNICEF, 2003). The special schools are concentrated more in the urban areas, with Mumbai having the highest number of special schools (Mukhopadhyay and Mani, 2002). The children in this study represent the very select group of children with disabilities who have attempted to transit from segregation to inclusion. These children with disabilities are among a minority who have secured admission to 'private inclusive school' and are being educated alongside their non-disabled peers. Mukhopadhyay (2003) reported that the private schools which are voluntarily providing inclusive education are mostly located in urban areas. There has been an expansive growth of private schools in the country due to the fact that government schooling has not been able to provide quality education (Nambissan 2003, Singal & Rouse, 2003).

This study was conducted among seven private schools in Mumbai which are providing 'inclusive education'. The practical demarcation between an 'integrated school' and 'inclusive school' is indeed subjective. The labelling of the so called inclusive schools has been done by the key practitioners in the field and their viewpoint was considered while selecting the schools.

## Demographics

This section would elucidate the essential demographics of the schools and research participants. The subsequent tables enlist the characteristics of schools, regular teachers, resource teachers, children with disabilities and mothers. Significantly, all the principals, regular teachers and resource teachers were females. Even the families of children with disabilities were represented by the mothers.

### *Introducing the Schools*

Table 3.4 illustrates the characteristics of the included schools. All the schools were private-unaided schools and were catering to children from the middle-income and high-income families. All the schools had the outlined infrastructure: resource room, resource teacher, library, playground, computer room and accessible toilets. Four out of the seven schools had elevators to support children with mobility problems, two schools made arrangements for conducting classes on the ground floor and one school did not admit children with mobility problems. On a similar trail two out of seven schools did not admit children with visual impairments and three schools did not admit children with hearing impairments. All the schools did not admit children with 'severe disabilities' and the decision on the 'severity' were made by the management, primarily the Principal. The schools do not give any fee concessions to the children with disabilities.

*School 1* is an independent co-educational ICSE day school, and is managed by a Educational Trust. It was conceived out of a realization for the need of an educational institution that would tap the innate intellectual curiosity of the child and channelize this sense of exploration to bring about an all round development. Since its inception in the year 2000, the school has blossomed from strength of 54 students to almost 640 students at present. The school nurtures an inclusive policy from the beginning. Each class from Nursery to Grade X comprises not more than 26 students. The school follows the ICSE curriculum.

**Table 3.4:** Characteristics of the Schools

| *School Code* | *Total Number of Students* | *No. of Children with Disabilities* | *No. of Regular Teachers* | *No. of Resource Teachers* | *Average Classroom Strength* | *'Disabilities' not Eligible for Admission* | *Fee Structure (Per Annum)* |
|---|---|---|---|---|---|---|---|
| School 1 | 700 | 30 | 45 | 09 | 28 | Blindness | Rs. 40,000 |
| School 2 | 1800 | 15 | 40 | 01 | 45 | Mobility problems | Rs. 24,000 |
| School 3 | 800 | 07 | 35 | 01 | 35 | — | Rs. 12,000 |
| School 4 | 1400 | 08 | 45 | 01 | 32 | — | Rs. 45,000 |
| School 5 | 1850 | 09 | 70 | 01 | 35 | Hearing impairment | Rs. 36,000 |
| School 6 | 1700 | 11 | 33 | 01 | 60 | Visual impairment | Rs. 15,000 |
| School 7 | 2200 | 10 | 36 | 01 | 35 | Hearing impairments | Rs. 30,000 |

*School 2* offers classes from Pre-primary to X grade. The aim of the school is to help the children to develop physically, spiritually and mentally. The school was established in 1985 by a Trust. The school is open to enrolling children with disabilities but cannot cater to children with mobility problem due to the unfriendly architecture. The school owns a resource room and has recruited a special educator to help children with disabilities. The school is affiliated to CBSE.

*School 3* was established in 1997 and is affiliated to the ICSE. The school provides education up to grade VIII. The school believes in dealing with students on an individual level. Therefore, special attention in the form of Remedial teaching is offered to students, who find it difficult to adjust to instructions in the classroom. The purpose behind this effort is to bring students who need individual assistance up to speed, and reinstating them back to their classroom. Counselling on the other hand, is open to not just students and teachers, but also to the parents of the school who have difficulties in understanding and resolving problems. The school Counsellor conducts regular meetings where teachers are encouraged to reflect on issues related to areas of work and interpersonal relationships, and resolve them. Parents are also encouraged to actively participate in their child's mental development.

*School 4* was established in the year 2000 and is managed by an Educational Trust. The school aims at creating a dynamic and interactive learning environment where lasting love for learning outside the school curriculum is cultivated. The school runs two parallel Boards—ICSE and Cambridge. It caters to around 1400 students and has average class strength of 32.

*School 5* is managed by a National Educational Society which has 127 schools under its management. The school started its service in 2001 and follows the CBSE curriculum. The school follows an inclusive policy since its inception and has adequate infrastructure to support enrolment of children with disabilities.

*School 6* is a 27 year old school established by the priest affiliated to the ICSE. The school believes in inclusive education and encourages admission of children with disabilities. The school has a resource room with special educators to help the children. The school fosters a culture of promoting extracurricular activities and own a playground and swimming pool.

*School 7* was started in 1967. It is affiliated to ICSE stream. The school recognizes the potential and uniqueness of each child and are committed to prepare them for their life ahead. Their approach is holistic and builds skills, values and self-reliance. The school has a range of extracurricular activities.

### *Introducing the Children*

Table 3.5 lays out the characteristics of the children with disabilities included in the research. The age group of the children was 7-15 years. The chronological ages of the children are not reflective of the grades in which the children studied because three out of the ten children have repeated their classes. We have specifically chosen to mention the 'impairment' rather than 'disability' in keeping with the social model of disability. In India, the 'disability' classification is laid out in Persons with Disabilities Act, 1995, which outlines seven kinds of 'disabilities', namely blindness, low vision, hearing impairment, locomotor, leprosy cured, mental illness and mental retardation. In this research, however, the category of mental retardation has been expanded to include learning disabilities (F81), Attention Deficit Hyperactivity Disorder (F84.4), Asperger's Syndrome (F84.5) Language and Communication Disorder (F80), and Slow Learner (F70) (The figures in the brackets indicate the ICD-10 codes). This is according to the International Classification of Diseases 10 (ICD 10) for Mental Retardation classifications of World Health Organisation and the fact that children with these special needs are categorized as 'disabled' and have the choice of either inclusive schools, regular schools or schools exclusively for children with disabilities. Children with disabilities comprise a heterogeneous group and the disabilities included in the research paper are not exhaustive. There is however a need to clarify our position; the findings relate to children with disabilities in general. The focus of the research is 'children with disabilities' and not the unique nature of their impairment. We believe that though the nature and severity of impairment could cause specific experiences and challenges, it must not overshadow the philosophy of inclusion which promotes equal opportunities to all learners. A brief case history of every child is presented for reference and understanding.

**Table 3.5:** Characteristics of the Children with Disabilities

| *Name** | *Sex* | *School Code* | *Age* | *Grade* | *Impairment* |
|---|---|---|---|---|---|
| Sania | Female | School 1 | 7 | II | Language and Communication disorder |
| Ishita | Female | School 1 | 9 | IV | Learning Disability |
| Aakash | Male | School 2 | 10 | IV | Asperger's Syndrome |
| Soham | Male | School 2 | 10 | IV | Slow learner |
| Nikhil | Male | School3 | 11 | V | Spina Bifida |
| Gaurav | Male | School 4 | 13 | VII | Attention Deficit Hyperactivity Disorder |
| Rakhi | Female | School 5 | 13 | IV | Spina Bifida |
| Tanmay | Male | School 6 | 13 | VII | Hearing Impairment |
| Simran | Female | School 6 | 15 | VIII | Visually Challenged |
| Harshit | Male | School 7 | 15 | VIII | Cerebral Palsy |

*Sania* is in Grade II of an inclusive school. She has language and communication disorder. She goes for her remedial class during school hours. She has a 4 months old brother. Her language disability began to surface when she joined school. Her mother used to worry when she did not speak words even when she was three. When she was admitted to the pre-primary classes, she started manifesting the problems. Her teacher always complained that she was not paying attention in the classes and would not understand simple instructions, like falling in line, getting water for herself or taking out notebooks. The school referred her to the psychologist for assessments. It was very distressing for the family to come to terms with the disease. The mother especially was disturbed after her diagnosis. Sania was born with a congenital hip dislocation. She underwent surgery for hip correction and had to remain in the hospital for many days. For this reason she dreads going to the hospital even after so many years for her surgery. The family attributed her delay in speech and language to this till she started going to school and started displaying more serious problems.

*Ishita* studies in Grade IV of an inclusive school. Ishita started manifesting learning problems in school. She has problems with the reading and writing. She is a shy girl and does not talk to anyone in the class. She goes for her remedial classes during her library and games period. She enjoys a good rapport with the resource teacher.

*Aakash* studies in class IV of an inclusive school. His twin brother, Vikas is also in the same grade in the school. Aakash has Asperger's Syndrome and he was diagnosed when he was in Grade II. His parents got worried when they began noticing his unusual behaviours in social situations. His behaviour was very awkward many a times. He would not be able to understand the non-verbal behaviours and complicated language. He would bear some strange expressions on his face. No one actually wanted to be his friend not even his brother. Vikas found him very selfish and annoying and would not like playing with him. Even when the interview was conducted, the brothers were not too close either at home or at school. They have different sets of friends at school and in the neighbourhood.

*Soham* studies in Grade IV of an inclusive school. He has been diagnosed as a slow learner in Grade II. Since then, he has been attending remedial classes in the same school. He is the only child of his parents. Soham attended a different regular school earlier where the teacher would always complain about Soham. In the previous school Soham did not fare well in studies. There were constant complaints from the teacher often in presence of other children and parents which was embarrassing for the parents. His mother then decided to change his school. He was admitted in the present school in Standard II. He needs help in completing his work. His comprehension is poor. He does not understand the question if it is twisted a bit also. However, the child is articulate and extrovert.

*Nikhil* studies in Class VIII of an 'inclusive' school. He has Spina Bifida and uses a wheelchair. The attendant (personal driver) stays in school to help him to commute between floors. Sometimes his peers help him with his wheelchair (they get to ride a lift in that case as told by one of his classmate). A couple of years ago he studied in a different school. He was compelled to leave the school when he reached the seventh standard. The classroom allotted to Standard VII was on the top floor and that building did not have a lift; it meant that the classroom was inaccessible to Nikhil. The student has problems with fine motor skills and therefore, is unable to take his own notes and therefore, borrows notebooks of his friends for photocopying.

*Gaurav* studies in Grade VII of an inclusive school. He had been diagnosed with Attention Deficit Hyperactivity Disorder (ADHD) when he was in Grade IV in the same school. The reported incidents of violence and aggression against his classmates made the parents think about the problem. Gaurav was subsequently taken to a Psychiatrist and was started on medications. The medications have to be administered daily and at school they are managed by the Resource teacher. Despite his regular medications sometimes he manifests some problem behaviours in the classroom. Due to some of his violent behaviours, some parents of the non-disabled children have questioned the authorities on Gaurav's admission status. The school has warned his parents that if Gaurav's behaviour does not show an improvement by the end of this term, they will expel him from school.

*Rakhi* studies in Standard IV of an inclusive school. The school staff and students have welcomed a student with Spina Bifida Meningomyocele. Rakhi has been attending this school for the past three years. Earlier she was attending another regular school, with very little support from the school authorities. She was expelled after she failed class II. The present school was optimistic about her inclusion and offered admission to Rakhi. The school where Rakhi is studying though is an 'inclusive' school there are not many children with disabilities. Even if there were a few, Rakhi's disability stands out conspicuously. She has to attend remedial classes on a regular basis.

*Tanmay* has a hearing impairment and had a cochlear implant. He has been challenge to the school authorities since he joined this school's pre-primary classes. He is presently in VII standard, his tenure in this school is now of 9 years. His successful inclusion is a combined effort of the school authorities, parents and most importantly the child. Tanmay had a congenital hearing impairment and underwent a cochlear implant a year ago when he was in Standard VI. His special teacher in the school had remarked, "Though his communication skills have improved since then, he still has to go a long way in terms of speech and language development".

*Simran* is a visually challenged child studying in Grade VIII of an inclusive school. She is of average intelligence and is very sociable. She has learned braille at a special school especially for the blind which has encouraged her to be independent. Her parents wanted that she should be educated in a regular school and therefore, admitted her to her present school in Grade IV. She is taught by the visiting teacher for the blind at regular intervals and is provided with audio cassettes which contains the learning material. She is provided with a writer in school.

*Harshit* has Cerebral Palsy. He is the only son of his parents. He studied in a special school till class VII till he was integrated in a regular school with efforts of the social worker. He has poor motor co-ordination and his speech is unclear. He however has average intelligence. Though the mother tried hard to send him to a regular school from the beginning, they did not succeed. The special school where Harshit studied was up to grade VII. Many of the students from this special school are integrated in the mainstream. Harshit's mother gives full credit to the special school for helping him secure admission in a regular school. Harshit's father had divorced his mother when he was 2 years of age. Harshit's mother informed that his father was abhorrent to him and wanted to send him away. Harshit is unaware of this fact.

### *Introducing the Teachers*

The characteristics of the regular teachers are presented in Table 3.6. It is important to mention that these teachers have not necessarily taught the children with disabilities included in the study. The sample is drawn from the included schools and the criterion was that they have children with disabilities in their classes. However, care was taken to include at least one teacher from each school and those who have taught the children included in the study. Their responses are therefore both generic and specific. Five out of the twenty regular teachers were untrained and the rest had undergone some formal training. Only one of the twenty teachers was trained in Integrated Education which equips the teachers to handle all kinds of learners in the classroom and has several comprehensive modules on disability.

Table 3.7 lists the characteristics of the resource teachers which were included in the study. They all had training in special education and were managing the resource rooms. Many of the teachers had a previous experience in special schools.

### Introducing the Mothers

Table 3.8 highlights the characteristics of the mothers of the children with disabilities. The children belonged to middle to high income families with an average monthly income Rs. 37,000. Mostly the mothers were housewives; some of them even mentioned about giving up their job in order to help their children in home and school.

This chapter was a prelude to the findings of the research under four themes; support systems, challenges, process and outcomes of inclusive education. The characteristics of the research participants would provide a background to the information that will be presented in subsequent chapter and help in interpreting the findings.

**Table 3.6:** Characteristics of the Regular Teachers

| *Name** | *Sex* | *Years of Expe-rience (in years)* | *School Code* | *Grade Taught* | *Subjects taught* | *Training* |
|---|---|---|---|---|---|---|
| Raina | Female | 2 | School 1 | Primary | English, Geography | BEd |
| Navneet | Female | 3 | School 1 | Primary | History and Computer Science | Untrained |
| Carol | Female | 1 | School 1 | VI, VII and VIII | Maths | Untrained |
| Gauhar | Female | 2 | School 1 | IX and X | Business Studies | BEd |
| Smita | Female | 2 | School 2 | Primary | Social Science, Craft | BEd |
| Nausheen | Female | 3 | School 2 | Primary | Maths and Science | BEd |
| Kauveri | Female | 5 | School 2 | VIII, IX and X | Maths and Physics | Untrained |
| Asmita | Female | 6 | School 3 | Primary and VI, VII | Hindi, Marathi | BEd |
| Sonia | Female | 12 | School 3 | IX and X | Science | BEd |
| Susan | Female | 1 | School 3 | Pre-primary | All subjects | ECCEd. |
| Dhara | Female | 3 | School 3 | VI, VII and VIII | History and Geography | DEd |
| Minal | Female | 4 | School 4 | Primary and Junior | Hindi, Marathi | Untrained |
| Kanya | Female | 2 | School 4 | VI, VII and VIII | Social Studies and Maths | BEd |
| Shivangi | Female | 3 | School 5 | III, IV and V | Maths and Science | BEd |

(*Contd.*)

**Table 3.6** (*Contd.*)

| *Name** | *Sex* | *Years of Expe-rience (in years)* | *School Code* | *Grade Taught* | *Subjects taught* | *Training* |
|---|---|---|---|---|---|---|
| Sonal | Female | 6 | School 5 | Primary | English | BEd. |
| Tripti | Female | 4 | School 5 | Primary | Social Studies | Diploma in Integra-ted Education |
| Pooja | Female | 3 | School 6 | Primary | Maths | BEd |
| Neha | Female | 1 | School 6 | Primary and Junior | Science | Untrained |
| Shaleen | Female | 5 | School 7 | Primary | English | BEd |
| Kavita | Female | 1 | School 7 | Primary | Maths | DEd. |

**Table 3.7:** Characteristics of the Resource Teachers

| *Name** | *Sex* | *Years of Experience #* | *School Code* | *Qualification* |
|---|---|---|---|---|
| Roopam | Female | 4 | School 1 | BEd. Special Education |
| Sagarika | Female | 2 | School 1 | BEd. Special Education |
| Shyamlee | Female | 6 | School 1 | BEd. Special Education |
| Geeta | Female | 7 | School 1 | BEd. Special Education |
| Sheetal | Female | 15 | School 1 | BEd. Special Education |
| Gauri | Female | 11 | School 1 | BEd. Special Education |
| Richa | Female | 7 | School 2 | BEd. Special Education |
| Kiara | Female | 6 | School 3 | BEd. Special Education |
| Preeti | Female | 8 | School 4 | BEd. Special Education |
| Fatima | Female | 6 | School 5 | BEd. Special Education |
| Shobha | Female | 4 | School 6 | BEd. Special Education |
| Kanti | Female | 5 | School 7 | BEd. Special Education |

# Not necessarily in the same school.

**Table 3.8:** Characteristics of the Mothers

| *Name and Age of the Mother* | *Child's Name, Gender, Age and Impairment* | *Education* | *Occupation* | *Family Monthly Income (in Rupees)* |
|---|---|---|---|---|
| Pramila | Sania /Female/ 7 yrs/ Language and Communication disorder | MA B.Ed. | Homemaker | 40,000 |
| Ratna | Ishita/ Female/ 9 yrs/ Learning Disability | BA | Homemaker | 35,000 |
| Malabika | Aakash/ Male/ 10 yrs/ Asperger's Syndrome | BSc | Homemaker | 45,000 |
| Uma | Soham/ Male/ 10 yrs/ Slow learner | BA | Homemaker | 30,000 |
| Nilam | Nikhil/ Male/ 11 yrs/ Spina Bifida | MA | Homemaker | 50,000 |
| Somya | Gaurav/ Male/ 13 yrs/ Attention Deficit Hyperactivity Disorder | XII | Homemaker | 25,000 |

*(Contd.)*

**Table 3.8** (*Contd.*)

| *Name and Age of the Mother* | *Child's Name, Gender, Age and Impairment* | *Education* | *Occupation* | *Family Monthly Income (in Rupees)* |
|---|---|---|---|---|
| Vimla | Rakhi/ Female/ 13 yrs/ Spina Bifida | BSc BEd | Lecturer | 30,000 |
| Kanaklatha | Tanmay/ Male/ 13 yrs/ Hearing Impairment | BA | Homemaker | 20,000 |
| Radhika | Simran/Female/ 15 yrs/ Visually Challenged | BA | Teacher | 50,000 |
| Sharmila | Harshit/ Male/ 16 yrs/ Cerebral Palsy | X | Homemaker | 45,000 |

* The names of all research participants have been changed to maintain anonymity.

# 4

# Study Outcomes

## 1 SUPPORT SYSTEMS

There were several supporting factors which helped the child with disability to continue in a regular school. The school has the primary responsibility for helping children learn alongside their typically developing peers. An inclusive school must enable education structures, systems and methodologies to meet the needs of all children, particularly those who face the greatest barriers to achieving their right to education (see also Save the Children, 2006).

Schools today need to be creative and responsive places, where collaboration among teachers leads to effective problem solving, shared learning, and a cooperative, welcoming school environment. Innovative school and classroom practices are required if education is to serve all students, including those with disabilities, in an effective way. Through participation and learning in the general education classroom, students with disabilities will have the opportunity to take their place as contributing citizens of communities.

The inclusive schools which have been included in this study have showed initiative in taking on the challenge. All the seven schools in this study have provided supportive mechanisms for their enrolled students with disabilities. The categories of support which have emerged from the analysis are academic, physical, psychological and parental support in the school (Figure 4.1). We have included the parental support within the school support system as this support was an integral part of the inclusive educational system in all the

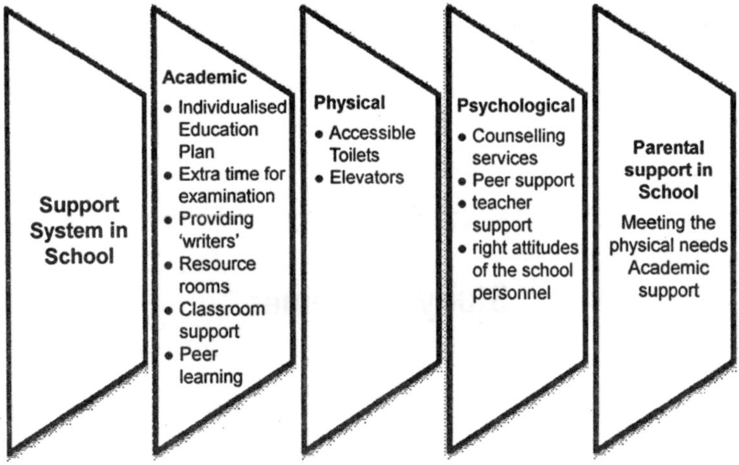


**Fig. 4.1:** Types of Support Systems for Children with Disabilities in Inclusive Schools

inclusive schools. The schools have recognised this support and count on it for maximising the educational experience of children with disabilities studying in the school. All the principals mentioned that the parents had to be involved as they have proved to be the 'best partners' in providing education to their children.

## Academic Support

The concept of 'supports' within classrooms is a particularly critical one and refashions inclusion as "supported education" (Snell and Drake, 1994). They include accommodations and modifications to enhance learning and acceptance in the regular educational system. Table 4.1 enlists the facilities provided by these schools to include children with disabilities. All children included in the study had spent at least two years in the school which suggest that the schools were responsive to their needs and were providing facilities to ensure continuity.

One of the schools (School 1) prepares *'Individualized Education Plan'* (see Appendix 1) for each of its children with disabilities. The illustrated IEP had five components, language and writing skills, number concepts and operations, science, general learning and inclusive activities. This particular IEP was developed for a 'slow

**Table 4.1:** Efforts of Schools to include Children with Disabilities

| *Child* | *Impairment* | *No. of years in inclusive school* | *Facilities provided at School* |
|---|---|---|---|
| Sania | Language and Communication disorder | 4 | Regular remedial classes with the resource teacher |
| Ishita | Learning Disability | 3 | Remedial classes with the resource teacher thrice a week |
| Aakash | Asperger's Syndrome | 5 | Counselling sessions for child and parents |
| Soham | Slow learner | 2 | Remedial classes with the resource teacher, exemption from one language |
| Nikhil | Spina Bifida | 2 | Remedial classes with the resource teacher, Provision of Writer, occasional counselling sessions |
| Gaurav | Attention Deficit Hyperactivity Disorder | 3 | Counselling sessions |
| Rakhi | Spina Bifida | 3 | Remedial classes with resource teachers |
| Tanmay | Hearing Impairment | 7 | Remedial classes with resource teacher, collaborative teaching in mathematics, exemption from one language |
| Simran | Visually Challenged | 2 | Remedial classes with resource teacher, collaborative teaching |
| Harshit | Cerebral Palsy | 5 | Provision of a writer |

learner'. In each of the sections curriculum is laid out in consultation with the Principal, parents and regular teacher by the resource teacher. An IEP is prepared for all children with disabilities studying in the school. The IEP is the blueprint of the curriculum which is followed for the child with disability by the resource teachers. The teaching and evaluations are based on the learning on the child on those defined areas.

The schools make the *'writer'* available to the children who may need their help. The 'writers' were usually children from lower grades who volunteer their services. Most schools had a policy to give *extra time* for children with disabilities to complete their examination.

In most cases the children with disabilities required personnel supports to allow them to benefit from placement in the inclusive settings in addition to instructional supports. All the inclusive schools had a resource room for students with special needs with at least one resource teacher. The research studies by Lingard (1994) and Martson (1996) show that a combination of resource and regular classroom teaching results in improved educational progress for students with mild disabilities. We perceived the 'Resource Rooms' to be the cornerstone of inclusion in private inclusive schools of Mumbai. They were the 'alibis' of inclusion, their presence meant that the school was open to enrol children with disabilities. (Here, we would like to add a word of caution for the audience. This is not a cynical statement; rather it is an observation which may have been affected by the "I" of the researchers). Almost all children need remedial teaching and the schools have made a provision of a resource room.

### *Resource Rooms*

The schools had set aside one room in the school premises which was referred as the 'resource room'. The room was equipped with various teaching aids and was managed by the resource teacher who was trained in special education. It is for the children with disabilities who need some special instruction in an individualized or small group setting for some part of the days.

Apart from one school where there were six resource teachers; rest of the schools had one resource teacher. For six resource teachers the workload was lesser in terms of number of students handled. It was the same school where an Individualized Education Plan (IEP) was prepared for the children with disabilities. Individual needs were supported in resource rooms as defined by the student's IEP. Here the children were handled on one-to-one basis. In the other schools, the students were either handled individually or in small groups depending on the nature of help required.

Many practitioners and researchers have advocated for supporting classroom teachers in integrated and inclusive settings (McLeskey & Waldron, 2002a; Mundschenk, Foley, & Swedburg, 2005; Simpson, de Boer-Ott, & Smith-Myles, 2003; Webber, 2005). All the schools were practicing the Resource Room Model of Inclusion and thus, the role of the resource teacher was of paramount importance. They were seen providing the maximum support in terms of helping the child with disability cope academically, socially and psychologically in inclusive schools.

We have endeavoured to summarize the role of the resource teacher based on the workload handled by them in various schools. Most of the resource teachers in schools are discharging these roles, however, in some schools a few roles were less important or totally absent. A resource teacher assists schools in providing support for children with special educational needs arising from disability by:

(i) Assessing and recording a child's needs and progress or calling for an assessment from a practicing psychologist;
(ii) Setting specific, time-related targets for each child and agreeing these with the regular teacher and principal;
(iii) Direct teaching of the children, either in a separate room or within the mainstream class;
(iv) Advising class teachers in regard to adapting the curriculum, teaching strategies, suitable text-books, use of Information and Technology and suitable software and a range of other related matters;
(vi) Meeting and advising parents, when necessary, accompanied by the class teacher, as necessary; and
(vii) Short meetings with other relevant professionals, in the children's interest—e.g. psychologists, speech and language therapists, visiting teachers, special school or special class teachers.

Resource teachers were mainly responsible to provide the extra support for students with disabilities in inclusive schools. The resource teacher handled the remedial workload, conducted counselling sessions with the child and parents, collaborates with the regular teachers to monitor their progress in class, and takes responsibility of the child during co-curricular activities. Their favourable attitude towards the children was evident during personal conversation with the researchers. All the children and their parents reported that the resource teacher would go the extra mile to make the child feel a part of the regular school. Almost all the children mentioned their resource teacher's name as their favourite teacher in school.

> *The resource teacher is very good, she takes lot of pains with Sania and keeps me informed of her progress. She even shares the board games she uses with her in school to be played at home. She is trying very hard for her to pick up the language (Pramila, Sania's mother)*

> *Rakhi has to attend remedial classes on a regular basis. She is very friendly with the resource teacher. The resource teacher ensures that Rakhi completes her class work on time and prepares her for the exams. The resource teacher works in collaboration with the regular teachers and updates on Rakhi's progress on a weekly basis. I am allowed to come to the school and have regular interactions with the resource and the regular teachers. She personally knows Rakhi's friends and she even persuades them to help Rakhi in classroom (Vimla, Rakhi's mother).*

> *I do not think Soham could have continued in the school if the Resource teacher was not there. Her made a great difference to Soham's life. She teaches, counsels, and plays with him. Soham thoroughly enjoys his remedial sessions and sometimes ask me why the other teachers are not like her (Uma, Soham's mother).*

The resource rooms of various schools were closely observed for the support they provided to the students with disabilities and it is

**Table 4.2:** School-wise Description of Resource Rooms

| | *General description* | *Consistency of help* | *Use of Teaching Aids* | *Provides opportunities to practice learning* | *Number of students handled per session* |
|---|---|---|---|---|---|
| School 1 | Small with L-shaped wooden plank and chairs. | Generally twice in a week, in some cases once | Depending on each child. More usage for abstract concepts | It is only a 40 minute session. Mothers are instructed for home teaching and practice. | One |
| School 2 | Fairly big room with tables and chairs. Cupboards for storage of teaching aids | Once in a week, sometimes 'zero periods' utilized for extra teaching | There is extensive use of charts, board games, mathematical games etc. | The classes and practice sessions are alternate. | Three-four |
| School 3 | Huge room decorated with charts. Table and chairs and also ground seating arrangement | Twice a week the remedial sessions are scheduled | Lot of teaching aids, computer and video-viewing arrangements | Recapitulation at the beginning. Home practice is advocated | Two from different grades |
| School 4 | Big room, ventilated housing the counsellor and the resource teacher | Once a week, twice for children in junior classes | Sand tray, board games, mathematical games, computer – lot of language training through interactive websites | Lot of practice activities is given. Home practice is also encouraged if the parents are interested. | Depending upon schedule; generally one at a time sometimes two or three |

(*Contd.*)

**Table 4.2** (*Contd.*)

| | *General description* | *Consistency of help* | *Use of Teaching Aids* | *Provides opportunities to practice learning* | *Number of students handled per session* |
|---|---|---|---|---|---|
| School 5 | Huge room, lighted and ventilated with table and chairs and mats. | Once a week | A lot of teaching aids, computer with interactive learning software | Lot of practice is provided during the year. Some sessions are only practice sessions | Three |
| School 6 | Small room with circular tables and mats | Once a week | Some teaching aids; most of them handmade by the resource teacher | Practice is an integral part of teaching and learning. Planned differently for each child. | One |
| School 7 | Small room | Once a week | Some teaching aids and games | Practice is simultaneous | One or two |

summarized in Table 4.2. All the schools have allocated rooms in the school premises which are called the resource rooms. The resource rooms of the schools were variedly equipped and all had some necessary teaching aids. Some of the schools encourage interactive learning through computers.

> *The internet is a storehouse of teaching material. Whenever I am free, I devote time to surf and download materials for my students with different needs. It gives me immense satisfaction when my strategy works with my students (Fatima, Resource teacher, School 5).*

> *Nikhil simply loves computer activity. He really enjoys learning on computer (Kiara, Resource teacher, School 3).*

Thus, maintaining resource rooms for children with disabilities emerged to be an important support that the schools were providing. Their presence in all the included school was indicative that it was a common belief that resource rooms with a resource teacher were essential component of an 'inclusive school' in the given context. Also the mothers of children with disabilities perceived it as an important support for their children.

### *Classroom Support*

This dimension relates to the rules, regulations and procedures that operate in the classroom. The 'home teacher' (in some schools called the 'class teacher') had established ground rules for the class and sporadically confirms that the students understand the rules and procedures developed for the classroom. For instance, it is for Tanmay that the students have been allowed to leave their seats to get his attention or assist him with the classroom activity. The teacher assigns a hearing peer to Tanmay through the week for assisting him with the classroom related work.

For Rakhi, the teacher's role was also to help her make connections with other students. The school believes that it was extremely important to give Rakhi an opportunity to learn things on his own, without the constant "shadowing" of a teacher/a particular friend. Her teachers and peers must always remain in the background, helping her with the class tasks. The peers were made responsible for helping Rakhi organize her homework and assignments, and to involve her in the group learning activities. Tests were written during class time as usual, but if Rakhi needed additional time, the peers from the lower classes would assist by offering their help as writers.

Such *support network of non-disabled peers* in the school is referred as the 'buddy system'. The 'buddy system' is quite popular in three of the schools where the non-disabled children are supposed to help the children with disabilities in the classroom and outdoor situations. The most striking feature of the 'buddy system' is the role of the teacher (regular or sometimes resource) in setting up a circle of friends or buddies to provide support.

> *The present school is quite different from the previous one. Here the students share their notebooks with me. I have a problem with fine motor skills and therefore, do not have legible handwriting. My friends lend their books for Xeroxing and later my mother helps me to complete his class and home work. One of my classmates is asked to help with my regular tasks. They help me to borrow books, take out books from my bag and sometimes even take me to computer class which is downstairs (Nikhil explaining 'buddy system').*

> *'Buddy system' ensures a particular kind of help needed by the child would be taken care of by his/her friends. The non-disabled children many a times do not consistently take responsibilities. We have seen that when we assign a 'buddy', the response is ensured (Principal, School 1).*

Some regular teachers were seen providing one to one attention to all the students in the class. This was mainly observed in schools where the average class strength was less (School 1, School 3, School 5 and School 7), indicating that the lesser number of children in classrooms facilitated the process of learning to a great extent. They ensure that the entire class participates in the classroom proceedings. For example, Nikhil's teacher Sonia ensured that Nikhil is no exception to the classroom activities and is involved as far as possible.

This indeed emerged as a factor influencing successful inclusion of students with a disability. If the classroom teacher makes sincere and genuine efforts to make the child feel a part of the class, it works in favour of inclusion. The child mentioned those teachers who made such efforts and the subjects taught by them amongst his preferences. The child felt more comfortable and confident in the company of those teachers.

> *Some teachers I found extremely caring and ensured that Nikhil followed everything done in class. These were those whom even Nikhil had named when asked about his favourite teachers in school. The teachers while taking rounds of the classroom gave personal attention to each of the student including Nikhil; inspecting the notebooks, observing the students while they were doing classroom assignments and asking sporadic recapitulatory questions (Observing in Nikhil's classroom).*

If we look at the contribution of the teachers in case of Tanmay, we come across some specific supports needed by him. One of Tanmay's teacher informed, "Children with hearing impairment need to have things carefully explained on a one-to-one basis because of the hearing loss. He needs extra help when learning new words and concepts. Physical objects normally do not pose problems, but abstract concepts such as time, feelings and thoughts are difficult to explain". When explaining things, the teachers try to use short, clear sentences and draw or use pictures, as required, to illustrate what they mean. She always talks to and asks Tanmay questions even though he has problems of hearing what she is saying. This was her strategy to encourage Tanmay to speak. She followed some simple strategies suggested by the resource teacher for Tanmay. The resource teachers encourage the regular teachers to prepare visually oriented materials to augment the oral information they provide in the classroom. They suggest making efficient use of the chalkboard to enhance learning for Tanmay. Certain subjects like Mathematics and Language pose greater problems for teachers. The teachers then take help of the resource teacher who makes herself available for these classes. She takes a seat next to Tanmay and ensures that the concepts explained in the classroom are followed by Tanmay. If the special teacher observes that Tanmay is having difficulty in following the classroom proceedings, she calls him for a remedial class for the subject. During the remedial class she ensures that he has followed the concepts presented in the class and helps him with the home assignments.

The most challenging aspect with Tanmay is to make that Tanmay participate in the communicational activities that is teacher to student, student to teacher and student to student. Also that he is able to handle the reading and writing demands of the class. While most teachers were aware and facilitated the process of the communication and extended their support in making him to cope with reading/writing necessary in the classrooms, some were indifferent to his needs. Some teachers (few of their names were mentioned by Tanmay under his disliking about the school) never bothered about his presence in the classroom. They would not make an effort to include him in the classroom. They thought Tanmay was the responsibility of the Resource Teacher and they had nothing to do with him. Tanmay's presence only slowed down the classroom proceedings and that they had to struggle to complete their course on time.

Another major consideration related to the physical set-up of the classroom is 'Seating'. The classroom teacher attempts to maximize learning for Tanmay by providing him an appropriate seat in the classroom. Tanmay is made to sit in the front row near the teacher's desk; this ensures that the teacher's speech could be followed by Tanmay. The classroom teacher remarked that it also helps in avoiding distractions for Tanmay.

A similar strategy is employed by Soham's class teacher. He is a slow learner and often needs a further explanation or extra and simpler instructions to carry out the classroom activities. He is, therefore, given a seat in the middle of the front row (see Figure 4.2). Unfortunately, in case of Soham it is a single seat. The other schools do not have such small classrooms and the students sit in pairs. This facilitates peer learning as in the case of Simran. The visual cues are quickly communicated to Simran by her partner who sits right next to her. While interviewing Neha who teaches Science in Simran's class, she shared her support strategy for Simran. She mentioned that her subject requires lot of visual inputs and it is not possible for her to give verbal instructions to Simran. She, however, finds time to

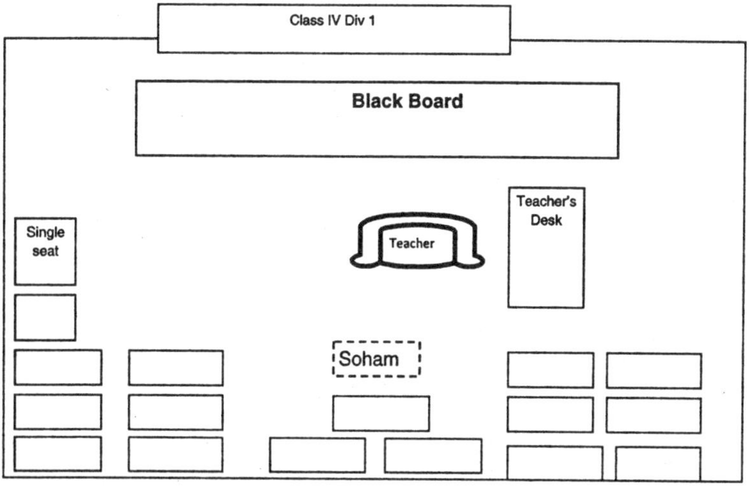


**Fig. 4.2:** Seating Arrangement for Soham (Slow Learner, 10 Years)

share her concerns with Shobha (the resource teacher) and often help her to prepare teaching material for Simran related to her subject.

Many a times a seating arrangement provides opportunities for greater attention of the classroom teacher for example in case of Tanmay and Soham. Even in the case of Ishita, the classroom teacher prefers to give her a seat in the front row and requests the subject teachers to inspect her notebooks during class exercise and involve her in classroom activities.

It was found that each school grapples with classroom issues depending on the student characteristics. The needs of the student are given prime importance and classroom management is altered to their favour. However, it is not practiced universally by all teachers.

## Physical Support

Physical support is an essential requirement for children with differing physical needs. In this research such support was particularly required by Nikhil and Rakhi and to a certain extent by Simran. We will take their case examples to illustrate how the school meets the physical needs of the children with disabilities. The research identified good practice in some organizational and social aspects of the schools visited. However, little good practice, except for the provision of elevators, was found with respect to physical issues in the schools.

> *Nikhil is a wheelchair user. The school building in which Nikhil studies has an elevator. The school does not employ ancillary staff to help the children with disabilities, rather seeks help from the family of the child. Whenever, there is need such as this the school authorities clarify it to the parents that they will have to arrange help for meeting mobility needs. In case of Nikhil, the family pays an extra amount to the driver who stays in the school for helping Nikhil reach his classes if on different floors. He also helps Nikhil with his toilet needs. The school though has a space crunch, has an accessible toilet for children who are wheelchair users. In fact, one of the toilets was redesigned when they admitted their first child who was a wheelchair user.*

> *Unlike the previous school where Rakhi studied, the school authorities allowed her to use special braced shoes. They also encourage her peers to help her with the wheelchair. Gradually, the school has done away with negative attitudes of parents of non-disabled children in her class. Keeping with its core values and mission, the school has taken Rakhi's case as a challenge and make every effort to include her in the normal activities of the school (Rakhi's mother). Rakhi's school is spread over a large area and is characterized by broad corridors and elevators. The school has always encouraged the non-disabled peers of the child to take responsibility of helping Rakhi with the movement from one classroom to the other if there is a need. The school has sought help from the mother for helping her with the catheter. She visits the school everyday to help the child meet her toilet needs.*

The most important goal for children with spina bifida is to provide them with the maximum level of mobility and independence possible. In adapting the school setting for the child with spina bifida, architectural factors should be considered. This can occur through structural changes (for example, adding elevators or ramps) or through schedule or location changes (for example, offering a course on the ground floor). Children with myelomeningocele need to learn mobility skills, and often require the aid of crutches, braces, or wheelchairs. It is important that all members of the school team and the parents understand the child's physical capabilities and limitations.

> *Simran needs some help to reach to the classes and the playground. The school encourages the peers without disabilities to help Simran and they take turns to help her (Neha, Simran's Maths teacher).*

Thus, it is seen that though an accessible physical arrangement would help the child in being mobile and independent some support mechanisms do help the child to continue with least difficulty in a regular school setting. However, the children with disabilities expressed their unhappiness over seeking help from others all the time. Rakhi for instance, felt guilty that the mother had to come to the school everyday for helping her. Nikhil as well felt that if the driver was not there or if he refused to help any day he would be stranded. Such apprehensions in children affect their self-concept and enhance dependence.

**Psychological Support**

The schools play an important role in providing psychological support to children with disabilities facing academic difficulties or other physiological or behavioural problems, and provide help to their parents to minimize apprehensions and anxieties related to their children. We shall examine this through an example from our respondent; with respect to Gaurav, the school faces the following problems with quite often (as told by Preeti, Resource Teacher, School 4); distractibility, impulsivity and restlessness/hyperactivity.

Because the school is considerate to Gaurav's needs, he is able to continue in a regular school. There are stringent complaints from parents of non-disabled children and many times, they are justified because their children have been gravely hurt by Gaurav. The Resource teacher manages his medication at school. When the reported incidents of aggression and restlessness increased the school even hired a part-time Counsellor to look into Gaurav's needs. She takes regular sessions with him and weekly sessions with his parents. The teachers have noted a marked improvement in Gaurav since his regular therapy sessions have begun.

The Counsellor even called his friends occasionally and counsels them on how they should behave with Gaurav. She has introduced a 'smiley' collecting scheme for the class. The whole class is made responsible for Gaurav's behaviour. The day any unsolicited incident is reported, one smiley is withdrawn from the class and *vice versa.*

There was only one school which had full-time Counsellor, one school had part-time Counsellor and two schools had Visiting Counsellors for the children. The visiting Counsellors visited the school once a week. They worked on a referral system; the regular teacher often referred cases to the counsellors. The Counsellor closely worked with the resource teacher discussing the cases and planning a course of action. Mostly, the caseload consisted of hyperactive children or slow learners. Sometimes, children with disabilities were also referred to the Counsellor if their parents expressed a need to the class teacher. The parents mostly complained about irrational behaviours, stubbornness, introvert or aggressive behaviour. The assessments were referred to practicing clinical psychologist in the school vicinity. A copy of the reports is retained by the school for further follow up and action.

The Counsellor administers behaviour therapy with the children and takes care to involve thc parents, resource teacher and regular teachers. The Counsellor periodically organized sessions with the regular teachers to sensitize them and guide them how to look for signs and symptoms for common problems in children. They also try to address the concerns of the regular teachers regarding children with disabilities. One of the Counsellors reported that the regular teachers are often in "complaining mode" and consider children with disabilities as additional burden. The Counsellors ensure that they help teachers overcome negative attitudes during the sessions they conduct with the teachers.

The counselling services are also availed by the parents of the children with disabilities. Whenever an appointment is sought, the school Counsellor and in some schools even the Resource teacher calls them at mutually convenient time. Many Resource teachers informed that mostly the parents need to 'ventilate' more than actually seeking any counselling help. They reportedly talk of incidents which made them feel hurt in school or community.

The Schools organized sessions for their teachers to develop right attitude and sensitivity towards the children with disabilities and their parents. A couple of resource teachers felt that such sessions facilitate understanding about 'disability' and create awareness about the related issues amongst members of the school community. It helps in building a conducive and empathetic environment for the children.

The psychological support is also provided the "good friends" of the children. Rakhi's peers are sensitive to her needs and help her wherever possible. This has been a result of Principal's and teachers constant endeavour to educate the non-disabled children on needs of their peers with disabilities. They often organize such talks during school assembly and sometimes on special events which are celebrated at school. The teachers have also introduced a system of "good points" and distributing 'smileys' and 'stars' when the non-disabled children help or involve their peers with disabilities.

While these schools were attempting to provide some facilities for children with disabilities, these facilities fall short of what was required. These gaps were filled by the mothers of the children. The mothers were found to execute their responsibilities with dedication and unrelenting spirit. Many (7 out of 10) children of the respondents identified their mothers as the main support provider even during school hours. We shall in the subsequent section highlight their role and responsibilities in their child's education.

The Counsellors were mostly housed with the resource teacher in the resource room. The Counsellors looked after the psychological needs of the children and the resource teachers concentrated on the academic needs. Thus, where the responsibility of children with disabilities was shared between the resource teacher and the Counsellor, the resource teachers did not complain about excessive workload. Also, the resource room was not only meant for children with disabilities as other non-disabled children with behavioural and emotional problems frequented the resource room to attend sessions with the Counsellor. This pointed towards the need for school Counsellors in the inclusive settings where they could effectively address the psychological needs of all children.

**Parental Support**

Parents also need to be involved in the education of their children, especially because they can provide the best source of information about their child's particular needs (Hornby, 1995:23). The home-school partnerships are widely accepted as important for success of inclusion for children with disabilities (Strickland & Turnbull, 1990; Lewis, 1992; Hayes, 1998). Parents provide a wealth of information about the child which the school could efficiently utilise for enhancing the education process (Hayes, 1998). All the seven schools heavily relied on the parents of children with disabilities for implementing inclusion. It was observed that predominantly all the mothers had taken on the responsibility to assist the children in the schools. There were ten mothers of children with disabilities who provided information on their roles in inclusion process. The demographical characteristics of the mothers have been earlier presented in Table 3.8 (chapter 3). Mostly the mothers (8/10) were housewives. The demands of caregiving were very high amongst mothers of children with disabilities.

However, none of the mothers expressed disappointment over father's inability to shoulder the responsibilities at school as they were main financial providers for the family. The fathers occasionally helped at the school when either the mother was engaged somewhere else or on their non-working days. Many of the mothers informed that the fathers helped with the homework or health related issues concerning the child. All the mothers demonstrated and mentioned about their strong commitment to providing their children with all opportunities which their non-disabled peers get to help them achieve their highest potential. They suggested that inclusive schools were the best placements for their children. There were three common beliefs among parents which made them believe regular school was the best possible decision they have made for their children and they will go to any extent to sustain the placement. Firstly, the desire of the mothers that their children lead 'normal' lives has motivated them to do their "extra bit" (Sania's mother).

> *I did not want that my son's life is restricted in any way, if he goes to special school he will get a chance and learn to*

> *communicate with only those who know and follow sign language. He has to learn to live in a world which is indifferent to people with disability. He has to find his own wayout in a world that is indifferent to special needs (Tanmay's mother).*

Secondly, they felt that it is their responsibility to share the "burden of school" (Gaurav's mother). Most of the mothers believed that the schools are "extending a favour" (Aakash's mother) by enrolling their children. The mothers, therefore, involved themselves in whatever capacities they could to facilitate the education of their child in the regular school. However, sometimes they got frustrated and blamed the school for not being sensitive to their child's needs. The following quote was an emotional account of a mother of the annual sports event where her daughter desired to participate. There is an evidence of twin perspective of the mother. She was caught between her daughter's desire and school's commitment to serve interests of all children. She has resigned to the fact that her daughter is not a part of all children, she is different from the rest. She believed that the school had extended a great favour to her by registering her daughter on roll. Her expectations from the school had to be minimal as her child was different she believed. This fact leads us to believe that parental expectations from the school are in someway subdued because they feel their children are unlike other children.

> *I almost picked up a fight with the School Coordinator, when she refused Rakhi's involvement in the Annual Sports Day. I had just requested for her participation in the "House March", I even volunteered to push her wheelchair. Rakhi was shattered that particular day. She cried the whole day because she wanted to participate with the other children. I am aware that my child is not like other children, she is not 'able-bodied' and hence, cannot run and play like her classmates. But she always wants to be like them. She wants to be a part of the school functions and a little cooperation from the school that day could have boosted her morale. Later, I realized that maybe I was wrong; the school cannot always prioritize my daughter's interest. I forgot that school honoured*

> *my request of admitting my daughter when no school accepted my child. I must remember the favour all through my life (Rakhi's mother).*

The third element which got evident was the belief that segregated settings could limit their children's potential. Some of the children had experience of studying in a special school before their enrolment in the current inclusive school. The following quote is a pointer to this belief system that the segregated settings did not provide ample opportunities for social development of their children.

> *Simran was in a special school for the blind. I felt that my daughter did not get enough opportunities to develop herself. Amongst the friends there was no one to share the sight of the world. Their conversations were often depressing. Just a few visits to the outside world does not make one fit to stay there. Now Simran is much more cheerful, wants to see the world through our eyes (Simran's mother).*

In order to enable the child with disability to attend a regular school, the family has to take on a proactive role even at school through providing additional support in not only caring for their physical needs such as eating, toilet care; but also in ensuring the child is able to keep up with the academic workload. There is a considerable involvement of the parents in the entire process of inclusive education. They are in constant touch with the teachers in the school who inform them about the child's progress. Nikhil's mother has taken this responsibility entirely. She visits his school once a week to complete his class notes, meets the concerned teachers and discusses the home teaching approach with the resource teacher. She always wanted to send the child to the regular school so that Nikhil gets a chance to interact with his non-disabled peers. She believed that special school setting could have been very depressing for the child as well as for the family. She believed that Nikhil can manage well in a regular school. She is satisfied with Nikhil's performance at school. Some mothers like those of Tanmay, Rakhi and Soham visit the school everyday for helping them while Gaurav's mother attends school on call.

*The resolution of helping Tanmay to cope in the regular school has brought in additional responsibilities for me. It is my routine to visit Tanmay's school during 'zero hours' or lunch time or at the end of the day to find out how the day has been for him. If there are any class notes which need to be photocopied, or assignments to be submitted next day or any assessment coming up, I have to keep track of everything. Sometimes it is difficult [sighs] but there is no choice. There is no one to share this responsibility with me, not even anyone in the family. There are no compromises anywhere, when it comes to discharging my duties as a mother or as a home maker. (Tanmay's mother)*

*My mother comes to school everyday during lunch time. She has to help me with the catheter. She never complains about anything. Sometimes, I ask Mummy whether I am a burden to her. She cannot go anywhere because of me, she always keeps worrying about me. She always tells me that she loves me and I am never going to be a burden. But she cries when she says this. (To researcher), Does she lie to me? (Rakhi, 13 years, Spina Bifida).*

*I have to go the school everyday otherwise Soham will not perform well. I have to complete his class notes, talk to teachers and his friends so that he feels comfortable. Soham always complains about behaviour of his friends or teachers and I have to ensure that everything is set right for the following day. Many a times it is his friends who tease and make fun of him and I have to inform this to the teacher or talk directly to the child whom Soham complains against. I know, I cannot always do this but a mother cannot see the child in pain. I am gradually preparing him to handle situations but it will take time. He is timid and very conscious of his low IQ." (Uma, Soham's mother)*

*I attend my sessions with the Counsellor and learn new activities for increasing Gaurav's attention span. I am satisfied with the school's efforts to include Gaurav. I had*

> *sought admission in many schools for Gaurav when there were repeated warnings from this school. She informed that no school is willing to put an ADHD child on roll. (Somya, Gaurav's mother)*

As the mothers were involved with the school, some of the mothers had to either quit jobs or dropped the idea of taking up one for the sake of their children. Only two out of the ten mothers were in service; Vimla and Radhika. The reasons they gave for continuing their jobs were also quite similar.

> *I had so many times thought of leaving my job but I couldn't because I am not working for building my career, I am working for my daughter. We have to buy a car for our daughter because it is difficult to take her around in public transport. Her father alone will not be able to fend for the needs of the family. It is very tough for me to handle everything but I have stopped thinking about my problems; my daughter is primary concern for me. (Vimla, Rakhi's mother)*

> *God has bestowed me with a beautiful daughter and I would like to give her the best. In today's material world, money is very important. It will help her even when we are not there. (Radhika, Simran's mother)*

## Conclusion

The major support systems as understood through the perspectives of the stakeholders are therefore the collaboration between resource and regular teachers; school-parent partnerships and fostering inclusive cultures in the school. Figure 4.3 depicts these three factors as interacting and trickling effect is the overall support required towards inclusive education. These factors are interacting because the stakeholders involved are not independent actors for example, the parents could not fulfil their role if the school, staff and non-disabled children do not cooperate. The analysis brought to the forefront that the resource teachers have an important role to play in

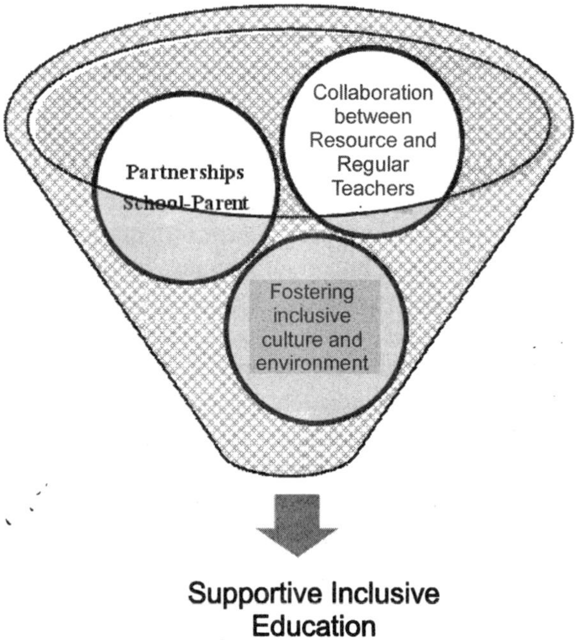


**Fig. 4.3:** Supportive Factors in Inclusion.

the current context of inclusive schools. Their effectiveness could be enhanced if their responsibilities are shared with the regular teachers of the school. Though in many schools some of the regular teachers made attempts to collaborate with the resource teachers and follow their classroom advice for children with disabilities as in the case of Tanmay, there are schools where regular teachers consider children with disabilities as "appendages" (Tripti, regular teacher, School 5) to the class. This 'collaboration' could be direct or indirect as the regular and resource teachers in the seven schools expressed in the interviews. They could collaborate within the regular classroom where both the teachers are present for assisting each other in the classroom proceedings. This would especially work in classes where the subject requires inputs which could be difficult for the child with disability to pick up for instance, Geometry and Geography classes for Simran where a lot of visual cues like diagrams and maps are used or language classes for Tanmay where he is required to pick up lot of audio cues. The resource teacher's presence in classes like these could certainly prove beneficial for enhancing academic gains for the child. The collaboration could be indirect when the teachers spend some time to discuss the classroom strategies for the child to enhance his/her learning like in the case of Gaurav who has short attention span and has to be frequently involved in classroom activities. Gaurav's History teacher, Kanya has shouldered this responsibility with the resource teachers and reports his behaviour to her. The inclusive schools have envisaged a new role for the special education teachers. Training and professional development opportunities must be utilized to ensure that teachers master the essentials of the "new" role (Florian, 1998).

Another factor which emerged as a very vital one was the partnership between schools and parents. In the current context the role of the mothers became apparent where they actively engaged in their child's education and contributed a great deal in terms of helping to continue in a regular school. Their support in meeting the physical and academic needs of the child is an indispensable one.

The school has a larger role to play in inclusion, its policies, culture and environment must support inclusion. The creation of this environment involves support from stakeholders within school. How the school helps in developing the right attitude amongst regular teachers, peers and parents of non-disabled children is crucial to understand.

Thus, we find that schools are practicing inclusion with their understanding, belief system, arranging resources, support from the resource teacher, regular teachers, non-disabled children and the parents of children with disabilities. We would build on the discussion in the subsequent themes and finally, present the contextual model for practice.

## CHALLENGES

In what follows, we present cases which helped us to effectively describe the social reality of an inclusive school and ascertain the challenges which the children with disabilities face in the school. The reason for selection of these case examples, out of many, is that they present to the reader a clear picture of our interpretative purposes, in examining how in India the policy of inclusive education is implemented in schools, and investigated whether some children are still marginalized, and if so, to identify factors supporting their marginalization and acting as a barrier to inclusion. These barriers could emanate from scarcity of resources, negative attitudes of teachers, non-disabled peers and their parents.

There were three distinct categories under which the responses fell; attitudes which included attitudes and behaviour of peers and of regular teachers, shortage of resources and capacity building. We shall discuss the responses under to build the analytical framework.

**Attitude and Behaviour of Peers**

The peers in school, being the closest on par, play an important role in the lives of the children with disabilities. There is general support for the hypothesis that children who are not accepted by peers are generally at risk for difficulties later in life (Ochoa & Olivarez Jr., 1995). Acceptance by peers provides a much greater challenge for children with disabilities. Children with disabilities are often an easy target for being teased and bullied by their non-disabled peers as reported by children interviewed in this study (see also Nabuzoka and Smith, 1993; Dawkins, 1996). Reynolds (2003:4) defined bullying as "the use of physical, psychological, or direct verbal means either individually or in a group, to cause physical or psychological distress to others."

Recent research findings suggest that vulnerability to bullying cuts across all types of disabilities (Mishna, 2003; Smith and Tippett, 2006). Seven children interviewed found it difficult to make friends with the non-disabled peers because they were made fun of and bullied. The children commonly reflected that they wanted to be accepted and have more friends in the class who understand them and involve them in their talks and play.

> *While talking to Nikhil he revealed that there are only a few students who claim to be his friends. But he knows within that his so called friends are faking their friendly behaviour because either they want small favours from Nikhil or appreciation from the teachers on being good to a child with disability. He recalled an embarrassing moment when a friend discovered that he uses diapers. The friend threatened Nikhil*

*of disclosing this to everyone in the class. Initially he was horrified but later he told him, "What you would have done if you were in my place" (Interview with Nikhil, 11 years, Spina Bifida).*

Nikhil is extremely conscious of the fact that he uses diapers. He does not want other students in the class to know of this. He feels even more vulnerable after one of his friends has discovered it. There are not many people other than his family with whom he can share his worries. Other problems that he faces in the classroom are that of teasing and bullying. Some children from other classroom call him, "lame" or ask him to run with them in sports. Such remarks hurt him but he resigns to the fact that he is disabled and that he will have to face this all through his life. The observations in the classroom supplemented what Nikhil and his mother informed me.

*Nikhil likes to make friends and shares good relationship with elder sister and his cousins. He wants to mingle with everyone even with those who want to use him. He comes to school in a car so many children want lift and therefore talk to him nicely. They are otherwise not bothered and would not show any friendly gesture. Those relationships are rather superficial. The other children have not accepted him completely. While children of his age call each other and visit each other, no one involves Nikhil in these activities (Nikhil's mother).*

*Observing the situation in the classroom, I could distinguish a certain apprehension in the eyes of the teacher and the other children that was directed towards Nikhil. The teacher avoided eye contact with Nikhil and concentrated on the delivery of the lesson planned for that day. The other observation was that during lunch times Nikhil would have his lunch alone in the classroom as other children went down to the ground floor.*

Soham also reported some incidents which had hurt him emotionally and which makes him feel that he does not have friends in the class. Apparently, there are two children in the class who play with him secretly and tell him that they are his friends. However, in presence of other children, they pretend that they are not his friends and mock at him. This signified that the class does not approve of 'friendship' with children with disabilities. Even Gaurav shared an incidents occurring in the classroom which make him angry and he resorts to violence after that provocation. Minal (Gaurav's Hindi teacher) informed that he is extremely violent when he is angry. He hits other children, sometimes ruins the charts and other decorations put up on the soft board in the fit of rage. On enquiring when does Gaurav normally gets angry, she mentioned that many a times it is his own classmates who tease him.

Sania also has experienced similar bullying by classmates and other children in the school. The children derive pleasure out of the fact that they can easily pass on the blame to her as she cannot communicate properly. Her mother reported the incident at school (mentioned below) and few which happen at her home when some children come home on her birthday party or other occasions. The other children would make a mess in Sania's room and later tell the mother that it was done by Sania.

> *I do not like children in my class because many of them say that I am 'stupid' and that my brain does not work. I know that they do not like me and no one wants to be my friend. I have two friends in the class but they also tell me that we are your friends and in front of the class we will act as if we are not your friends (Soham, 10 years, Slow Learner).*

> *They (classmates) know that I get angry easily because of my problem, however, they tease me to such an extent that I get angry. Sometimes they tell me, that Vaibhav (classmate) has made my cartoon in his English notebook or they complain to the teacher that I have not done my work or I am talking. They want me to get angry so that I get scolded by the teacher (Gaurav, 13 years, ADHD).*

> *Sania wants to play with other kids in the school but other kids shun her. Because she is not able to speak, other kids*

> *make her scapegoat. They also do not involve her with their games or laugh at her. The school organized some games for an outdoor picnic. It was sheer insensitivity on the part of the school management to organize 'dumbcharades' and Chinese whisper. When someone would whisper something in her ear, Sania was not able to replicate the message. Even while doing actions for words, she would do something out of context and all children would laugh at her and say that 'she is mad'. I witnessed everything because I had volunteered to help out the teachers (Sania's mother).*

Despite the bullying and teasing the children with disabilities want to continue their friendship because they nurture a desire to have more friends. The mothers also avoid complaining against other classmates for the fact that then it might lead to 'total rejection' (Pamila, Sania's mother) or 'more bullying' (Nikhil's mother). However, some of the mothers had reported the matter to the Principal, resource teacher, and class teacher but they felt that the effect was temporary. Somewhere the issues like these were not taken cognizance of by the authorities. Pramila was concerned about the impact these issues may have on Sania as she is not able to 'ventilate'. She expressed that she may know only 'twenty-five per cent' of what Sania faces.

The data suggests that bullying and classmate acceptance of children with disabilities is a serious challenge and has to be prevented for successful inclusion. The students with disabilities are particularly vulnerable to the peer victimization and anxiety about harassment bothers all children and their mothers.

### Attitude of the Regular Teachers

Another strong barrier which the children perceived was the attitude of regular teachers. Several studies using both quantitative and qualitative studies have examined teachers' beliefs, attitudes, and perceptions about students with disabilities and inclusive education (e.g. Agbenyega, 2007; Wall, 2002; Opdal & Wormnaes, 2001; Balboni and Pedrabissi, 2000; Chiang, 1999; Cornoldi *et al.*, 1998; Brantlinger, 1996; Minke *et al.*, 1996; Villa *et al.*, 1996; Fulk & Hirth,

1994; Giangreco *et al.*, 1993; Gerber, 1992). These studies conclude that attitudes and concerns of teachers affect their acceptance and commitment to implementing inclusion.

There were three general attitudes which surfaced from our interviews as being challenges for children with disabilities in inclusive schools. Firstly, regular teachers considered children with disabilities as the responsibility of the resource teachers. Secondly, they felt children with disabilities to be a 'disturbance' to the class and as causing distractions which delayed course completion. Finally, the lack of sensitivity on part of the regular teachers towards children with disabilities also acts an attitudinal barrier. Therefore, they choose to ignore their presence and concentrate on execution of their lesson plans. The following quotes depict these three general attitudes which surfaced during interviews.

> *I cannot waste the time of the entire class in giving special attention and guidance to Soham. I have to look after the interest of all my students. Besides, Soham gets remedial education at the Resource centre. The special teachers are there to look after his special needs. (Class Teacher of Soham, 10 years, Slow Learner).[Signifying that 'Soham' is responsibility of the resource teacher.]*

> *I have no personal problem with Aakash but it is difficult to teach with him in the class. For how long, could one ignore his distractive behaviours. Sometimes, he taps his pencil on the table continuously. Some other time he is reading a different book in class. Sometimes he even starts to talk to himself. The other children in the class get distracted and a lot of time is wasted (Class Teacher of Aakash, 10 years, Aspergers Syndrome). [Signifying that 'Aakash' is a disturbance to the class.]*

> *My teachers like me except my maths teacher. My maths teacher does not even understand me. He always asks my friend to repeat whatever I tell him. (Harshit, 15 years, Cerebral Palsy) [Signifying 'lack of sensitivity'.]*

*The regular teachers do not cooperate with us from their side. It is always anyone amongst us who takes initiative and action for children with special needs. The child could really benefit if we teachers are able to work together. There is a great difference in our ideology in terms of dealing with children with special needs. (Resource teacher of a school which had nine resource teachers.)*

*Soham's class II teacher took pride in the fact that it was she who discovered that he was a slow learner. She mentioned it to me everytime I met her during Parent-teacher meetings. She talks about it even today when Soham has reached Std. IV (Uma, Soham's mother).*

*Radhika (Simran's mother) supports inclusion but she feels that there are some serious drawbacks. She has had some bitter experiences with the teachers who are simply ignorant and never attempt to understand that it is extremely difficult to do academic activities without vision. Some teachers think that Simran is using her blindness as an excuse. Simran has greater problems in understanding subjects like Algebra and Geography because there is an extensive usage of visual cues which do not translate well verbally. There are some teachers in school who obviously wish that they did not have to deal with a student who is blind, but there are some who do everything to make Simran a part of their class. Her role in subjects where the teachers are less cooperative increases considerably (summarised from Interview with Radhika).*

These are the challenges faced by children with disabilities who have secured admission in inclusive schools. Children with disabilities aspiring to study in inclusive school have the greater challenge in their attempt to secure admission. The eligibility criteria of these schools are stringent; the nature and severity of disability is the foremost concern of the school authorities. It was observed that most inclusive schools only enrol children with mild disabilities. The schools also assess the parental support during the time of admission. They give preference when parents are willing to take on the extra responsibility for their child in terms of sharing the workload with the resource teachers (in some schools), meeting the child's physical needs (if any), visiting the school regularly to monitor and facilitate child's progress, and arranging transport (as there are few inclusive schools, in many cases the child's home is distantly located) and the child is accordingly granted admission.

We looked at the general attitude of the peers and the regular teachers which acted as a barrier to inclusive education. Six out of ten children felt hurt and segregated by some interactions at school, particularly with regular teachers and peers. These attitudes could be categories as of two kinds—*intentional attitudinal barriers* and *unintentional attitudinal barriers* (see also Pivik *et al,* 2002).

Amongst the intentional attitudinal barriers, some of the students in the interviews reported instances of isolation, physical bullying, or emotional bullying. Isolation took the form of either being ignored or having difficulty building friendships. Physical bullying usually related to people pushing the student's wheelchair without permission (as in the case of Nikhil) or engaging in constant fights (as in the case of Gaurav). The most frequent attitudinal barrier mentioned was that of emotional bullying. The students indicated that this was the most hurtful and included name calling, pointing, being labelled as "stupid," condescending attitudes by teaching staff, and generally being treated differently from other students. For example, Harshit reported that his peers "just stare at me and point and then whisper to each other. perhaps they discuss my disability."

The unintentional attitudinal barriers related to a lack of knowledge, education, understanding, or effort on the part of the educational system or staff. From the entire sample, the most frequently reported barrier was a lack of understanding by teachers and support staff. This took the form of being given inappropriate substitute work when the other students engaged in something that was a limitation for the child with disability. When the whole class was busy practicing for the sports day, Rakhi was made to sit in the library and study or when the students go to the gymnasium or dance class Nikhil is sent for the remedial class. The children liked to engage in equally interesting activity during the time others engaged in co-curricular activities in which they could not participate. Nikhil's mother shared that he faces problems on an everyday basis as all his efforts to cope in a regular school despite the numerous problems are never acknowledged or appreciated. The mother was worried about the attitude of the regular teachers who would never go a step forward to include Nikhil in the activities of the class. This leads her to wonder whether the 'inclusion' process is a one-sided effort. She suggested that there could be some group counselling sessions which may lead to better acceptance by the students and fight these unintentional attitudinal barriers. We would like to present the case of Nikhil in greater detail to bring out the issues involved.

Nikhil's mother was made a part of these deliberations and inquired about the challenges her idea of 'inclusive school'. The highlights from the interview would bring out certain concerns and issues for building the discourse further. Nikhil studied in another renowned school in the city earlier. He was the only child who suffered from a disability. Though the school had lifts and some of the physical support for the child, they were unwilling to let him continue in the same school after class VII. They reasoned that they were short of some basic resources like a resource room or ancillary staff to help Nikhil. The mother had made up her mind to find a regular school for her child and therefore, approached many schools for his admission. Unfortunately, no school was ready to admit her child because of his physical disability. She disappointedly noted that though Nikhil has average intelligence, he was never given a fair and equal chance at school.

The experiences of a previous school were shared in the process bringing some facts to the forefront. The schools are hesitant to take responsibility of a child with disability. Their unwillingness and negative attitude deter parents to keep the child in the same school. In the first place, no school admits a child with disability to their school and even if they allow him/her admission there are problems in continuing with the school. The abilities of the child were sidelined and ignored by the school, what mattered to the school was his 'disability'.

Due to this he became demotivated and has become apathetic to studies. He displayed mood swings and resorted to excessive video gaming. The mother blamed this to his adolescent age. The parents face a lot of worries about his future. They know that there is lot of struggle ahead. Nikhil is good in science and he wants to pursue his interest but there is little hope that he would be able to continue studying science. At higher level of education he may or may not get the support he needs.

The Principal of the earlier school was not very encouraging about Nikhil and many times counselled parents to send their child to special school. The parents believed and insisted that Nikhil attends a regular school as he was faring well in studies. The parents also had to put their patience to test when their child was used as an 'exhibit'. During a sports day function the Principal would go and pose with Nikhil in front of the Press to prove that the school gives equal opportunity to all his children. He was given a small role on stage everytime during an annual function so that the other parents would appreciate the efforts of school in providing a chance to a child with disability as well.

The parents have had experience of school of high repute which boasts of their inclusive culture in their brochures, but denied admission to Nikhil. They tend to equate a physical disability with a mental disability which was very disheartening for the parents and the child. The following extracts from the interview with the mother had reported an incident and recommended strategies to help her child continue 'willingly and happily' in the school.

> *In the current school, the child should be given chance to participate in all academic and extra-curricular activities of the school. The child was discouraged to stand for elections in the school. The mother however felt that this was injustice done to him. If given a chance he could prove his leadership skills. There is a lot of bullying. This particular school where the child was studying lacks strict discipline. Children are over-friendly with their teachers which is good in some sense but the children should be taught some discipline. Due to this indiscipline, the child with a disability suffers more. The child has learnt lot of violence, he hits his classmates and* vice versa. *Many a times, he would gravely hurt himself while indulging in fights. The mother is confused at this behaviour, one hand it has made him tough and he is learning to fight while on the other, he is engaging in misbehaviour.*

*I suggest that a few sessions with the entire class by regular teachers and Counsellors could help in better acceptance of the child in school. At the beginning of the new session all the children should be given a chance to introduce them to their friends in the classroom wherein they could share their abilities and differences. This may help in better understanding of the problems that a child with differential ability faces in a regular classroom (Nikhil's mother).*

When this vignette was analyzed for emergent findings, we came across some barriers to effective inclusive school systems. The parents had a bad experience with previous schools where the child was asked to discontinue due to his disability. Nevertheless, these schools would not lose out on an opportunity to gain popularity as inclusive schools in presence of media or other school events. Even in the classroom what appeared was a situation of non-acceptance by the peers and the teacher. The child would sit alone in the classroom during lunch hours and even during class sessions he would be excluded from the peer conversations and play. Nikhil was not allowed to contest school elections due to the nature of his disability. The children with disabilities are constantly exposed to these challenges which may cause a negative outcome (more in the Section 4)

If we look at the section which we have presented there is an evident catch. In our study the children with severe disabilities, Nikhil and Rakhi face greater attitudinal problems from their peers than say children with less apparent disabilities like Soham and Gaurav. 'Regardless of context or age of participants, society tends to view the physically attractive as inherently better than those of less physical attractiveness' (Patzer 1985; Erwin 1993). Physical attractiveness does unfortunately also play an important role when it comes to making friends. Though none of the non-disabled peers mentioned it, the children with disabilities were concerned about the physical appearance and athletic competence as factors affecting their friendships and inculcating negative attitudes amongst their classmates (more details in Section 4).

For teachers however greater attitudinal problems arise when the children with disabilities pose instructional problems. Though again not specifically mentioned by any of the teachers, their examples had names of children with disabilities who either disturb the proceedings of the class or require extra instructions/special attention during activities.

**Shortage of Resources**

This study contends that the resources owned by the school facilitate the inclusion process of children disabilities, their absence however does not deter inclusion (see also Stubbs, 1997; Alur, 2006). A particular impairment in a child restricts his ability to perform if the environment is not conducive. We will share the experiences of the children who participated in the study and faced challenges sometimes on an everyday basis in the school. Nikhil has some specific needs. If those needs are met he could continue in the regular school as any other child with least problems.

> *It was a pre-lunch hour in July 2008 soon after we began our data collection in schools. We were waiting for the Special Teacher to introduce us to some children who had gathered near the front office at her behest. One of the children who came was Nikhil, accompanied by his driver who volunteered to help him during school as an attendant. After our introductions, the special teacher told us that he is an average student but they could not have admitted him to the school without an assistant. She informed, "It is very difficult for the school to meet his needs. His complete immobility makes him completely dependent on the assistant.*
>
> *Nikhil needs architectural friendliness. The broad corridor and few ramps could enhance his mobility in school. He undergoes emotional distress which often goes unnoticed by the regular teachers.*

A school would be able to successfully include Nikhil only when they have adequate infrastructure and organization. Nikhil was admitted to the school only on the condition that the parents provide for an attendant during school hours to help him commute between classrooms. This points towards the inadequacy of the school to make its own arrangements to help the child. This means that a child hailing from a family which could afford providing a full-time attendant may experience inclusive environment while other children may not.

The human resource is a major constraint. Six out of the seven schools had only one resource and all the Principals expressed their concerns over it. They felt that more number of resource teachers could facilitate the process. One of the resource teacher mentioned that, "my job profile is very different from the regular teachers. I am required to give more time to student but I feel constrained due to excess workload."

Some teachers and resource teachers also felt that appointment of ancillary staff for children who are wheelchair users would be welcome gesture from the school. Other resources like availability of school transport could help some of the students who are located distantly from the school. We must reiterate here that the city of Mumbai is a metropolis with large number of schools (for details refer Section 1) out of which very few are inclusive. Also, the public transport is not disabled friendly (for e.g. see Shetty, 2006), the architecture of the local stations and the models of the buses encourage the children with disabilities to make self-arrangements like a personal car or an assistant to help them to reach school.

## Capacity Building

Out of the twenty regular teachers, fifteen felt that they were not trained for handling children with disabilities in the classrooms. They expressed that even when they wished to help children with disabilities in their respective classes they felt inadequately qualified to do so. They desired to learn more about inclusive education. To quote few teachers who expressed concerns like these are mentioned below:

> *I have done my regular teacher education. It does not equip me to deal with child with disability. I do not know what to do with him. I feel frustrated.*
>
> *I am not trained to teach children with disabilities. They have been forced on us. It wastes the time of the entire class (Dhara, Regular teacher, School 3)*

> *Though we keep having these trainings at our school, I do not think it is sufficient for us to handle children with special needs. The manifestations of these needs are so varied, there are no ready solutions. Our minds do not work like resource teachers.*

During our discussions with the regular teachers, Ms. Gauhar (Sania's teacher) provided additional information which contributed a great deal in interpreting the proceedings. Ms. Gauhar informed that she did not feel equipped to handle a 'special child'. She considered it to be the job of a special teacher. She did have a very cordial relationship with the Special Teacher; she felt the special teacher was more of an 'interfering kind'.

The interviews with regular teachers revealed that the teachers did not have appropriate exposure in dealing with children with disabilities during their preservice training and therefore, lacked appropriate attitude and sensitivity. The teacher training courses across India are varied and approach inclusive education from the 'deficit perspective'. Apart from an optional paper on 'children with special needs' there are no formal inputs on inclusive education which could prepare the teachers to handle diversity in the classrooms (Singal 2005 cited in Giffard-Lindsay 2007). The standard Bachelor in Education programme has a course on educating children with special needs in India. However, teachers when confronted with the practical challenge of teaching in inclusive classes lacked the skills to deal with the situation and mostly ignored children with disabilities as being the responsibility of the resource teachers alone. Most (15 out of 20 teachers) teachers interviewed during the study expressed their inability to deal with children with disabilities. Thus, the concern of inadequate training of teachers to handle diversity in their classroom emerges. Specifically, in numerous surveys, teachers have reported that they have insufficient skills and training to adequately serve students with special needs (see also Lieber *et al.*, 2000; Schumm *et al.*, 1995; Houck & Rogers, 1994; Schumm & Vaughn, 1991; Semmel, Abernathy, Butera, & Lesar, 1991). To facilitate confidence and competence, teachers need systematic and intensive training that includes research-based best practices in inclusive schools. Moreover, critical to sustained change is staff development that is ongoing and participatory, for example, establishing study groups, teacher collaboratives, and long-term partnerships (Little, 1993; Wenitzky, Stoddart, & O'Keefe, 1992).

During the analytical process which began almost simultaneously with data collection, teacher training started emerging as a very vital issue in terms of handling children with disabilities in the classrooms. Therefore, in order to strengthen this component in the research the teacher trainees of an 'Integrated teacher training course' which is one of its kind in India were interviewed and perspectives were also obtained from the Director and teaching staff of the institution.

This course upholds that all children are special and may have variations in capacities and talents, pace of learning, extent and limits to learning, and inputs needed for their learning. It was considered necessary to adopt a unitary approach to education, where teaching and training fell within the same organizational system and structure to incorporate the planning of schools and the professional development of teachers. The course addresses the educational needs of children as well as the professional needs of teachers. The course aimed to develop knowledge of diverse needs, disabilities and giftedness, appropriate skills, ability to teach at elementary level in multiple settings amongst the aspiring teachers.

It was interesting to find out what motivated the teacher trainees to opt for the course. There were twelve teacher trainees enrolled for the course. Though some of them were not sure what motivated them to join the course, few drew inspiration from earlier unsuccessful experiences with children with disabilities and a couple of them had someone in the family who had suffered due to insensitivity of the educational system due to their disability. Nonetheless, all mentioned that they were confident about dealing with children with disabilities in the regular classrooms after this training. Our interviews and experience with the teacher trainees just strengthened the direct relationship between the pre-service training and the attitude of the teachers. The statement by one of the teachers which summarizes the following quotes and the discussion to quite an extent is, "because we have knowledge we look at the "special" children as "normal". The other teachers, however, see them as different and a liability".

*When I was teaching in a school, I had an ADHD child in the*

> *class. He was unlike normal children so I did not know how to handle the child and therefore I was looking out for a course which would equip me with the expertise to handle such children. I really had a tough time handling the ADHD child. She would show variable behaviour, today she will drop a table, tomorrow she would run around the school, she would think that it is a playground. For being a good teacher you require immediate reaction which was earlier absent in me (narration by a teacher trainee).*

> *Earlier we used to get scared looking at such children, now for us it is normal to have such difficulties and we feel equipped to handle children with special needs in the classroom (Teacher trainees).*

> *Our faculty always stress that it is not that our curriculum is very different from the regular teacher training curriculum it is just that it is taught differently. There the focus is on some children while we focus on all children. The similarities in children are many and differences are only few (one of the teacher trainee).*

It was interesting to find Tripti, a regular teacher with School 5 who had undergone training as an 'integrated teacher'. She shared that the training curriculum has helped to face all children in the classrooms. She was mostly concerned about the attitudes of the teachers towards the children with disabilities. She felt that they relied on the resource teachers even for things they could have easily addressed in the classroom settings.

> *I truly feel blessed to have undergone integrated teacher training. It has prepared me to handle all children in my class, unlike the other teachers. I often share my learning with the other teachers but they do not seem interested. I am concerned about the children with disabilities enrolled with us. Except the principal and few teachers, no one actually cares for them (Tripti, School 5).*

Thus, capacity building of the teachers emerged as an important concern. It could help in combating negative attitudes, help them acquire essential knowledge and develop relevant skills for handling diversity in their classrooms.

## Conclusion

Through this research three main challenges surfaced in the inclusive set-ups. We have endeavoured to depict them diagrammatically (Fig. 4.4) for a vivid understanding. The biggest share of the challenges was negative attitudes of the regular teachers and peers (see also Stubbs, 1997). The reason for this suggestion is that all the Principals mentioned that that they were actually struggling to bring about an attitudinal change in the regular teachers. One of the Principals dramatically put forward this concern as the *"Sensitivity, Sensitivity and Sensitivity,* these are the only three things I require from my teachers to help the school function better". The Resource teachers (8 out of 12) also mentioned that the attitude of the regular teachers needs to undergo a change for collaboration and planning better outcomes for children with disabilities.

The smaller share is given to resources and capacity building in terms of illustrating priority not magnitude. The schools are functioning with some resources and there is little doubt over the fact that some additional resources could prove extremely beneficial; whether we consider human resources like resource teachers or material resources like teaching aids and enhancing accessibility. One of the schools had employed nine resource teachers and certainly was doing better in terms of number of children with disabilities and quality of remedial teaching provided. Even the mothers from that school experienced less burdened with academic activities.

The other challenge was the pre-service and in-service training of the regular teachers. The capacity building is sure to bring about the necessary attitude change as well (Beh-Pajooh, 1992; Shimman, 1990) and thus the arrow showing the relationship. The two concepts of resources and capacity building are also related. The training shall also strengthen the human resource component and facilitate understanding of minimal use of resources for inclusion.

When a school introduces an inclusive environment, it would be

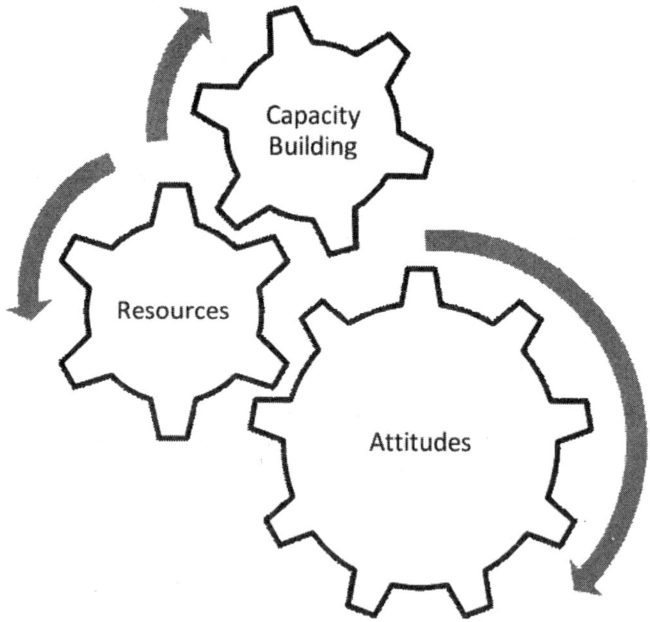


**Fig. 4.4:** Challenges Faced in Inclusive School

beneficial for at least the teachers who would be handling inclusive classes to be given some orientation to equip them to deal with relevant situations. The individual schools might find it beneficial to organise special training workshops at regular intervals for teachers who might be interested and involved with children with disabilities could improve satisfactory outcomes for both the children and the school. In fact, prior to planning the training sessions, there could be training needs analysis which would identify areas in which the teachers seek help. At the macro level, as more public and private schools might become inclusive, the teachers training curriculum could include a special module to train on inclusive education. This module might also provide an internship period in inclusive schools. The government bodies responsible for designing teacher education curriculum is National Council for Teacher Education (NCTE) and National Council for Education, Research and Training (NCERT). There have been recent attempts to redesign the teacher education curriculum to respond to changing educational context and a Draft Curriculum

Framework for Teacher Education in India (2006) has been published (the website currently displays the draft document for discussion, retrieved from *http://www.education.nic.in/Elementary/NCFTE-31.08.2009.pdf* on 2nd Sept. 2009). However, this may take a long time to get finalised and implemented as other policy documents.

This theme has identified a number of important systemic barriers to implementing inclusive education. The elucidation of the challenges of inclusive education in the given context would help us in constructing the model which could affect practice. The clear understanding of these issues helps in formulating and implementing concrete strategies to effect real and lasting change.

## PROCESS

The framework for the analysis of the process of inclusive education was adapted from the Index of Inclusion designed by Tony Booth and Mel Ainscow (2002). There are three dimensions of the inclusive education process—Cultures, Policies and Practices. The process of inclusion involves the experiences of the staff, students, parents and the community. The data generated from the schools in Mumbai were fed into the analytical framework; the consequential findings are herein presented.

### Cultures

The first dimension is that of Cultures; it requires upholding the beliefs and values that create a secure, accepting, collaborating and stimulating community for all students (National Curriculum Council 2002). Paula Kluth (2005) suggests that school philosophy or mission statement must support inclusive education. All the schools which admitted children with disabilities had committed themselves to the philosophy aligning with inclusive education. The philosophical statements concern the overall goals for the organisation. These statements must reflect that the school takes responsibility of the children with varying needs and abilities and shall endeavour to provide a stimulating educational environment to all its learners.

Some examples which truly align with the inclusive philosophy have been presented below. The first two quotes have specifically laid out their inclusive philosophy through statements like "student's schedule to be tailored to his special needs, strengths and interests". The mission statement of School 1 is quite comprehensive and takes into account the special needs of the children and achieving excellence through an inclusive development programme. Similarly, School 3 emphasizes the worth of every child and its learning abilities. This is much in alignment with the child right philosophy embodied in the Convention of the Rights of the Child which upholds that all children can learn and must be provided equal opportunities.

> *The course and the system of education at the school allow a* student's schedule to be tailored to his special needs, strengths and interests *[emphasis added]. Excellence in education through an all-round inclusive development programme is the guiding belief of 'the school'. The main objective is to propagate and advance education to the fullest possible degree, by incorporating quality principles in all areas (School 1).*

> *The school philosophizes that* every child has equal worth and can learn *[emphasis added]. Children learn best when they are in emotionally secured environment and all individual needs of the child must be addressed utilizing the multiple intelligences (School 3).*

> *The school garners a belief that learning is a shared responsibility between students, teachers and parents. Learning should be meaningful, relevant and life-long for the learner and teacher. The school should feed the child's innate curiosity, stimulate creativity and concern through actual hands—on developmentally appropriate experience and reflection (School 4).*

Some of the schools, however, remained silent on inclusive issues despite practicing inclusion. There is an ambiguity in the philosophical statement of School 3 with respect to inclusion; it is unclear whether the term "every child" signifies all children in general including children with disabilities or it meant every child enrolled in the school.

For instance, School 4 centres the learner and does not categorically spell out 'child with special needs' or 'all learners'. Table 4.3 illustrates the usage of the inclusive terminologies by the schools in their mission statements.

These statements acquire special importance as during the interviews with the Heads of the Schools, they often cited the school's guiding philosophy and how it has affected their functioning and administration.

> *I derive my strength from our school's philosophy and often quote it in staff and parent meetings to reiterate our belief systems and motivating the staff (Principal, School 1).*

> *As you have read, our school believes that every child can learn and we abide by this simple yet most powerful statement. It guides us make appropriate policies, to acquire the necessary resources and sensitivity required to manage an inclusive statement. We practice what we uphold (Principal, School 3).*

The indicators of inclusive culture as proposed in the index of inclusion were "*Building Community*". The more specific implications which emerged were whether the first contact of the

**Table 4.3:** Usage of the Inclusive Terminologies

| Inclusive Terminology → School ↓ | "Children with Special Needs" | "All Learners" | "Inclusive Environment" | "Every child can Learn" | "Equal worth" | General Philosophical Statements |
|---|---|---|---|---|---|---|
| 1 | √ | | | | | |
| 2 | | | | | | √ |
| 3 | | | | √ | √ | |
| 4 | | | | | | √ |
| 5 | | √ | √ | | | |
| 6 | √ | | | | | |
| 7 | | | | | | √ |

student or the parent or the community was welcoming and friendly, and there were indications of positive rituals for the welcome or marking their leaving.

In most of the schools (5 out of 7), a seminar or a welcome event is organized at the beginning of the new session. In some schools the parents are also invited for the event where the school's inclusive philosophy is reiterated through speech, role plays, empathy exercises etc. to educate the students and parents (in some cases). The School Principals believed that it was an extremely benefitting exercise and it helped the students to be more responsive to their peers with special needs. The children with disabilities also felt welcomed through this initiative of the school. The two schools which did not organize annual event like this at the beginning ensured that the newly admitted students and their parents had been briefed about the school's stance on inclusion and clarified to the parents whatever concerns they had regarding this. Mostly the concerns that the parents of the non-disabled peers raised were related to the fact that whether such an arrangement is practical and if it implied any harm to their children's academic interests. Such concerns were addressed at the beginning by the Principals and in some cases the Counsellors or Resource Teachers employed with the school. Nonetheless, despite an orientation these issues crop up many times during an academic year and such sessions are conducted whenever the need arises.

The Principals of the school were 'torchbearers' of inclusion (see also Singal, 2008). Their commitment towards including children with disabilities in their school, their effort to sensitize the teachers through personal meetings and training, their concern about the sustenance of the child whom they have enrolled and personally looking their matters were significantly pointing towards their dedication to the cause.

The Principal of School 1 had adopted the "open door policy", which meant that her doors were deliberately kept open for the parents, teachers and students. She said that it helps to address concerns which sometime arise on an everyday basis. She believes that if people get into the intricacies of taking appointments then people tend to avoid or blanket the issue. She is of the opinion that it has kept her more informed and aware about the school issues and rendered her more approachable and democratic.

There were many indicators in the Index which did not have a 'data match'. Let us discuss those to understand what was missing from the 'cultures'. Some of the indicators which feature in the "establishing inclusive cultures" section were, *high expectations for all students, all students are equally valued, staff seek to remove barriers to learning and participation in all aspects of the school and the school strives to minimise discriminatory practices (details in Appendix II).* Though there were no evidences on abstract indicators of whether the schools have high expectations from all learners or value the learners equally from this research, the theme on 'Challenges' discussed the barriers which exist in the school and not many efforts directed towards addressing those concerns. It is interesting to note that though the school has an inclusion policy and some support mechanisms are in place, there are some 'latent' influences which perpetuate discriminatory practices. We have a reason to call these influences 'latent' as the school culture and authorities do not approve of them and if brought to notice, they take stringent actions like for instance in case of 'bullying' the parents of the accused child are called and warned that repeated activities like these could result in expulsion (School 1), or if the regular teacher refuse to take responsibility or shows indifference then a memo is issued (School 5). However, these barriers continue to exist in the school situation despite the measures adopted by the principals in case of non-compliance.

**Policies**

The second dimension is that of Policies, which entails the introduction of explicit aims for promoting inclusion in school development plans and other guidelines for practice in the management, teaching and learning in the schools (National Curriculum Council 2002).

The first step towards sustaining inclusion by the schools was the recruitment and staff development programmes. All the seven Principals emphasized that they ensure that the newly recruited teachers fit the desired criteria of an 'inclusive teacher'. All the principals believed that the new teachers take special interest in children with disabilities and sometimes are successful in involving them and satisfying the parents of the children with disabilities. However, with time a few Principals reported that their enthusiasm dies down. Some of the reasons which we got as explanations to this were: "the experienced staff colour their perception" (Principal, School 3), "the extra effort becomes burdensome" (Principal, School 1) or "the probation time is over" (Principal, School 5).

> *I normally get a good response from the new teachers. They try to follow instructions, collaborate with the resource teachers and do a fine job. The parents of children with disabilities have expressed this often in personal meetings with me. (Principal, School 4)*

The recruitment policy in all schools gives preference to pre-service training (it is not a mandatory requirement), years of experience, skill set, personal characteristics of the teacher which can be assessed during interviews like willingness to teach 'all' learners, professionalism, way of communication and confidence (summarized from the interviews with the principals).

Five out of the seven schools believe in staff-development through periodic in-service training ranging from two to five times in a year on various aspects of teaching-learning. At least one workshop deals specifically for teaching children with disabilities and maximizing their involvement in class. The five principals strongly believed that these in-service workshops and training helps the teachers in better classroom management, advancing their teaching skills and handling diversity. Some of the training programmes conducted by the schools for the regular teachers were entitled, "Enhancing sensitivity", "Involving children with special needs", "Make every child learn" etc. The two school principals who did not organize these in-service trainings for the teachers expressed shortage of resources. They, however, encouraged their teachers to participate in external short-term trainings offered by other institutions.

## Practices

The third and the final dimension is that of *Practices* which calls for practices that reflect inclusive school cultures and policies by ensuring that classroom and extra-curricular activities encourage the participation of all students and draw on their knowledge and experience outside the school (National Curriculum Council, 2002). This dimension was the most concrete and tangible. We will attempt to look at practices adopted by the school and the teachers in details so as to understand the 'process of inclusive education'. The Principal (School 5), summarized the practices as "training the teachers to be receptive and non-judgmental and creating a student centre environment which encourages independence and facilitates learning which is centred around each student's individual learning style". Before, we consider the practices it would be pertinent to look at the curriculum which is followed in the schools.

***Curriculum***

Curriculum is what is learned and what is taught (context); how it is delivered (teaching-learning methods); how it is assessed (exams, for example); and the resources used (UNESCO, 2004). All the schools were following the "formal curriculum," on a prescribed set of educational outcomes or goals. Because this formal curriculum may be prescribed by authority, teachers feel constrained and often implement it rigidly. Teachers feel that they cannot make changes to or decisions about this type of prescribed curriculum including the predetermined textbook selection. As a result teachers are bound to teaching from the textbook and to the "average" group of students. It often becomes essential as the system is examination and performance oriented which the students must pass. The teacher success is also measured by students' performance on these examinations.

The included schools were following the ICSE and CBSE curriculum, however, a couple of the schools had parallel teaching for the NIOS Board. The National Open School (NOS) was set up by the Government of India, Ministry of Human Resource Development (MHRD) in 1989 with a view to provide education through distant mode to those who cannot attend regular schools. Since its inception, the NOS discharged the responsibility to promote the entire range of school education through open learning system in the country. It performed a significant role for defining standards in open schooling, experimenting with innovations, assisting State level organisations with professional resource support and expertise, and dissemination of tested innovations, curriculum and materials. In July 2002, the National Open School (NOS) was re-christened as the National Institute of Open Schooling (NIOS).

For programme delivery, NIOS had adopted multi-media approach. The Self Learning Materials are provided to all enrolled students in printed form. The NIOS books of Secondary stage have been put on the Internet. CDs of NIOS books are available at a price. The Audio Cassettes of NIOS are particularly useful for blind students. The Media programmes of NIOS are telecast and broadcast regularly every month. The audio and video cassettes are made available to the Study Centres of NIOS.

The most significant barriers to learning for learners in a regular school is the curriculum as expressed by the regular teachers. The barriers to learning arise from different aspects of the curriculum, such as the content (what is taught), the language or medium of instruction, how the classroom or lecture is organised and managed, the methods and processes used in teaching, the pace of teaching and the time available to complete the curriculum, the learning materials and equipment that is used and how learning is assessed.

The evaluation of child's performance in school is done through examination and periodic class tests. For children with disabilities, some concessions are offered in all schools, e.g. extra time, provision of writers etc. In one school (School 1), separate question papers are set for children with disabilities in consonance with their IEPs. In many of the schools the children with disabilities were exempted from doing one language if there were difficulties in language and communication. Some teachers also preferred to take oral tests for children with writing problems.

### *Pedagogy*

The next relevant issue is the pedagogy adopted in the inclusive schools. The pedagogical experience for children in inclusive schools is indeed a different one. All learners have to made part of the teaching-learning exercise. Mitler (2000) contends that inclusive pedagogy is not an appendage to poor pedagogy; the initial point has to be good pedagogy.

Amongst the twenty regular teachers who were interviewed, fifteen of them informed that there is no specific pedagogy that they adopt for children with disabilities in the classroom. However, five out of them made specific reference of children with disabilities in their daily lesson plans and tried to introduce the topic in a simpler manner so that it is universally followed. These teachers endeavoured to make some modifications in their teaching style in order to involve everyone. The schools adopt tailor made practices for their enrolled children with disabilities. There are no uniform set of guidelines to guide pedagogy and curriculum for the children. It is "more on a case to case basis" (Principal, School 2).

This pedagogical component was found to include successful classroom management, effective instructional techniques and appropriate accommodative practices. It would be interesting to present each of these with illustrations from the experiences of children and teachers. The areas covered are diagrammatically represented in Fig. 4.5 for clear understanding of related concepts.

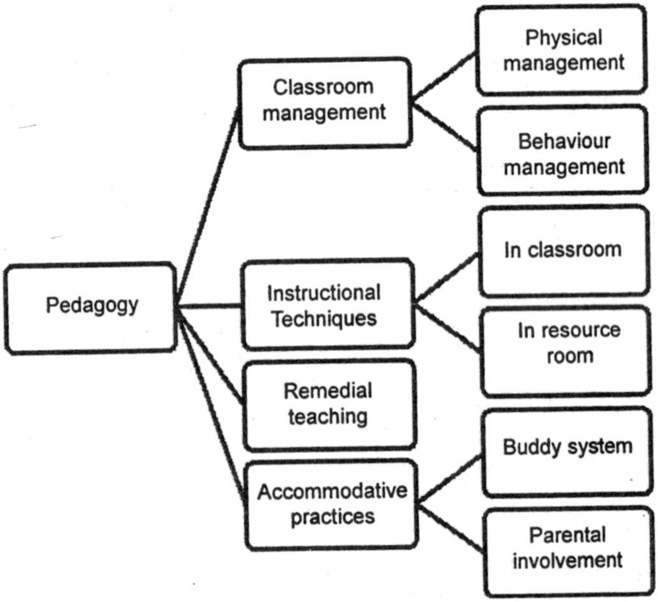


**Fig. 4.5:** Pedagogy of inclusive Schools

*Classroom Management*

Every classroom environment has several elements that have a profound impact on effectiveness of instruction and learning (Doyle, 1986). One important element which emerged from this study was the physical management. The arrangement of all classrooms were observed and found to be 'traditional expository teaching seating plan' (Loreman, Deppler and Harvey, 2006), where children were seated in rows of tables and desks facing the teacher who provides instruction from the front. Teachers thought carefully about allotting seats to the children with disabilities. Seating the children with disabilities in the front row was a common practice across schools. For example, for Tanmay the first major consideration is the 'Seating'. He occupies a permanent place in the first row near the teacher. Berry (1995) also suggested that the children with hearing impairment must be positioned to avail advantages of all visual cues.

The other issue concerning physical management was that of 'accessibility'. This surfaced with regard to Nikhil and Rakhi who use wheelchair. In the schools where these children studied the classrooms were cramped and there was not enough space to move about. This meant that they are mostly stationed at one place throughout the day. However, the door space was large enough for entry with wheelchairs.

Another important area of classroom management was management of those specific behaviours which may disrupt classroom environment. Here we would like to present Gaurav's case which would elucidate how behaviour management techniques are being effectively used. Gaurav was diagnosed with Attention deficit Hyperactivity Disorder. The school faces the following problems with Gaurav quite often (Preeti, Resource teacher)—

- Inability to perform everyday tasks/distractibility
- Impairment to control impulses/impulsivity
- Restlessness/hyperactivity

The Resource teacher in the school had regular sessions with the child and according to the parents it has helped to some extent. She even helped the parents and arranged several counselling sessions for the parents. It was she who carried out initial assessments and referred the Gaurav to the psychiatrist. Gaurav was helped through the group management techniques employed with the help of the resource teacher, classroom teacher and school Counsellor. For implementation, the classroom rules are explained to the class and also displayed with the help charts and the consequences for breaking the rules. The resource teacher and Counsellor informed that it is possible to enforce two-three rules at any point in time. Depending on the behaviour Gaurav displayed in the classroom, the rules were changed. The rule most strictly adhered to was 'no aggressive/violent behaviour'. Gaurav had a short temperament and had gravely hurt some of his classmates in the past. The students are positively reinforced through "smiley's and stars" when there are no occurrences of fights. The entire class was made responsible for Gaurav's behaviour and if anyone indulged in provocative behaviour was punished. Though this had reduced the frequency of unfavourable events in the classroom it had not completely stopped.

It was observed that most of the unsolicited behaviours were reported during the free time or lunch time. Gaurav was, therefore, strictly instructed to report to the resource room during 'free times' and 'recess'. The resource teacher usually gave him some activity or allowed him to access the computer. He usually found it interesting and sometimes got a couple of his friends to the resource room to play with him.

The resource teacher had instructed the regular teachers on certain ground rules for Gaurav's class, scheduling activities to be completed within the given time, not to assign any other activity if the student finishes before allotted time, he is assigned a group where his friends belong, use behaviour management techniques with Gaurav and provide him with positive feedback.

In consultation with the mother target behaviours were determined for instance, when we were around the mother had complained that Gaurav did not finish his lunch. The resource teacher and the Counsellor then set this target for that week. If Gaurav finished his lunch during recess, she made a note in his diary. Generally, the classroom teacher stayed in the class during recess and therefore, they requested her to be attentive with Gaurav. If he continued to show good behaviour for the entire week, the resource teacher allowed him to access the computer for half hour. During that week he finished his lunch four times in six working days of the week.

> *Sometimes a particular positive reinforcer fails to work. I therefore, believe in involving the child when the reinforcer is decided so that he is motivated to sustain good behaviour. Till now it has worked wonders (Preeti, Resource teacher).*

Gaurav's mother was also involved in planning activities for him so that she could even engage him at home. She visited the school at least twice a week to appraise and assist the resource teacher. Gaurav's mother also handed over the responsibility of administering medication to him. The resource teacher has scheduled an alarm for the same and makes him have his medicines.

> *The medication has helped to control his unsolicited behaviours and improve his concentration (Preeti, Resource teacher).*

Gaurav, thus, sustained in the school through a support network created by the resource teacher, Counsellor, mother and to some extent by the regular teachers. The case illustrated how practice entailed increasing desirable behaviours, decreasing undesirable behaviours, promoting generalization and maintenance and enhancing self-management.

Sania's mother provided many examples (one presented below) as to how the resource teacher had been helping Sania to continue in the school. According to the mother the other teachers were 'apathetic' to her and she does not even have many friends. The resource teacher had been an instrumental in the entire process of helping Sania to learn the language, help with the curriculum and other concerns.

> *One day Sania just refused to go to the school. She would throw tantrums in getting up early for school and would cry. When this continued for two-three days, the mother shared it with the resource teacher. The resource teacher made a behavioural contract with Sania. She said that if you come to the school and will not make your mother angry in the*

> *morning for three consecutive days, you will be given a "treasure". She would ensure going to Sania's classroom in the morning and ask if I was 'happy' (the teacher uses a sign) or 'sad' in the morning and would confirm with me when I visited the school in the afternoon. Sania's behaviour improved a great deal after this exercise (Sania's mother).*

Thus, the behaviour management for children with undesirable behaviours is often initiated by the resource teacher. Nevertheless, for effective management and maintenance it is important to involve the regular teachers and parents as well as it was evident from the case examples.

*Instructional Techniques*

All of the dimensions discussed in this chapter are associated with instructional outcomes. However, here the focus is specifically on the instructional techniques which may help the children with disabilities in regular classrooms. Not only did the resource teachers used multisensory techniques for children with disabilities in the resource room setting, they also encouraged the regular teachers to employ certain instructional techniques in the classroom.

> *As part of my responsibility I share and sporadically reiterate what will work with him in the classroom situation. She had instructed the teachers to "provide short clear instructions, keep their faces visible to Tanmay, avoid movement in the classroom, try to speak clearly and 'normally', use lot of gestures and facial expressions, use of charts, writing on the blackboard, and occasionally check on Tanmay."(Tanmay's resource teacher).*

Despite the instructions and initiative taken by the resource teacher she informed that the major responsibility of Tanmay is shared between the mother and her. During the remedial class conducted twice a week, she works on his subjects. She often has to make Tanmay wait after his school hours for completing the course. She uses interactive mathematical games and computers to teach him.

The resource teachers were seen taking considerable responsibilities of these children and devising ways and means to facilitate instruction in classroom. We would like to exemplify it through another case example. Aakash's resource teacher, Richa had communicated certain behaviours and strategies for the classroom to the regular teachers who teach Aakash. She recommended that the teachers must provide warning before suddenly switching over to other activities. She reminded teachers about using simple and clear language rather using complex phrases which might cause confusion to Aakash. Generally, the teacher provided Aakash with simple instructions individually. The resource teacher commented that the regular teachers are not consistent with their ways of teaching and including Aakash in all the activities.

The instructional techniques may vary according to the need of the child, however there were some common instructional techniques like learning in groups which some of the schools actively used and favoured. Some teachers mentioned that learning in groups is effective for all students and especially useful for children with disabilities.

### *Remedial Teaching*

Remedial teaching was a universal phenomenon for all children with disabilities. All the children attend remedial classes by the resource teacher. Three children, Harshit, Ishita and Soham attended remedial sessions after school hours and remained in the classrooms for entire day. The educational problems of these children were looked after by the Resource teachers and there were no specific techniques which the resource teachers followed. They used lot of activity based learning, computers and interactive learning techniques with the students during remedial teaching.

With Aakash, the resource teacher made the following attempts when he visited the resource room—

- Giving him clear guidelines on what activities they will be carrying out in the scheduled time.
- Specific teaching of social rules/skills, such as eye contact and social distance.

- Encourages computer based learning as Aakash enjoys learning using the computer.
- Sometimes when she is free she sits with Aakash in the classroom and helps him with some activities.
- She also had educated the classroom peers about his condition and encourages them to help him.

These examples are indicative of the role of the resource teachers in the process of education delivery for the enrolled children with disabilities. Their understanding of the disabilities and associated needs help them to facilitate learning.

### *Accommodative Practices*

These practices are additional to the curriculum and pedagogical practices wherein some extra efforts are made for accommodating children with disabilities in regular schools. The practices found in this respect were cooperation elicited from the peers and the parents.

#### *'Buddy' System*

An important goal of an inclusive educational system is to prepare the non-disabled children to understand and assist their peers with disabilities. Some of the schools had introduced the 'buddy system' to augment this process of inclusion for children with disabilities. This system involves non-disabled children to help their friends with disabilities in classroom and other school activities. Though the 'buddy system' ensured that children with disabilities are rendered a helping hand by some students, the behaviour is not guaranteed by all classmates. Apart from few friends, all children are not sensitive to the needs of their peers with disabilities (refer theme on challenges). The 'buddies' were usually assigned to the children with disabilities by the classroom teacher for few days or weeks.

The system was useful for Simran to quite an extent. Simran has a visual impairment and presents a range of educational needs. The primary need for Simran is to be completely familiar with the physical layout of the classroom. The classroom teacher along with the resource teacher has ensured that Simran is well versed with the classroom arrangement and take care that it is not disturbed through the academic year. The classmates were sensitized to her needs and the teacher encourages everyone to help Simran. The head teacher had instructed not to force responsibility of Simran on other children. The teacher informed that they never had problems with addressing her mobility needs especially to the computer laboratory or the playground. Some students in the class voluntary take that responsibility for her and carry it out successfully.

> *Her classmates are extremely sensitive and caring. Some of them give directions to her as guides. One day her friend Jagriti told me that she wants Simran to move around on her own and that is why she helps her understand the school architecture as well (Simran's class teacher).*

Similarly, Nikhil and Rakhi expressed that this system is quite helpful to them as they borrow notes from them, help in accompanying them to different classes and interact with them. The 'buddy system' works on rotation and reportedly the non-disabled children carry out the responsibility well.

*Parental Involvement*: The schools were involving willing parents as teachers which was benefiting the child. Furthermore, most parents had already been teaching their children for years. It is the parents who inculcate the behaviours and manners in children even before they enter the school. The resource teachers were found to provide framework and strategies to help them better teach their child. There are two settings where parental involvement is crucial, at home and at school. At schools the parents were given more of secondary roles like providing physical assistance (if needed), completing class notes and facilitating the process of inclusion. At home, their role was magnified as teachers, helping the child with the homework, teaching desired behaviours and maintenance and reinforcing what is taught in school.

In case of Tanmay, the mother is also a proactive stakeholder in his education. She visits the school everyday to complete class notes, meet regular and resource teacher on activities to be done at home. She also meets the visiting school Counsellor periodically to deal with the social and emotional problems of the child.

For Nikhil and Rakhi, the parents are in constant touch with the teachers in the school who inform them about the child's progress. Nikhil's mother has taken this responsibility entirely. She visits his school once a week to complete his class notes, meets the concerned teachers and discusses the home teaching approach with the resource teacher. She always wanted to send the child to the regular school so that Nikhil gets a chance to interact with his non-disabled peers. She believed that special school setting could have been very depressing for the child as well as for the family. She believed that Nikhil can manage well in a regular school with some support.

Thus, parental involvement is a vital component of the process of inclusive education as they were found shouldering responsibilities of their wards in the school ranging from meeting their physical needs to helping them with the classwork and homework.

***Role of Administration***

The minimum requirements for the school to implement the inclusion policy in the current context which emerged from the study was setting up of a resource room equipped with adequate teaching aids and managed by qualified special educators, ensuring accessibility to classrooms, other areas like library, playground and activity areas and upholding an inclusive philosophy.

The Principals as administrative heads were found to play an important role in the entire process. The Principal of the school 3 ensured that children with disabilities are made to feel a part of the school. She organized regular meetings with the resource teachers, regular teachers and parents. She implemented an inclusive policy in school and made it clear to every child seeking admission and his/ her parents at the beginning.

Similarly, the Principal of school 6 informed that apart from the academic inputs and focus on performance there were some other goals which the teachers were encouraged to achieve. The school promoted 'activity based learning' and the teachers are expected to create a positive, supportive and nurturing environment, encourage involvement of each child, help them develop problem solving skills, and making themselves available for students if they have any problems. This creates an overall learning environment and the

Principal ensured compliance through classroom inspection, talking to the students and parents. According to the principal, the children with disabilities enrolled in the school were adjusting well and had gained acceptance among their classmates and teachers. However, she lamented that if they get support from all the teachers then the experience of inclusion could be more successful.

> *Some teachers are reluctant to take the responsibility of a blind child. They do not give their 100 per cent in the teaching. I try to sensitise them, even at times warn them but I have not been able to see much improvement* (Principal, School 6 giving example of Simran).

The other staff of the school were not directly involved with the children on an everyday basis. However, the mothers of Nikhil and Rakhi mentioned that the peons or the guard were sensitive to them and helped them to get in the vehicle.

## Conclusion

While presenting the information on culture, policies and practices it seems that the practice component was more dynamic. The practices were more specific than universal. If we look at the history of inclusion in schools it is a recent phenomenon and the eligibility criteria entail the nature and severity of disability, family support and 'educability' of the child. All the principals clarified that they discourage very severe cases as they feel unequipped to handle them. "We believe in enrolling those whom we can serve (Principal, School 1). Thus, practices were tailored to suit individual needs of the child, as we observed in each of the cases. Fig. 4.6 depicts the 'not so fixed' aspect of the process of inclusive education.

In conclusion, it may be valuable to look at certain common and some individualistic practices. For children with disabilities all schools emphasized on seating practices. The common belief that the seat 'right under the nose' of the teacher was the best arrangement prevailed in all schools. For some children, undoubtedly this was the best possibility to maximize their abilities like Tanmay, Soham and Simran. Another common practice was the remedial sessions by the

**Fig. 4.6:** Process of Inclusive Education

resource teachers in various schools. Sending the children with disabilities to the resource centres for any help that they may require or enhance learning was followed by all schools. The prevalence of 'buddy system' in some of the schools could also be categorized as common. The 'buddies' help the children with disabilities in areas where they may require help for instance helping them finish class work, helping in physical mobility and addressing small concerns like repeating the instructions or demonstrating instructions.

There are some disability specific needs which are catered to in someway by the schools. For example, if we analyse the two cases of Nikhil and Rakhi the issues related children with spina bifida surfaced. School programmes should be flexible to accommodate the special needs of children. The most important goal of treatment of children with spina bifida is to provide them with the maximum level of mobility and independence possible through optimized therapeutic concepts. This complex disease therefore requires a transdisciplinary effort. Early intervention with children who experience learning problems can help considerably to prepare them for school. Successful inclusion of a child with spina bifida into school sometimes requires changes in school equipment or the curriculum. In adapting the school setting for the child with spina bifida, architectural factors should be considered. This can occur through structural changes (for example, adding elevators or ramps) or through schedule or location changes (for example, offering a course on the ground floor). Children with myelomeningocele need to learn mobility skills, and often require the aid of crutches, braces, or wheelchairs. It is important that all members of the school team and the parents understand the child's physical capabilities and limitations. Physical disabilities like spina bifida can have profound effects on a child's emotional and social development. To promote personal growth, families and teachers should encourage children, within the limits of safety and health, to be independent and to participate in activities with their non-disabled classmates.

The children who exhibit specific needs are mostly catered to by the resource teachers in the schools. In most cases we observed that it was the resource teachers extending the additional help required for the students. Though they attempted to collaborate with the regular teachers by sharing the strategies which they adopt with the children, they did not get the desired response from them. The practice component of the process thus, depended on the resource teacher to the large extent. The children were pulled out of the regular classroom during the free time or hobby classes to attend the remedial sessions with the resource teacher. Sometimes, the resource teacher also attended the classroom sessions with the children to provide special attention. The role of the resource teacher was flexible and multidimensional. It largely was dependent on the student characteristics, needs and family support available to the student.

## 4 OUTCOMES FOR CHILDREN

This theme delves on the outcomes of inclusive environment on children with disabilities. Here we understand and perceive outcomes as achievements which need to be seen and celebrated within the context of the child's abilities and potential. All the children included in the study had spent at least two years in the inclusive school. Their experiences in the inclusive schools were indicative of their self-development and personality. Thus, when we were categorizing the data under the themes, strong connections with the self-concept began to emerge which we decided to portray as a sub-theme. Self-concept enables the children to form healthy relationships, become independent and contribute actively to the society as they mature into adulthood; thus playing a vital role in their development (Harter 1998). Self-concept at school seems to be influenced by the image that other significant persons (teachers, parents, peers) have of the pupil (Burns, 1982; Harter, 1986) and by social comparison with others in the same setting (Rogers, Smith, Coleman, 1978).

The outcome indicators for this research were thus the development of the *self-concept* which was arrived at by the interviews with the children and significant others, and other indicators like enjoyment and achievements education and learning, self-care and life skills and positive contribution, the information on which was largely provided by the mothers and teachers.

**Inclusive Environment and Self-Concept**

Self-concept is defined as a person's view about oneself (Harvey and Greenway 1984). Self-concept is based on accumulated perceptions throughout the lifespan and is strongly influenced by the interplay between their own actions, the reactions of others, and one's perceptions of the events and their surrounding behaviours and outcomes (Byrne, 1996; Davis-Kean and Sandler, 2001; Marsh *et al.*, 1983). We have aligned our discussions with this understanding of self-concept.

A study by Ittyerah and Kumar (2007) focused on four components of the self-concept; body image, life experiences, skills/ abilities, and social interaction patterns for children, adolescents and adults with disabilities. The narratives from children (7-13 years) included in the study showed that schools were viewed as "place of reformation" (p. 109). Children interviewed in this study had highest mean scores for positive statements on self-concept and adolescents with disabilities in the age group of 14-20 years, had least. Children with disabilities also had the highest mean scores for the negative statements illustrating their tendency to respond in extremes. In inclusive settings self-evaluations provides a measure for comparisons with peers without disabilities. Thus, exploring the school experiences of children with disabilities in inclusive schools and the impact of these experiences on self-identity becomes relevant.

Out of the ten children we interviewed, two of them (Simran and Harshit) were slightly older than the other children and may be considered belonging to the adolescent group. We have not generalised our findings to children with disabilities and have specifically provided their chronological age in the quotes keeping in mind that the self-concept develops with age (Damon & Hart, 1982; Papalia & Olds, 1992). As indicated in the quotes below, most students with disability ranked low in their academic performance, which they perceived as a shortcoming.

> *I do not understand many things in the class and therefore, I borrow their notebooks. They then tease me and everyone in the class tells me that my brain does not work like theirs (Soham, 10 years, slow learner).*

> *I never perform well in my examinations. My teachers, parents and my tutor are always unhappy with me (Ishita, 9 years, learning disability).*

> *My disability distinguishes me from the rest of the class. I am not very good at studies but there are others in the class who are also not. But I am known in the school, in the neighbourhood and everywhere else as a 'special child' (Nikhil, 11 years, Spina Bifida).*

Children with disabilities were found to be conscious of their physical self and develop poor self-image. All the four girls and one boy were concerned about their physical self and were comparing themselves with other children in the class on standards of physical beauty. Two of the girls who considered themselves 'pretty' (others had told them so) were very conscious of their physical self and tried to enhance their appearance by choosing clothes for themselves matching it with appropriate accessories. It appears that the girls were more conscious of their physical self than boys; the data however is insufficient to generalize.

> *Sania is very conscious of her physical self. She is pretty and she spends quite a lot of time in front of the mirror. She is fond of dresses, kids' jewellery and nice shoes. She picks them herself in stores and tries them passionately when she reaches*

*home. She spends a lot of time everyday in choosing what she decides to wear. (Sania's mother)*

*I have never seen myself, but my parents and friends tell me that I am very pretty. It makes me happy when people tell me I am pretty and I like this about myself (Simran, 15 years, visually challenged).*

However, children with physical disabilities or physical traits which were not considered as attributes of physical beauty, like obesity (example Ishita) or a squint (Soham as below) had low physical self-concept.

*They do not like me because I am not as pretty as other girls like 'Nirisksha' (Another girl in class). I feel sad in the school. All the children have fun and they play but I sit alone in the classroom. If I go with them, they say "See, football is coming with us" and they laugh. So I do not go out with them. (Ishita, 9 years).*

*I am a girl having a disability. I look very different from everyone, I use long shoes and cannot walk and roam around in the school. I am also not as pretty as my friends (Rakhi, 13 years, Spina Bifida).*

*I have a squint eye, so I do not look like other children. I am not as smart as they (Soham, 10 years, Slow Learner).*

All the boys and one girl (Sania) seemed to give more importance to athletic competence. The child's physical capabilities and performance were fundamental to the formation of physical self-concept (see also Stein, 1996). Children with physical disabilities mentioned that they were unable to perform well in sports and it bothered them. This is consistent with Appleton *et al.* (1994) finding that young people with spina bifida in the UK regarded themselves as less socially accepted and less athletically competent than did able-bodied controls.

> *I am very different from all the other kids in the classroom. I use a wheelchair. I am not able to run and play like other kids (Nikhil, 11 years, Spina Bifida).*

However, those children who displayed athletic competence were happy about it and it seemed to give them a lot of confidence.

> *I love outdoor activities. I am good at Judo, Basketball, Cricket and Athletics. I want to be a sportsperson, someone like Sachin Tendulkar (Gaurav, 13 years, ADHD).*

Two children (Nikhil and Rakhi) who had mobility problems and were unable to join the rest of the class during sports activities felt dejected about it. They usually remained in the classroom or spent time in the library while their classmates were away.

> *In school, I am not so active. I usually read books during games period because I cannot do much. All my friends go down and play during lunch hours and games period. At home, I do lot of things like playing computer games, playing board games with my sister and watching television (Nikhil, 11 years, Spina Bifida).*

In most cases (6 among 10 students), children with disabilities perceived problems for social interactions. They expressed that their 'disability' caused social isolation. They desired to have more friends and be involved in normal activities with their friends. However, they expressed dissatisfaction in their relationships with their non-disabled peers.

> *I do not have many friends in school. No one likes to be my friend because I cannot perform well in studies or sports. They do not call me to their home for birthday parties and other events. I want to be friends with my classmates. I always call them for my birthday party. I even drop them home in my car. But it seems that they do not reciprocate. (Nikhil, 11 years)*

> *Sania wants to play with other kids in the school but other kids shun her. Because she is not able to speak, other kids*

*make her a scapegoat when they are chided for some mischief. (Sania's mother)*

*I do not like talking to people in the class. They are not good and they make fun of me (Ishita, 9 years).*

All 10 children were openly appreciated for their abilities at home as well as in school, which made them happy. However, two of the children informed that their special talents were ignored or not nurtured by the teachers, peers and families. These children were not as confident about their special abilities as other respondents who received encouragement from their family. Some parents (Aakash and Tanmay) accompany their children to the stadium and special sports training camps in school during vacations as they aspired to provide the necessary support for nurturing their special talents. This extra effort towards their children's special abilities was not a common finding as in an inclusive school; parents (particularly mothers) are very involved as care providers. The discussions with resource teachers in schools revealed that mothers were vital actors in inclusive education. Most mothers visit the school daily or at least once a week to keep track of their child's progress, complete class notes, and help him/her with physical needs (if any). These visits are in addition to their household responsibilities and helping the child at home. This pressure sometimes results in their inability to groom their children's abilities by providing the needed support like in the case of Rakhi who had a good voice and wanted to sing but was disappointed that she was not able to take music lessons, or Sania who had special gymnastic talent but did not have the opportunity to develop this.

*I like singing and I want to learn music. I cannot learn music now because my mother will have to take me to the music class and be there with me. We cannot call the music teacher home because they will take too much money. But I will learn music one day and become a singer (Rakhi, 13 years).*

*I do not get time to play with Sania (7 years) or take her to special gymnastics classes. I know she can do very well in sports but I struggle with finding the time to manage*

> *everything. Her father too does not have time for her. (Sania's mother)*

It was observed that some children with physical disabilities like Nikhil and Harshit had accepted their disability and appeared resilient but 6 out of 10 children lamented about their disability.

> *I am not as capable as other kids when it comes to studies and sports. But I feel I am mentally stronger than them. I go through tough times everyday. I have a severe disability, and the other kids can never understand what I go through, I am happy with whatever I am able to do under the circumstances (Nikhil, 11 years).*

> *Though I know that things are not going to change for me and I have to spend my whole life with this disability, I do not lose hope and try my best to make myself strong to face the challenges (Harshit, 15 years).*

> *I never understand anything in the school. All children make fun of me. I cry at home everyday. (Soham, 10 years).*

> *My friends ask me how I can live such a difficult life. I tell them that I was born like this so I have to live this life. Now I have got used to it. But truly speaking, I have lot of pain. I do not know why God has not made me like my friends (Rakhi, 13 years).*

Some studies have shown that children with disabilities want to be seen as 'normal' (Priestly *et al.*, 1999), stay healthy, to have friends and interests, to be part of the local community, to acquire social and self-care skills and future independence, to feel confident and respected by others, and to experience success and achievement (Beresford *et al.*, 2007). Burchard's (2005) research shows that disabled young people in UK have high ambitions and display desires for education, to gain qualifications, get high-status jobs and earn a good wage. For many children feeling 'normal' was important and was linked to being accepted by their peer group. 'Looking good', wearing similar clothes to others and being able to use attractive equipment (boots, wheelchair etc.) contributed to how they felt about themselves. Parents wanted services to be more sensitive to the child's identity and social integration when issuing with equipment, making sure that it is attractive whilst still offering appropriate support. They also stressed the importance of the child experiencing success, and having their achievements recognised.

The study also shows that the children with disabilities aspire to be like their non-disabled peers. These children too expressed ambitions for doing well in their academic work, in sports and they also wanted to look attractive. Therefore, it is important that children with disabilities be provided with opportunities to perform and develop their skills to the best of their abilities.

**Outcomes from the 'Other' Perspective**

In most cases mothers provided this perspective, however, in some cases there were opinions from the teachers as well. In some sense, they were the most convincing explanations as they were also analyzing their decision to have chosen inclusive over special schools. Most mothers were happy about their decision on inclusive placement as their children were getting experiences of the "real and normal" world. Tanmay's mother excitingly noted that his ten years of being in a regular school has learnt to communicate with his hearing friends. The mother feels ecstatic to see him play with children in the neighbourhood. The mother informed that he has confidence to face the hearing world now. Sania's mother, however, had apprehensions about her being in an inclusive school. Sania's mother informed, "She is getting to see the mean side of her friends most of the time". However, she has few friends in the class and the mother feels that she will anyway has to face this in the outside world. She has to learn to communicate and find her way out. Anderson and Anotak (1992) reported that if the person who has a disability had problems with communication, they are seen in a negative light and rejected by their non-disabled peers. Johnson Jr. (1998) found that "students with disabilities often suffer rejection in the regular classroom" (p. 40).

For children who had problems with communication, *being able to communicate* was seen as fundamental to meeting desired outcomes in other areas of life for all groups. The parents highlighted the importance of other people who had regular contact with the child (including parents and siblings, teachers, carers and peers) having the knowledge and skills to understand the child's means of communication. Apart from giving the child a 'voice', having the ability to communicate was seen as opening doors to more opportunities, such as socializing, being active and becoming more independent, which in turn help promote a child's feeling of security and self-esteem.

The outcomes in terms of *enjoying and achievements* in inclusive schools were also interesting to note. As we observed even while building the subtheme on 'self-concept' that children nurtured a desire of having more friends. Even the parents were apprehensive and worried about the social circle of their children. They also wanted them to have more friends so that they enjoy their time in school. The lack of contact with school friends out of school was seen as a barrier to achieving friendship across all groups, and was a source of considerable frustration for some children especially Nikhil and Sania. All the parents irrespective of the differential abilities of their children expressed that it is vital that the children enjoy with their friends because it was a factor which motivated them to come to school. For some like Simran, Ishita, Harshit the classmates did render their support to them but they could not be called 'friends'. Harshit reported that the classmates were sensitive to him, would talk to him and helped him with his work if required but they all had different sets of friends. Even Weiserbs and Gottlieb (2000) concluded that non-disabled children favour helping individuals with disabilities more than forming friendships with individuals who have disabilities.

Achievements were both academic and extra-curricular in nature. For some students who did not lack in intellectual abilities for instance, Harshit who scored had performed well even in academics. However, many of the children had low academic performance and were ranked low in the class. We would dwell on some cases to discuss the academic and non-academic achievements for children with disabilities (Box 4.1).

Another indicator of 'outcomes' as emerged from this research was *activities and experiences* having interests and being able to participate in activities was something all parents wanted for their

**Box 4.1: Case-wise Information on Participation Indicators**

*Nikhil's* teacher ranked him as an average student who manages to pass most of his examinations with the help of a writer. He does fairly well in language but is not very good with computer studies, mathematics and social studies especially geography. In his last final exams he secured 58 per cent marks which made him rank 19th in the class of 24 students. His presentations are good and he has good vocabulary. He participates in story writing, elocution, drama but his performance is average. He is a sensitive and introvert kid who is well behaved in class. He likes to be independent and does most of the things like taking out his notebooks, writing his homework diary on his own. His handwriting is not very legible, but he manages to understand his own handwriting and could read from his notebooks.

*Aakash* stood 20th in a class of 28 students and scored 62 per cent marks. Vikas scored 86 per cent and stood 5th. Aakash like participating in quiz and his team has won a prize a couple of times. The school has helped Aakash to a great extent. The Resource teacher in the school has regular sessions with the child and according to the parents it has helped to some extent. Aakash is allowed to continue in the school due to efforts of the parents, Principal and Resource teacher. The parents are always scared that their child might face expulsion at a later stage if he does not improve his social skills, but they are worried that if he is sent to a special school then he would be labelled as a special child in the community. The parents feel that it might spoil his future and he might develop an inferiority complex. Till now they feel that he does not feel he is different from others.

*Gaurav* has been an average student. He scored 65 per cent marks in his last examination and was ranked 18th in class of 28 students. Of late, he has started having problems in Mathematics. The teacher opines that he has started having problems with his concentration. Gaurav is very good in outdoor activities, he takes active interest in sports. He performs very well in athletics and has represented school in inter-school competitions as well. He does not have many friends in the class. He indulges in quarrels and fights in classroom. He is articulate and expresses his feelings well.

*Rakhi* has a learning disability as well. The teachers informed that she cannot write but she tries her best to understand. According to the teachers she is a shy and introvert girl. She secured 48 per cent marks in her last annual examination and was ranked 26th in a class of 28 students. She is good at Hindi language and History. Rakhi sings well and has won many prizes in singing at the school level.

*Soham* scored 55 per cent in his last final examination and ranked 20th in a class of 22. He displays problems with his comprehension. He is good at remembering things but if the problem is twisted he does not understand. According to many of the teachers in the school, he is a lovable sweet child who is well behaved in class. The resource teachers had reported a marked improvement in his performance since he had started taking remedial lessons (2 years ago). He is a talkative child and tries to draw attention of the teacher

(*Contd.*)

by trying to answer their questions. Though his answers are wrong most of the time, he does not give up.

*Sania* remained at the bottom of her class always but the feel(s) mother that she understands a lot of things now. She follows simple instructions at home and school. She is improving. She attempts to communicate using few words. She is doing very well in sports and painting and we make every effort to encourage her.

*Harshit* had average intelligence and he manages well in his classroom. He needs a writer for his examination and the school has made this provision for him. He scored 63 per cent marks in his final examination and stood 18th in a class of 30 students. According to his teacher, he is a sensible child and never disturbs the class. He is attentive in class and sometimes ask questions. He does not have many friends and mostly remains quiet.

*Tanmay* scored 42 per cent marks in his last annual examination and was the lowest scorer in a class of 35. Though his academic achievement has substantially declined as he reached the higher grades, yet his improved social skills are encouraging for the parents and school. He enjoys the company of his friends during the lunch hours and 'zero' hours. The peers were seen extending their full support to Tanmay. The peers were aware of Tanmay's limitations and make an effort to communicate in a manner which everyone in the group including Tanmay follows. The mother saw it as a preparation to lead a normal adult life because he is improving with time and she is hopeful that he would manage quite well.

*Simran* scored 65 per cent marks in her last final examination and she was ranked 21st in class of 35 students. The teachers describe her a vivacious girl with lot of aspirations. She is a talkative girl with a lot of friends. She is good at reciting poems. She has good memorizing skills and follows the sessions well. She is inquisitive and asks lot of explanatory questions. Sometimes, the teacher even volunteers to answer them outside class when it starts disrupting the ongoing session.

*Ishita* did not perform well in her last annual exams. She failed in most subjects and ranked last in the class of 34 students. She is good at painting but the talent is not getting nurtured at home or school.

child. Many were concerned that their child's 'world' was restricted to home and school and they wanted their child to have greater variety and opportunities. Most parents expressed the desire for their children to participate in mainstream activities in their local community. The exception were some parents of children with impairments who reported their children were not able to cope with such situations like Nikhil's mother was always afraid sending her child to the playground with the domestic help. She observed that he always returned depressed from there or any other place where he would find other children playing with their friends. Similarly, Rakhi's mother also feared situations like these when she would feel disheartened due to her 'disability'.

Many children also expressed a desire to be 'doing more'. The lack of accessible or appropriate facilities and/or the lack of support to assist the child meant that taking part in mainstream activities was often very difficult. Rakhi wanted to join regular singing class, Sania's mother was unable to make her join the gymnastics class and Nikhil would have enjoyed a special computer class where he could learn more about it. Nikhil complained that in school, the computer teacher spent more time teaching study material than giving them time to explore things which he liked to do on the computer. He likes to play activity games and try out new ways in various programmes like Microsoft Word or MS Paint and Powerpoint.

*Education and learning*: Parents' aspirations for their child's education varied according to the severity of the condition and associated learning difficulties. All parents wanted their child to fulfil their learning potential. For those with limited cognitive abilities, acquiring self-care and living skills and enjoying a stimulating environment was often prioritised over academic achievements as in case of Nikhil and Rakhi. However, for children with greater cognitive abilities, parents wanted their child to at least achieve basic skills such as reading, writing and number skills. Children with complex health conditions did not want their schoolwork to be affected by having time off due to ill-health or for treatments. Rakhi's mother noted the need for educational goals to be appropriate and responsive to her child's abilities. Box 4.1 which contains qualitative performance statements for all children depicts that most students rank low in academic performance, however, most of them pass their examinations. This is also reflective of the school criteria of eligibility. The school prefers admission of those who could manage to pass examinations with the available resources. The students with intellectual impairments were declined admission.

*Self-care and life skills*: While for non-disabled children independence is often seen as the child being able to do something without help, for many disabled children, this is not achievable in certain areas of their lines. Managing self-care tasks as independently as possible, with or without support, was a key priority among some children and parents. Two children out of the ten had urologic difficulties and this was a major concern with the parents.

> *I normally discourage Rakhi to visit her friends' places as the environment may not be friendly and encouraging. I have had tough time to manage her when I took her for a birthday party to a friend's place. Many of the children were staring at Rakhi and I was the odd one out as the party was only for the kids (Rakhi's mother).*

Some parents were concerned about learning in the area of life skills. Independence was seen in terms of children reaching their potential in carrying out daily tasks or without support. The life skills children wanted to acquire included being able to make snacks, go out alone, handle money and manage unforeseen circumstances when out. In Sania's case the mother wished that she acquires basic communication skills to manage her life circumstances.

> *I cannot accompany her everywhere, nor can I help her in all life circumstances. She needs to learn to defend herself when she is made a scapegoat or bullied. This learning I only expect in a regular school and I am working towards it with the resource teacher. She will learn soon (Sania's mother).*

*Being part of the local community*: Having the same access to opportunities and activities as non-disabled children and being part of the local community was important to many children and parents. Many of the parents felt that sending their child to a regular school has in someway helped. The children learn to face the world and take initiatives to be a part of the 'normal' world. Mothers of Nikhil and Rakhi reported that it was difficult for the children to gain acceptance amongst others because of the severity of the disability. Though in the school they have gained confidence and feel that they are like other kids, they feel saddened with the attitudes of children in the neighbourhood. The school's decision to enroll them has helped them to understand that they were more similar than different from the other children.

*Feeling involved and having the opportunity to exercise choices*: Being involved in decisions that affect their lives was important for many children and their parents. This ranged from choices about what to wear, how and where they spent their time, planning for the future and decisions about their care and treatments. Many parents observed that their children were keen on making their decisions and talking about things which affect them. Though the parents were not sure whether this was a consequence of regular schooling but they believed so. They thought that their increased participation in things could have been due to social learning. When they observed the other children talking about the decisions they make like choosing their own clothes, making plans for vacation etc., they are also encouraged to think that way. They are thus able to break that 'dependence shell' (Sania's mother).

*Preparation for Adult Life*: All the parents were worried about the future. Every mother was concerned about their children having a job and earning money in adulthood. Firstly, it was important for the children to get accustomed to the normal worldly life. This was the biggest outcome of the regular education they were looking forward to. Secondly, many parents were apprehensive about them being able to find 'normal' partners. They were concerned about the expression of their sexuality in years to come. Thus, many parents felt that this was one area where the school must initiate programmes for awareness and training. They recommended that the schools must nurture the talents or inculcate skills in the students which might prove helpful when the children grow up.

*Feeling loved, valued and respected*: The schools have helped the children to feel that they were loved and that what they wanted mattered. The parents mentioned the Principals and the resource teachers as being instrumental players in this. Treating the child as an individual, involving the child in making decisions about his/her life, and respecting the child's privacy (in a way appropriate to their age) were among things said to make children feel valued. Some of the children shared these experiences and felt extremely good about them.

> *Today the Principal called me on the stage and said that she was proud to have me in the school. She said that we all must*

*learn patience and perseverance from Tanmay (reported by Tanmay to his mother).*

*Ma'am always asks me what I want to do each day. She wants to know what I like (Rakhi about the Resource teacher).*

**Conclusion**

It is not possible to generalize the subjective experiences of the children with disabilities and their parents in inclusive schools. However, we would attempt to present some common experiences through Fig. 4.7; on one side of the balance are the negative experiences of the children and on the other positive. This analysis is based on the reporting by the majority because for some students the 'outcome placement' could be reversed. For instance, for Sania and Simran who were physically attractive, had developed a positive

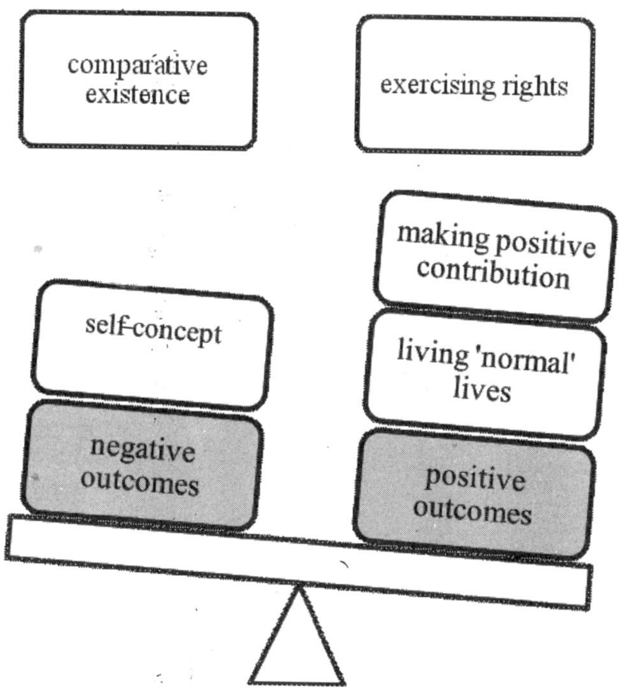


**Fig. 4.7:** Weighing Outcomes

concept about their physical self. However, in many of the discussed areas of self-concept; physical, academic, social and active self-mostly the children had developed negative self-image. In a regular school all the children were leading a 'comparative existence'. The parents reported that the children were in constant comparison with the peers and would often debate on certain issues which the parents avoid, like many of them would question why they cannot be sent to their friends' home, why do other children behave in certain 'unwanted' ways etc.

On the other hand, almost all parents were satisfied that the children were admitted and continuing in a regular school. This to them was "the beginning of normal existence" (Tanmay's mother). All the parents felt that this prepared the children to face the 'normal' world. Some of the parents reported that it has helped in their increased participation in the 'normal daily' activities which could have been restricted in a segregated setting. This would also help them to exercise their rights as equal human beings. The parents had noticed greater involvement of their children in making decisions regarding their lives. Some children like Nikhil, would even participate in the medical decisions about visiting the doctor, asking questions to the doctor etc.

There were outcomes which were achieved while some were expected through the process of inclusive education. For each child the experience of the 'inclusive school' was different and so were the outcomes. It was dependent on the nature and severity of the disability, support mechanisms in inclusive schools, and environment and culture of inclusive culture.

# 5

# The Inclusive Model

## Modelling the Theory: Philosophical Basis

In this chapter, the final research objective of model development is addressed via the findings from inclusive schools. While considering modelling inclusive education in India, we will also discuss how barriers to equal participation in teaching and learning can be overcome. This study seeks to contribute directly to the improvement of the education environment in India and elsewhere by enabling stakeholders to overcome obstacles to the implementation of inclusive education. In addition, it seeks to enable teachers to identify and deal with those factors that act as barriers to the provision of equal education opportunities for all children in their classrooms.

There are three basic principles which govern the inclusive education model. We have derived these principles from the international and national policy documents. These according to us are the basis of inclusive education. For any school to be inclusive, it must adhere to these three principles. It is important to have strong philosophical base for implementing a concept like this, as we have seen from this research. The schools which had explicitly laid out their inclusive policy were more committed in terms of providing support for the enrolled children with disabilities.

- All children have a right to education (Right to Education Act, 2009).

- An inclusive school welcomes children with all backgrounds and abilities (MHRD 2005).
- All children benefit from inclusion.

## The Working Model

To put these principles and findings into action, the model was designed to offer an understanding of contextual practice of inclusive education. We have used the input-process-outcomes (IPO) framework to elucidate the process of inclusive education. In the IPO model, a process is viewed as a series of boxes (processing elements) connected by inputs and outputs. Information or material objects flow through a series of tasks or activities based on a set of rules or decision points (Harris & Taylor, 1997). Flow charts and process diagrams are often used to represent the process (Harris & Taylor, 1997). What goes in is the input; what causes the change is the process; what comes out is the output (Armstrong, 2001). The IPO model provided the general structure and guide for the direction of the study. Substituting the variables of this study on the IPO model, the researchers came up with the following model. Fig. 5.1 illustrates the basic model the elements of which will be subsequently described. The conceptual map developed for conducting the research served as the blueprint for the model.

Input and resources denote all aspects provided to the system to achieve a certain outcome. In the field of inclusive education, inputs and resources could not only be for example, financial resources, or legislation related to education, but also the qualification level of teachers or any infrastructural issues. Education processes transform these inputs and resources into outputs and outcomes. While outcomes describe efficiency measures such as participation rates or curricular achievements, this research highlights the relevance of outcome

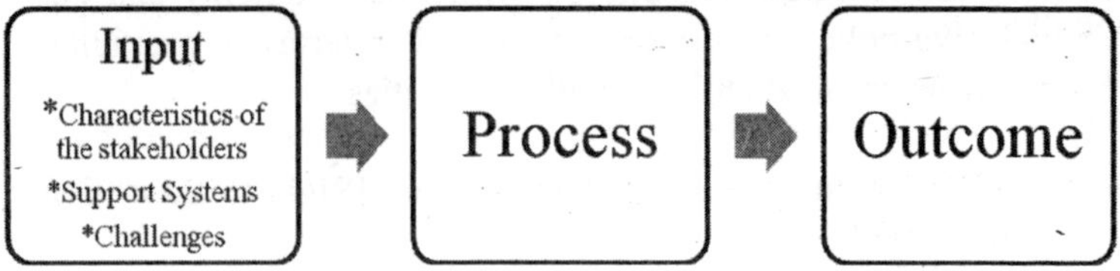


**Fig. 5.1:** Model of Inclusive Education

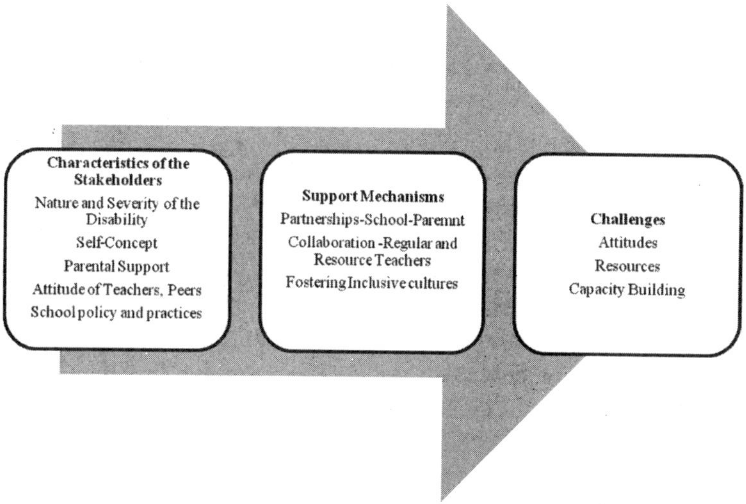


**Fig. 5.2 (*Part A*):** Substituting the Findings in Model. Part A Input Variables.

aspects that emphasise the effects, impact or consequences of input and processes, e.g. academic and functional literacy, independence, or citizenship. Process finally refers to all educational activities including procedures, school policies and culture, or classroom instructional practice. The Parts A, B and C of the Fig. 5.2 illustrate the substitution of findings of the research to the parts of the model for clarity and discussion.

At the core of the Inclusive Education Model is the child with disability. The background characteristics of the child play a significant role in child's education in a regular school. Firstly, the eligibility criteria followed by schools for enrolment of the child in the school is in itself indicative of the interplay of the child's and familial characteristics. The nature and severity of disability was the primary concern among the decision-makers in schools. The school essentially admitted only those children for whom it had enough resources to provide for the special needs arising out of their 'disability'. The school emphasized and sought parental cooperation at the time of admission. The other input variables pertaining to child which played a vital role in the entire IPO cycle were IQ and self-esteem which helped in admission and continuity. The parents had decided in favour of sending their child to inclusive school when they had felt the desire in the child to be a part of the 'normal' community. The other factors which influenced the process and the outcomes were the parental support, financial resources, attitude of the teachers and the school environment in general.

### *Part A—Input Variables*

The child is supported by the Resource Programme and classroom programming which, in turn, is supported by the school administration. Collectively, these people work as a team to play an integral part in the child's development and learning. The Resource Programme is run by the Resource Teacher who offers the following services to classroom teachers and to families of children with special needs on a child-by-child basis: direct classroom support; direct family support; curriculum enhancements and modifications; teaching methods enhancements; coordination and assimilation of specialized support services, such as occupational, physical, and speech and language therapy; and, leadership in the community with ideal practices for inclusive education. The other support factors (see Fig. 5.2 Part A) have been favourable attitude of the peers, their support in classroom and school activities, and positive relationships in school.

The main challenges which emerged were teasing and bullying by the peers, attitude of the teachers, the training of the teachers to handle diversity and the scarcity of resources. The challenges were the negative aspects of the model and would share an inverse relationship between the quality of teaching-learning and expected outcomes for the children with disabilities.

### *Part B—Process of Inclusive Education*

The process of the inclusive education was studied within three dimensions of culture, policies and practices (findings illustrated in Fig. 5.4 Part B). The practice component of the schools was found to be dynamic with respect to the children with disabilities. While some of the practices were common for all children with disabilities enrolled in the school, most were tailored to suit individual needs of the children and thus, were presented case-wise. The practices were

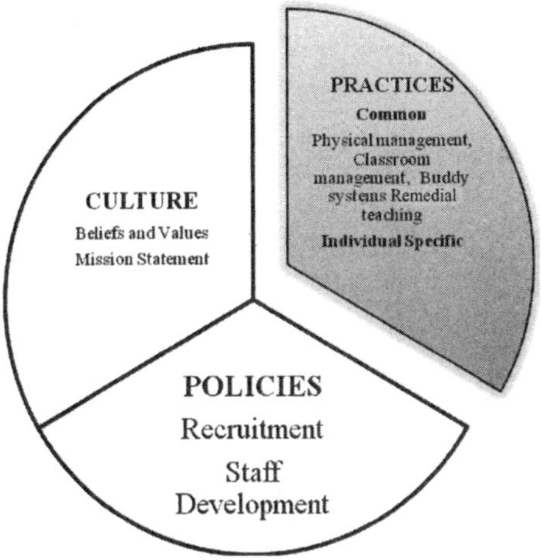


**Fig. 5.2 Part B:** Process of Inclusive Education

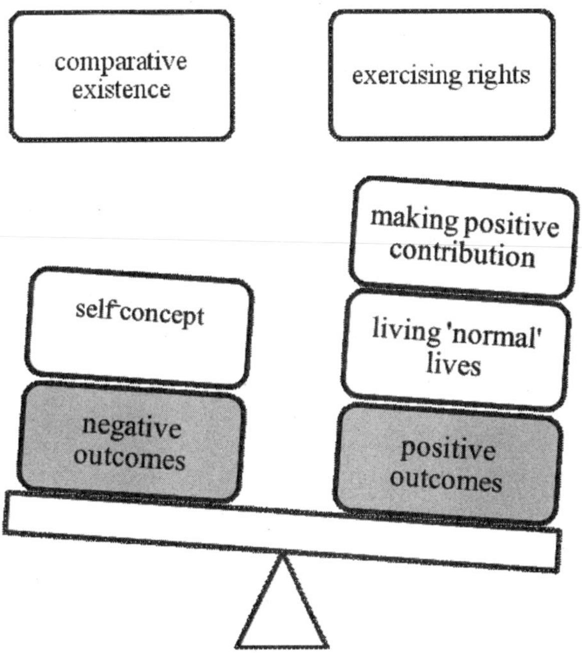


**Fig. 5.2 Part C:** Outcomes for Children with Disabilities.

largely teacher-centric with some inputs from the resource teacher. In the resource room, the practices were more or less uniform in all the schools as they were managed by resource teachers.

### *Part C—Outcomes for Children with Disabilities*

The outcomes for children with disabilities as also depicted in Part C of the Fig. 5.2 were most positive and negative. Mostly the parents and the children aspiration of 'normal' life got fulfilled to a great extent. This has given the children confidence to face the world and they hope and strive towards positive contribution to the society. However, a constant interaction with the non-disabled peers forces the children in comparative existence. They cannot help but compare themselves with the classmates in various areas of school life which sometimes was frustrating for the children. The areas of self-concept where they lacked also set in negative feelings in the children. Though these outcomes were not measurable but we have still chosen to tilt it towards the positive outcomes; probably because the interviews with the parents revealed that the children had disliked their segregation and always endeavoured to be a part of the 'normal world'. This experience prepares them for a 'healthy and normal' life ahead and that sense of achievement was evident with the children and the parents.

Thus, through this model we get to understand the process of inclusive education in the given context. It would be pertinent to lay out certain recommendations which might provc useful in improvising the current practice.

## Implications for Practice and Research

As the issue undertaken for this research is rooted in the ecosystemic layers, we would also like to encompass its relevance and implications for national policy as well. India is still grappling with the issue of achieving "...compulsory education for a majority of children takes precedence over meeting the needs of those with disabilities..." (Ainscow *et al.,* 1995 cited in Singal, 2005b: 338), change for children with disabilities will continue to be sporadic and painfully slow. Inclusive education is a matter of their right rather than a special privilege. Currently, there are not many schools which have taken this responsibility of educating children with disabilities alongside their non-disabled peers. The legislations which promote inclusive education in India, the PWD Act 1995 and the most recent Right to Education Act 2009 await strict implementation. Though the latter is a recent legislation, the former was enacted fifteen years ago still requires a legal enforcement mechanisms (Alur, 2002).

The research showed that many children felt hurt and segregated due to insensitivity of the treatment at school, particularly by regular teachers and peers. The regular teachers lacked training in dealing with children with disabilities and therefore, lacked appropriate attitude and sensitivity. The evidence from the study showed that the regular teachers were unprepared to handle children with disabilities in their classrooms and highlighted their unfavourable attitudes. Teacher development has to be the heart of initiatives for developing inclusive practices in schools (Aniscow, 2003). This necessitates building competencies of all "regular teachers" to deal with diverse population of students and to learn pedagogical strategies that facilitate the learning of all students in their classroom. The inclusive education system requires a more knowledgeable, highly skilled teaching force (see also Panda, 2005). The teacher training must aim to impart necessary skills and develop favourable attitudes towards children with special needs in inclusive classrooms. The standard Bachelor in Education programme has a course on educating children with special needs in India. However, teachers when confronted with the practical challenge of teaching in inclusive classes lacked the skills to deal with the situation and mostly ignored the children with disabilities as being the responsibility of the resource teachers alone. Most (15 out of 20 teachers) teachers interviewed during the study expressed their inability to deal with children with disabilities. When a school introduces an inclusive environment, it would be beneficial for at least the teachers who would be handling inclusive classes to be given some orientation to equip them to deal with relevant situations, if the school organises training workshops at regular intervals, there could be improved outcomes. In fact, prior to planning the training sessions, there could be training needs analysis which would identify areas in which the teachers seek help. At the macro level, however, the teachers training curriculum must encompass the required areas of inclusive education and must have an internship period in inclusive schools.

In the study it was observed that all schools except one had one resource teacher for all children with special needs in the school (ranging between 20-25 children). This meant that the proportion of resource teacher to student was very low in most of the schools. A similar finding has also been reported by Sreekumari (2003), that the number of children with disabilities under one resource teacher is high which acts a barrier. For the Integrated Education for Disabled Children (IEDC) scheme the ratio of resource teacher to student has been decreased to 1:6 (Mukhopadhyay and Prakash, 2004). It is important to have resource teachers in the school to be proportionate with the needs of the children with disabilities in order to provide adequate support. Sometimes, children with disabilities display some needs which may require a constant collaborative effort of the regular and resource teacher in the classroom, for instance, a child with an acute hyperactivity disorder may require the presence of a resource teacher in the classroom. This would only be possible if there are enough resource teachers to share the workload. The one school which was an exception had hired nine resource teachers for around thirty-six children with disabilities, the ratio thus worked out to be one resource teacher for four children with disabilities. It was observed that the resource teachers in this school were satisfied with their ability to keep up with the needs of the children and the children benefited greatly from the level of care and support available to them. The parents of children with disabilities from this school had to come to the school less frequently and were appreciative of the school's efforts towards inclusion of their child. Thus, the recruitment policy of resource teachers in inclusive schools must ensure that the ratio of resource teachers is commensurate with the extent of disabilities of children enrolled.

Peers could be sensitised by the regular and resource teachers through group sessions where they learn about disability and empathy. A constant effort by the school personnel to include the child with disability in normal activities of the school could certainly bring about a change in behaviour of non-disabled peers towards their classmates with disability.

Children with disabilities have an equal right for education as laid out by CRC. Therefore, any School offering education to children with disabilities should be able to provide equal facilities to children with disabilities on par with facilities offered to their non-disabled peers. While the disabled children in this study have had access to their right to education along with their non-disabled peers, our analyses show that the facilities provided to the disabled children fall short of their needs. Therefore, the inclusive schools need to make efforts to introduce and provide for relevant alternative activities for children with disabilities when their classmates engage in activities which disabled children cannot participate in. Computer games, art and craft classes, additional music classes or any special skill class where the child displays interest could be arranged as alternative activities.

Based on the study, the schools are impelled to develop comprehensive inclusive policies and procedures and direct resources to that effort. Principals need to ensure that their schools are fully inclusive and take a lead role in modelling inclusive attitudes and behaviours. Teachers need to ensure that they have the knowledge and skills to adapt their teaching to include all children and the willingness to learn about the experiences of children with disabilities. Finally, we all need to acknowledge and respect the students with disabilities to better understand their realities. With its structures, rules, and objectives, a school is like a microcosm of our world. We have the opportunity to provide schools that model the behaviour and attitudes that we want our children to take with them into the real world. In order for the actions to reflect the words, the schools need to provide the necessary effort, educational policies, resources and minimise challenges to ensure that their values and principles are met.

What emerged from the research that the schools were practicing inclusion in their own ways. The schools were catering to some specific kinds of disabilities depending on their resources and expertise bank. Thus, we propose the schools practicing inclusion to come together to form an association where a pool of experience, practices and resources could be created. This would help in enhancing the inclusion process as well as strengthen the belief and practice. These recommended changes in policy might prove beneficial for children with disabilities who have taken on the challenge of studying in inclusive schools as well as being rewarding to the schools which have taken on the challenge of providing inclusive education.

This study portrays the experiences of children with disabilities in inclusive school settings. The focus of this research was not one any particular kind(s) of disability. It meant to capture the social reality of inclusive schools with children who had varied needs. It, however, emerged that nature and severity of disability did play a role in inclusion processes. Further research is needed to examine the experiences of children with other types of disabilities and learning styles. Also exclusive studies on various aspects of inclusive education like process, outcomes, facilitators and barriers could be undertaken for bringing out other facets which may not have surfaced due to the context and sample size. As the field is advancing there would be numerous new things which would emerge, it is imperative to keep track and document these practices through research. Also, the study on inclusive education could be approached through centring other stakeholders which would help in understanding different perspectives. We also need national level studies which may provide statistical input to small-scale studies. Large scale surveys on inclusive schools, their resources, enrolment ratios, drop-out ratios are required in States which would help in building a comprehensive national picture for policy and action.

*Appendix I*

# Individualized Educational Plan (I.E.P.) 2009-10

*(Procured and Published with Permission from School 1)*

Name of child:

Grade: III

## Part 1: Language-Reading and Writing Skills

- Identify parts of a book
- Short vowel sounds
- Rhyming words
- Read and write his/her own name and telephone number—Give child a wide variety of opportunities to write out or trace his/her name (clay, soap, crayons, sand)
- Alphabetize to the first letter
- Identify and read basic sight words and vocabulary words
- Retell, dramatize, or dictate a story
- Recognizing action and naming words
- Copywriting
- Writing basic sight words and three letter words
- Picture talk
- Answer questions based on picture/story
- Match picture with words/sentence

## Part 2: Number Concepts and Operations

- Calendar skills—tell date and write in notebook

- Concept of more and less—using numerals
- Concept of before and after
- Rote counting up to 300
- Telling time—counting by 5
- Addition and subtraction—3 digit with carryover/borrowing
- Use of calculator
- Recite and recognize days of week and months of year
- Number names
- Money—identify notes and coins, money value
- Measurements
    1. Sort objects by size
    2. Draw line using ruler
    3. Concept of fractions—full, half, ¼ and ¾.

**Part 3: Science**

- Show awareness of the five senses
    1. Tactile—rough, smooth, hard, soft
    2. Taste—sweet, sour, bitter, spicy, salty
    3. Kinaesthetic—balance, throwing, catching, cutting, tearing, pasting
    4. Auditory—differentiation of various sounds, rhythm (auditory perception)
    5. Sight—near, far, primary and secondary colours
- Climate and Seasons
    1. The 3 seasons—climatic conditions (rain walk)
    2. Clothes we wear
    3. Seasonal fruits
- Transport
    1. Water
    2. Land (bus ride)
    3. Air—(visit to Hangar)
    4. Traffic Rules
- Health and nutrition
    1. Meal times

2. Healthy/Junk Food

**Part 4: General Learning**

- Visual and Auditory perception (Following multiple/sequence instructions)
- Good Habits
- Cleanliness
- Map of Beacon High/Map of India (outline)

**Part 5: Inclusive Activities**

- Music
- Art
- Craft
- Computers

# Appendix II

## Index for Inclusion

**The indicators**

| | |
|---|---|
| | **indicators**<br>**DIMENSION A Creating inclusive CULTURES** |
| **A.1** | **Building community** |
| **INDICATOR A.1.1** | Everyone is made to feel welcome. |
| **A.1.2** | Students help each other. |
| **A.1.3** | Staff collaborate with each other. |
| **A.1.4** | Staff and students treat one another with respect. |
| **A.1.5** | There is a partnership between staff and parents/carers. |
| **A.1.6** | Staff and governors work well together. |
| **A.1.7** | All local communities are involved in the school. |
| **A.2** | **Establishing inclusive values** |

***Questions springing from one indicator***

| | |
|---|---|
| | **dimensions, indicators and questions**<br>**DIMENSION A Creating inclusive CULTURES** |
| **A.1** | **Building community** |
| **INDICATOR A.1.3** | ***Staff collaborate with each other*** |
| **i)** | Do staff treat each other with respect irrespective of their roles in the school? |
| **ii)** | Do staff treat each other with respect irrespective of their gender? |
| **iii)** | Do staff treat each other with respect irrespective of their class or ethnic background? |
| **iv)** | Are all staff invited to staff meetings? |
| **v)** | Do all staff attend meetings? |
| **vi)** | Is there wide participation in meetings? |

**The indicators**

| INDICATOR | |
|---|---|
| A.2.1 | There are high expectations for all students. |
| A.2.2 | Staff, governors, students and parents/carers share a philosophy of inclusion. |
| A.2.3 | Students are equally valued. |
| A.2.4 | Staff and students treat one another as human beings as well as occupants of a 'role'. |
| A.2.5 | Staff seek to remove barriers to learning and participation in all aspects of the school. |
| A.2.6 | The school strives to minimise discriminatory practices. |

indicators
DIMENSION B Producing inclusive

**Questions springing from one indicator**

| | |
|---|---|
| vii) | Are all teachers and classroom assistants involved in curriculum planning and review? |
| viii) | Is teamwork between staff a model for the collaboration of students? |
| ix) | Do staff know who to turn to with a problem? |
| x) | Do staff feel comfortable about discussing problems in their work? |
| xi) | Are regular supply staff encouraged to be actively involved in the life of the school? |
| xii) | Are all staff involved in drawing up priorities for school development? |
| xiii) | Do all staff feel ownership of the school development plan? |
| FURTHER QUESTIONS | •<br>•<br>• |

dimensions, indicators and questions
DIMENSION B Producing inclusive

**The indicators**

| | POLICIES |
|---|---|
| B.1 | **Developing the school for all** |
| INDICATOR B.1.1 | Staff appointments and promotions are fair. |
| B.1.2 | All new staff are helped to settle into the school. |
| B.1.3 | The school seeks to admit all students from its locality. |
| B.1.4 | The school makes its buildings physically accessible to all people. |
| B.1.5 | All new students are helped to settle into the school. |
| B.1.6 | The school arranges teaching groups so that all students are valued. |
| B.2 | **Organising support for diversity** |
| INDICATOR B.2.1 | All forms of support are co-ordinated. |
| B.2.2 | Staff development activities help staff to respond to student diversity. |
| B.2.3 | |

***Questions springing from one indicator***

| | POLICIES |
|---|---|
| B.2 | Organising support for diversity |
| INDICATOR B.2.2 | ***Staff development activities help staff to respond to student diversity*** |
| i) | Do all curriculum development activities address the participation of students differing in background, experience, attainment or impairment? |
| ii) | Do all curriculum development activities address the reduction of barriers to learning and participation? |
| iii) | Do staff development activities support staff in working effectively together in classrooms? |
| iv) | Is partnership teaching, followed by shared review, used to support teachers to respond to student diversity? |
| v) | Do staff observe each other's lessons in order to reflect on the perspectives of students? |
| vi) | Do staff receive training in devising and managing collaborative learning activities? |
| vii) | Are there shared opportunities for teachers |

| The indicators | Questions springing from one indicator |
| --- | --- |
| inclusion policies.<br>**B.2.4** The Special Educational Needs Code of Practice is used to reduce the barriers to learning and participation of all students.<br>**B.2.5** Support for those learning English as an additional language is co-ordinated with learning support.<br>**B.2.6** Pastoral and behaviour support policies are linked to curriculum development and learning support policies.<br>**B.2.7** Pressures for disciplinary exclusion are decreased.<br>**B.2.8** Barriers to attendance are reduced.<br>**B.2.9** Bullying is minimised. | and classroom assistants to develop more effective collaboration?<br>**viii)** Are there opportunities for staff and students to learn about peer tutoring?<br>**ix)** Do teaching and support staff learn about using technology to support learning (such as cameras, television, video, overhead projector, tape-recorders, computers/internet)?<br>**x)** Do staff explore ways of reducing disaffection by increasing the engagement of students in curricula?<br>**xi)** Is disability equality education provided for all staff?<br>**xii)** Do all staff learn how to counter bullying, including racism, sexism and homophobia?<br>**xiii)** Do staff and governors take responsibility for assessing their own learning needs?<br>**FURTHER QUESTIONS** •<br>•<br>• |

***The indicators***

| | indicators<br>**DIMENSION C Evolving inclusive PRACTICES** |
|---|---|
| **C.1** | **Orchestrating learning** |
| **INDICATOR C.1.1** | Teaching is planned with the learning of all students in mind. |
| **C.1.2** | Lessons encourage the participation of all students. |
| **C.1.3** | Lessons develop an understanding of difference. |
| **C.1.4** | Students are actively involved in their own learning. |
| **C.1.5** | Students learn collaboratively. |
| **C.1.6** | Assessment contributes to the achievements of all students. |
| **C.1.7** | Classroom discipline is based on mutual respect. |
| **C.1.8** | Teachers plan, teach and review in partnership. |
| **C.1.9** | Teachers are concerned to support the |

***Questions springing from one indicator***

| | **dimensions, indicators and questions<br>DIMENSION C Evolving inclusive PRACTICES** |
|---|---|
| **C.1** | **Orchestrating learning** |
| **INDICATOR C.1.4** | ***Students are actively involved in their own learning*** |
| **i)** | Are students encouraged to take responsibility for their own learning? |
| **ii)** | Do teachers explain the purpose of a lesson or group of lessons? |
| **iii)** | Do the classroom environment, displays and other resources help independent learning? |
| **iv)** | Does the support given to students help them to move on in their learning while drawing on the knowledge and skills they already possess? |
| **v)** | Are curriculum plans shared with students so that they can choose to study at a faster pace or in greater depth? |
| **vi)** | Are students taught how to research and write up a topic? |

| The indicators | Questions springing from one indicator |
|---|---|
| learning and participation of all students. | vii) Are students able to use the library and information technology resources independently? |
| **C.1.10** Teaching assistants support the learning and participation of all students. | viii) Are students taught how to take notes from lectures and books and organise their work? |
| **C.1.11** Homework contributes to the learning of all. | ix) Are mechanical copying activities avoided? |
| **C.1.12** All students take part in activities outside the classroom. | x) Are students taught how to present their work in spoken, written and other forms, individually and in groups? |
| **C.2** **Mobilising resources** | xi) Are students encouraged to summarise what they have learnt verbally and in writing? |
| **INDICATOR C.2.1** Student difference is used as a resource for teaching and learning. | xii) Are students taught how to revise for tests and examinations? |
| **C.2.2** Staff expertise is fully utilised. | xiii) Are students consulted about the support they need? |
| **C.2.3** Staff develop resources to support learning and participation. | xiv) Are students consulted about the quality of lessons? |
| **C.2.4** Community resources are known and drawn upon. | xv) Are students involved in finding ways to overcome their own and each other's difficulties in learning? |
| **C.2.5** School resources are distributed fairly so that they support inclusion. | xvi) Are students given a choice over activities? |

| The indicators | Questions springing from one indicator |
|---|---|
| | xvii) Are the interests, knowledge and skills acquired independently by students valued and drawn upon in lessons?<br>FURTHER QUESTIONS •<br>•<br>• |

# References

Affleck, J.Q., Madge, S., Adams, A., Lowenbraun, S. (1988). Integrated classroom versus resource model: Academic viability and effectiveness. *Exceptional Children*, 54, (4), 339-348.

Agbenyega, Joseph (2007). Examining Teachers' Concerns and Attitudes to Inclusive Education in *Ghana International Journal of Whole Schooling*, Vol. 3, No. 1. 2007.

AIHW (Australian Institute of Health and Welfare) (2004). Children with disabilities in Australia. AIHW cat. no. DIS 38. Canberra: AIHW.

Ainscow, M. (1995). Education for All: Making It Happen. Keynote address presented at the International Special Education Congress, Birmingham, UK, 10-13 April 1995.

Alexander, E., Rennick, J.E., Carnevale, F. and Davis, M. (2002) Daily struggles: living with long-term childhood technology dependence. *Canadian Journal of Nursing Research* 34 (4), 7-14.

Altman, Barbara M. (2001). Disability Definitions, Models, Classification Schemes and Applications. In Gary L. Albrecht, Katherine D. Seelman and Michael Bury (Eds.), *Handbook of Disability Studies*. Thousand Oaks (Cal.): Sage Publications.

Alur, M. (2002). Special Needs Policy in India, in Seamus Hegarty and Mithu Alur (Eds.) *Education and Children with Special Needs—From Segregation to Inclusion*. New Delhi: Sage Publications Inc.

Alur, Mithu and Marcia Rioux (2006). *Included: An Exploration of Six Early Education Pilot Projects for Children with Disabilities in India*. Unpublished Project Report sponsored by UNICEF and Canadian International Development Agency.

American Youth Policy Forum (AYPF) and Centre on Education Policy (CEP) (2001). *Twenty Five Years of Educating Children with Disabilities: The Good News and the Work Ahead.* Washington DC: Author.

Anderson, J.L. (2003). School wide supports for inclusive education: Restructuring for effectiveness. In B. Bartlett, F. Bryer, and D. Roebuck (Eds.), *Reimagining practice: Researching Change*. (Vol. 1, pp. 1-15). Brisbane, Australia: School of Cognition, Language, and Special Education, Griffith University.

Appleton, P.L., Minchom, P., Ellis, N.E., Elliott, C.E., Bol, V., and Jones, P. (1994). The self-concept of people with spina bifida: *Developmental Medicine and Child Neurology*, Oxford: Mackeith Press, Blackwell Scientific Publications.

Argyropoulos, Vassilious and Marina Stamouli (2006). A collaborative action research project in an inclusive setting: Assisting a blind student. *British Journal of Visual Impairment,* 24(3), pp. 128-134.

Armstrong, M. (2001) *A Handbook of Human Resource Management Practice* (8th edition), page 534, Kogan Page (UK).

Arnesen A-L., Lundahl L. (2006) Still Social and Democratic? Inclusive Education Policies in the Nordic Welfare States. *Scandinavian Journal of Educational Research* Vol. 50, No. 3, pp. 285–300.

Artiles, A.J., Kozleski, E.B., Dorn, S., and Christensen, C. (2006) Transformative Agenda Learning in Inclusive Education Research: Remediating Theory and Methods with a Transformative Agenda. *Review of Research In Education* 30; 65.

Ayres, P., Sawyer, W., and Dinham, S. (2004). Effective teaching in context of a Grade 12 high stakes external examination in New South Wales, Australia. *British Education Research Journal*, 30(1), 141-165.

Baer, D. (1981). A Hung Jury And A Scottish Verdict: "Not Proven." *Analysis and Intervention in Developmental Disabilities*, 1, 91–98.

Bailey, D.B., Jr. (1994). Working with families of children with special needs. In M. Wolery and J.S. Wilbers (Eds.), *Including children with special needs in early childhood programmes* (pp. 45-70). Washington, DC: National Association for the Education of Young Children.

Bain, A. and Dolbel, S. (1991) Regular and special education principals perceptions of an integration programme for students who are intellectually handicapped, *Education and Training in Mental Retardation*, 26(1), 33–42.

Balasundran, P. (2005). The journey towards inclusive education in India Presented at Seisa University. Ashibetsu shi, Hokkaido, Japan, 9th July 2005 available at *http://www.gtid.net/global_trend/4_The_Journey_Towards_Inclusive_Educa_India.pdf* (Accessed on 11th June 2009).

Balboni, G. and Pedrabissi, L. (2000). Attitudes of Italian teachers and parents towards school inclusion of students with mental retardation: the role of experience, *Education and Training in Mental Retardation and Developmental Disabilities*, 35, 148–159.

Balboni, G. and Pedrabissi, L. (2000). Attitudes of Italian teachers and parents towards school inclusion of students with mental retardation: the role of experience, *Education and Training in Mental Retardation and Developmental Disabilities*, 35, 148–159.

Banerji, M. and Daily, R.A. (1995). 'A Study of the Effects of an Inclusion Model on Students with Specific Learning Disabilities', *Journal of Learning Disabilities*, 28 (8), 511.

Barton, L. (1997). Inclusive education: romantic, subversive or realistic? *International Journal of Inclusive Education*, 1(3), 231–242.

Barton, L. (1998). Markets, Managerialism and Inclusive Education. In Peter Clough (Ed.), *Managing Inclusive Education: From Policy to Experience*. London: Paul Chapman Educational Publishing. pp. 78-92.

Barton, L. (2003). *Inclusive education and teacher education: A basis for hope or a discourse of delusion*. London: Institute of Education, University of London.

Baumgart, D. and Giangreco, M. (1996). Key Lessons Learned About Inclusion In D. Lehr and F. Brown (Eds.), People With Disabilities Who Challenge The System (pp. 79–97). Baltimore: Paul H. Brookes. Key Lessons 205.

Beh-Pajooh, A. (1992). The effect of social contact on college teachers' attitudes toward students with severe mental handicaps and their educational integration. *European Journal of Special needs Education*, 7(2), 87-102.

Bender, R. (1970). *The Conquest of Deafness*. Cleveland: Western Reserve University.

Bennett, T., Lee, H., and Lueke, B. (1998). Expectations and concerns: What mothers and fathers say about inclusion. *Education and Training in Mental Retardation and Developmental Disabilities*, 33(2), 108-122.

Bent Flyvbjerg (2006). Five Misunderstanding about Case Study Research. *Qualitative Inquiry*, Vol. 12, No. 2, April 2006, pp. 219-245.

Bentley, J. (2000). School effectiveness, School Improvement and Assuring Quality. In S. Dinham and C. Scott (Eds.), *Teaching in Context* (pp. 154-169). Victoria: The Australian Council for Education Research.

Beresford, B., Rabiee, P. and Sloper, P. (2007). *Priorities and Perceptions of Disabled Children and Young People and Their Parents Regarding Outcomes from Support Services*. Social Policy Research Unit, University of York.

Biklen, D. and Knoll, J. (1987). The Disabled Minority. In S. Taylor, D. Biklen and J. Knoll (Eds.), *Community Integration for People with Severe Disabilities* (pp. 3–21). New York: Teachers College Press.

Bishop, M. (1995). Inclusion: Balancing the Ups and Downs, *Momentum*, 26 (3), 28-30.

Blaikie, Norman (2000). *Designing Social Research: The Logic of Anticipation*. Cambridge: Polity Press.

Booth, T. and Ainscow, M. (2000). *Index for Inclusion: Developing Learning and Participation in Schools.* Bristol: Centre for Studies in Inclusive Education. *http://www.inclusion.uwe.ac.uk*

Booth, T., and Ainscow, M. (2002). *Index for inclusion: Developing learning and participation in schools* (Rev. ed.). Bristol: CSIE.

Booth, Tony and Ainscow, Mel (eds.) (1998) *From Them to Us—An international study of inclusive education.* London, Routledge.

Borg, W.R., and Gall, M.D. (1989). *Educational Research* (5th ed.). White Plains, NY: Longman Inc.

Bouma, R. and Schweitzer, R. (1990). The impact of chronic childhood illness on family stress: a comparison between Autism and Cystic Fibrosis. *Journal of Clinical Psychology* 46 (6), 722-730.

Brewer, J., and Hunter, A. (1989). *Multimethod research: A synthesis of styles*. Newbury Park, CA: Sage.

Brown, L., Long, E., Udvari-Solner, A., Davies, L., VanDeventer, P., Ahlgren, C., Johnson, F., Gruenewaid, L., and Jorgensen, J. (1989a). The home school: Why students with severe intellectual disabilities must attend the schools of their brothers, sisters, friends and neighbours. *Journal of the Association for Persons with Severe Handicaps* 14(1), 1-7.

Brown, L., Long, E., Udvari-Solner, A., Davies, L., VanDeventer, P., Ahlgren, C., Johnson, F., Gruenewaid, L., and Jorgensen, J. (1989b). Should students with severe intellectual disabilities be based in regular or special education classrooms in home schools? *Journal of the Association for Persons with Severe Handicaps*, 14(1), 8-12.

Brown, L., Ford, A., Nisbet, J., Sweet, M., DonneUan, A. and Gruenewald, L. (1983). Opportunities available when severely handicapped students attend chronological age appropriate regular schools. *Journal of the Association for the Severe Handicapped*, 8(1), 16-24.

Bruder, M.B. (1994). Working with members of other disciplines: Collaboration for success. In M. Wolery and J.S. Wilbers (Eds.), *Including children with special needs in early childhood programmes* (pp. 45-70). Washington, DC: National Association for the Education of Young Children.

Burchardt, T. (2005). *The education and employment of disabled young people.* Bristol: Policy Press.

Burns, R.B. (1982) *Self-concept development and education.* London: Holt, Rinehart and Winston.

Burrell, G. and Morgan, G. (1979). Sociological Paradigms and Organisational Analysis. Aldershot, England: Arena.

Byrne, B.M. (1996). Measuring self-concept across the life-span: Issues and instrumentation. Washington, DC: American Psychological Association.

Cambra, C. (2002). Acceptance of deaf students in regular classrooms, *American Annals of the Deaf*, 147.

Cambra, C., Silvestre, N. (2003). Students with special educational needs in the inclusive classroom: social integration and self-concept, *European Journal of Special Needs Education*, 18, 197-208.

Cates, J. (1991) Self-concept in hearing and prelingual, profoundly deaf students, *American Annals of the Deaf*, 136, 352-359.

Census of India (2001). Government of India. http://censusindia.gov.in/

Chadha, A. (2003). *Perspectives in Special Needs Education in India: A Journey from Isolation to Inclusion*, Janshala Volume VI Issue 1 January-March 2003 Joint GOI-UN System Education Programme.

Chiang, L.H. (1999) *Secondary Teachers' Perceptions of Regular Education Initiative*, paper presented at the Midwestern Educational Research Conference, Chicago, IL, October 1999.

Chib, Malini (2002). In Seamus Hegarty and Mithu Alur (Eds.), *Education and Children with Special Needs—From Segregation to Inclusion*. New Delhi: Sage Publications Inc.

Clough, P. (1988), Bridging "mainstream" and "special" education: a Curriculum problem in *Journal of Curriculum Studies*, 20(4), pp. 327-38.

Comer, J.P., and Haynes, N.M. (1991). Parent involvement in schools: An ecological approach. *Elementary School Journal*, 91(3), 271-277.

Comer, J.P., Haynes, N.M., Joyner, E.T., and Ben-Avie, M. (1996). *Rallying the whole village: The process for reforming education*. New York: Teachers College Press.

Cook, L., and Friend, M. (1995). Co-teaching: Guidelines for creating effective practices. *Focus on Exceptional Children*. Vol. 28 (3), Love Publishing Co.

Cornoldi, C., Terreni, A., Scruggs, T.E. and Mastropieri, M.A. (1998). Teacher attitudes in Italy after twenty years of inclusion, *Remedial and Special Education*, 19, 350–356.

Creswell, J.W. (1994). *Research design: qualitative and quantitative approaches*. London: Sage Publications.

Damon, W., and Hart, D. (1982). The development of self-understanding from infancy through adolescence. *Child Development*, 53, 841–864.

Danby, J. and Cullen, C. (1988). Integration and mainstreaming: a review of the efficacy of mainstreaming and integration for mentally handicapped pupils. *Educational Psychology*, 8, 177-195.

Davern, L. (1996). Listening to Parents of Children With Disabilities. *Educational Leadership*, 53(7), 61–63.

Davis-Kean, P.E., and Sandler, H.M. (2001). A meta-analysis of measures of self-esteem for young children: a framework for future measures. *Child Development*, 72, 887–906.

Dawkins, J.L. (1996). 'Bullying, physical disability and the paediatric patient', *Developmental Medicine and Child Neurology*, 38, 7, 603-612.

De, A., Majumdar, M., Samson, M. and Norohna, C. (2002). Private Schools and Universal Elementary Education. In R. Govinda (Ed.), *India Education Report*. New Delhi: Oxford University Press.

Demchak, M. and Drinkwater, S. (1992). 'Preschoolers with severe disabilities: The case against segregation'. *Topics in Early Childhood Special Education* 11(4): 70–83.

Denzin, N.K. and Yuonna S. Lincoln (2000). Introduction: The Discipline and Practice of Qualitative Research in Norman K. Denzin and Yuonna S. Lincoln (Eds.), *Handbook of Qualitative Research*: Second Edition. Thousand Oaks: Sage.

Denzin, N.K. (1989a). *Interpretive interactionism*. Newbury Park, CA: Sage.

Denzin, N.K. (1989b). *The research act* (3rd ed.). Englewood Cliffs, NJ: Prentice Hall.

Department of Education. (2004). *Overview. Annual report, 2004–2005*. Retrieved from *http://education.nic.in/Annualreport2004-05/ar_en_05_cont.asp* on February 11, 2008,

Deppeler, J., and Harvey, D. (2004). Validating the British Index for Inclusion for the Australian context: Stage one. *International Journal of Inclusive Education*, 8(2), 155-184.

Deppler, J.M. (1998). *Professsional Development Workshops: Supporting People with Disabilities*. Melbourne: Impact Printing.

Dick, B. (1995). Session 5—The change process and action research, *Action Research and Evaluation On-Line*. St Lucia: Bob Dick. URL *ftp://psy.uq.edu.au./lists/arlist/areol_session05.*

Dinham, S., Cairney, T., Craigie, D., and Wilson, S. (1995). School Climate and Leadership: Research into three Secondary Schools. *Journal of Educational Administration*, 33(4), 36-58.

Edelen-Smith, P., Prater, M., and Siloe, T. (1993). The impact of current issues in teacher education on the preparation of special educators. *Issues in Special Education and Rehabilitation*, 8(1), 7–15.

Eleweke, C.J. and Rodda, M (2002). 'The challenge of enhancing inclusive education in developing countries', *International Journal of Inclusive Education*, 6:2, 113-126.

Erwin, E.J. (1993). *The philosophy and status of inclusion*. The Lighthouse, 1-4.

Erwin, P. (1993) *Friendship and peer relations in children*, Wiley and Sons, Chisester.

Farber, B. (1960). Family organization and crisis: Maintenance of integration in families with a severely retarded child. *Monographs of the Society for Research in Child Development*, 25, 1-95.

Farrel, P. (2000). The impact of research on developments in inclusive education. *Int. J. Inclusive Education*, 2000, Vol. 4, No. 2, 153-162.

Feinberg, E.A. (1985) Stress in pediatric home care. *Caring* 4 (5), 38–41.

Fielding, N.G., and Fielding, J.L. (1986). *Linking data*. Beverly Hills, CA: Sage.

Filmer, D. (2005). *Disability, Poverty and Schooling in Developing Countries: Results from 11 Household Surveys*, World Bank Discussion Paper.

Flick, U. (1992). Triangulation revisited: Strategy of validation or alternative? *Journal for the Theory of Social Behaviour*, 22, 175-198.

Florian, L. (1998). Inclusive practice: What, why, how? In C. Tilstone, L. Florian, and R. Rose (Eds.), *Promoting inclusive practice* (pp. 13–26). London: Routledge/Falmer.

Forlin, C. and Cole, P. (1993). Attributions of the social acceptance and integration of children with mild intellectual disabilities, Australia and New Zealand. *Journal of Developmental Disabilities*, 19, 11–23.

Forlin, C., Douglas, G. and Hattie, J. (1996). Inclusive practices: how accepting are teachers, *International Journal of Disability, Development and Education*, 43(2), 119–133.

Forlin, C., Tait, K., Carroll, A., and Jobling, S. (1999). Teacher education for diversity. *Queensland Journal of Educational Research*, 15(2), 207–226.

Fourgeyrollas, P., Cloutier, R., Bergeron, J., Cote, G., Michel, S.T. (1999). *The Quebec Classification: Disability creation process*, Quebec, INDCP/CSICIDH, p. 162.

Fryxell, D. and Kennedy, C. (1995). 'Placement along the continuum of services and its impact on students' social relationships'. *Journal of the Association for Persons with Severe Handicaps* 20: 259–69.

Fulk, B.J.M. and Hirth, M.A. (1994). Perceptions of special education programme effectiveness and attitudes toward inclusion, paper presented at the Annual Meeting of the *American Educational Research Association*, New Orleans, LA, April, 1994.

Garcia, S.M.Y. and Alban-Metcalfe, J. (1998). Integrated or inclusive education versus interactive education: the need for a new model. *European Journal of Special Needs Education*, Vol. 13, No. 2, pp. 170-179.

Gartner, A., and Lipsky, D.D. (1987). Beyond Special education: Toward a quality System for all students, *Harvard Educational Review*, 57, 367-385.

Gerardi, R.J., Grohe, B., Benedict, G.C. and Coolidge, P.G. (1984). IEP—More paperwork and wasted time, in *Contemporary Education*, 56(1), pp. 39-42.

Gerber, P. (1992). Being learning disabled and a beginning teacher and teaching a class of students with learning disabilities, Exceptionality: *A Research Journal*, 3, 213–231.

Ghosh, Nandini (2005). *The Concept of Disability*. Unpublished Pre Doctoral Paper. Mumbai: Tata Institute of Social Sciences.

Giangreco, M. and Putnam, J. (1991). Supporting the Education of Students with Severe Disabilities in Regular Education Environments, in L.H. Mayer, C. Peck, and L. Brown (Eds.) *Critical Issues in the Lives of the People with Severe Disabilities* (pp. 245-270). Baltimore: Paul H. Brookes.

Giangreco, M.F., Cloninger, C.J., Dennis, R.E. and Edelman, S.W. (1993). National ExpertValidation of Coach: Congruence With Exemplary Practice and Suggestions For Improvement. *The Journal of the Association for Persons with Severe Handicaps*, 18, 109–120.

Giangreco, M.F., Dennis, R., Cloninger, C., Edelman, S. and Schattman, R. (1993). "I've Counted Jon": Transformational Experiences of Teachers Educating Students With Disabilities. *Exceptional Children*, 59, 359–372.

Goel, S. and Rao, I (2008). Special and inclusive educational services in India. In M. Puri and G. Abraham (Eds.), *Handbook of Inclusive Education for Educators, Administrators and Planners: Within Walls Without Boundaries*. New Delhi: Sage pp. 35-43.

Goodman, J.F. and Bond, L. (1993). The individualised educational programme: A retrospective critique in *Journal of Special Education*, 26(4), pp. 408-22.

Gouveia, D. (1997). The Benefits of Inclusive Education. Con Val School District available at *http://www.conval.edu/sped/Programs.html* (accessed on 24th March 2009).

Graziano, A.M. and Raulin, M.L. (1993). *Research Methods: A Process of Inquiry*. New York: Harper Collins.

Groschl, Stefan (2005). Persons with Disabilities: A Source of Non-traditional Labour for Canada's Hotel Industry. *Cornell Hotel and Restaurant Administration Quarterly*, Volume 46, Number 2, 258-274. New York: Cornell University.

Guba, E.G. and Lincoln, Y.S. (1989). *Fourth generation evaluation*. Newbury Park, Ca.: Sage.

Halvorsen, A.T., and Neary, T. (2001). *Building inclusive schools: Tools and strategies for success*. Needham Heights, MA: Allyn & Bacon.

Harris, A. (1999). *Teaching and Learning in the Effective School*. Aldershot: Ashgate Publishing Company.

Harter, S. (1986). Processes underlying the construction, maintenance, and enrichment of the self-concept in children, in: J. Suls and A. Greenwald (Eds.) *Psychological perspectives on the self* (vol. 3,137-181). London: Lawrence Erlbaum.

Harter, S. (1998). The development of self-representations. In N. Eisenberg (Ed.), *Handbook of child psychology*, Vol. 3 (pp. 553–617). New York, NY: Wiley.

Harvey, D.H.P., and Greenway, A.P. (1984). The self-concept of physically handicapped children and their non-handicapped siblings: an empirical investigation. *Journal of Child Psychology and Psychiatry, and Allied Disciplines*, 25, 273–284.

Hasazi, S.B., Johnston, A.P., Ligget, A.M. and Schattman, R.A. (1994). A qualitative policy study of the least restrictive environment provision of the IDEA, *Exceptional Children*, 60, 491–507.

Hayes, A. (1998), 'Families and disabilities: Another facet of inclusion' in *Educating Children with Special Needs*, A. Ashman and J. Elkins (eds.), Sydney: Prentice Hall, pp. 39-66.

Hegarty, S. (1993) Reviewing the literature on integration. *European Journal of Special Needs Education*, 8, 194-200.

Hegarty, S. (1993). *Meeting Special Needs in Ordinary Schools: An Overview*. London: Cassell.

Heiman, T., and Margalit, M. (1998). Loneliness, depression, and social skills among students with mild mental retardation in different educational settings. *Journal of Special Education*, 32(3), 154-164.

Helmstetter, E., Peck, C. and Giangreco, M.F. (1994). Outcomes of Interactions With Peers With Moderate or Severe Disabilities: A Statewide Survey of High School Students. *The Journal of the Association for Persons With Severe Handicaps*, 19, 263–276.

Helper, J.B. (1997). Social development of children: The role of peers. *Social Work in Education*, 19(4), 242-256.

Holroyd, J. and Guthrie, D. (1986). Family stress with chronic childhood illness: cystic fibrosis, neuromuscular disease, and renal disease. *Journal of Clinical Psychology* 42, 552–561.

Hornby, G. (1995). Working with parents of children with special needs. Cassell.

Houck, C.K., and Rogers, C.J. (1994). The special/general education integration initiative for students with specific learning disabilities: A "snapshot" of programme change. *Journal of Learning Disabilities*, 27, 435–453.

Huebler, F. (2007). *International Education Statistics, Analysis* by Friedrich Huebler, Retrieved from *http://huebler.blogspot.com/2007/11/india-has-21-million-children-out-of.html on 12th September 2009.*

Hunt, P., Staub, D., Alwell, M. and Goetz, L. (1994). Achievement of All Students within the Context of Cooperative Learning Groups. *The Journal of the Association for Persons with Severe Handicaps*, 19, 290–301.

Inos, R. and Quigley, M.A. (1995). *Research Review for Inclusive Practices. Pacific Resources for Education and Learning.* Available at *http://www.prel.org/products/Products/Inclusive-practices.pdf* (Accessed on 12th June 2009).

International Save the Children Alliance (2001). *Children's Rights: A Second Chance*. Available Online at *www.savethechildren.net/alliance/resources/child_second.pdf*

Ittyerah, M. and Kumar, N. (2007). The Actual and Ideal Self-concept in Disabled Children, Adolescents and Adults. *Psychology Developing Societies*, 19, 1, pp. 81-112.

Jambor, E., Elliott, M. (2005). Self-esteem and Coping Strategies among Deaf Students, *Journal of Deaf Studies and Deaf Education*, 10, 63-81.

Jangira, N.K. (1995). *Rethinking Teacher Education. Prospects*, vol. XXV, No. 2, June 1995.

Janney, R. and Snell, M. (1996). How Teachers Use Peer Interactions to Include Students With Moderate and Severe Disabilities In Elementary General Education Classes. *The Journal of the Association for Persons with Severe Handicaps*, 21, 72–80.

Jones, H (2000). Disabled Children's Rights and the UN Convention on the Rights of the Child. *Disability Studies Quarterly*, Fall 2000, Volume 20, No. 4.

Julka, A (2005). *Including Children and Youth with disabilities in Education: A Guide for Practitioners. http://ncert.nic.in/sites/inclusiveeducation/Draft%20manual_DEGSN.pdf* (Accessed on 17th July, 2007).

Julka, A. (2005). *Educational Provisions and Practices for Learners with Disabilities in India.*

Kashyap, L. (1991). Research on families with disabled individuals: review and implications. In Murli Desai (Ed.), *Research on Families with Problems in India*, Volume II. Mumbai: Tata Institute of Social Sciences.

Kaul, V. (2002). Early childhood care and education. In R. Govinda (Ed.), *India education report. A profile of basic education* (pp. 23–34). Oxford, England: Oxford University Press.

Kersten, S. & Ison, R. (1994). Diversity in Yearly Calendars on Pastoral Properties in Western NSW : a Constructivist Perspective. *The Rangeland Journal*, 16(2), 206-220.

Kholi, T. (1993). Special education in Asia. In. P. Mittler, R. Brouillette and D. Harris (eds), *Special Needs of Education* (London: Kogan Page), pp. 118-129.

Koelle, W., Convey, J.J. (1982). The prediction of achievement of deaf adolescents from self-concept and locus of control measures, *American Annals of the Deaf*, 127, 769-779.

Kozleski, E.B. and Jackson, L. (1993). Taylor's Story: Full Inclusion In Her Neighbourhood Elementary School. *Exceptionality*, 4, 153–175.

Kuth, P. (2005). *Is your school inclusive*? Available at *http://www.paulakluth.com/articles/schoolinclusive.html* (accessed on 14th April, 2009).

Lancaster, Julie and Bain, Alan (2007). 'The Design of Inclusive Education Courses and the Self-efficacy of Preservice Teacher Education Students', *International Journal of Disability, Development and Education*, 54:2, 245-256.

Leeman, Y. and Volman, M. (2001). Inclusive education: recipe book or quest. On diversity in the classroom and educational research. *International Journal of Inclusive Education*, 2001, Vol. 5, No. 4, 367-79.

Leigh, I., Stinson, M. (1991). Social environments, self-perceptions and identity of hearing-impaired adolescents, *Volta Review*, 93, 7-22.

Lerner, J. (1993). The Influence of Child Temperamental Characteristics on Parent Behaviours. In Luster, T. Okagaki, L. (Eds.), *Parenting: An Ecological Perspective*. Hillsdale, New Jersey: Lawrence Erlbaum Associates.

Lewis, M. (1992), *Parental Involvement in the Special Education Process: A Synopsis of Exemplary Models*, Bloomington, IND: Indiana University.

Lieber, J., Hanson, M.J., Beckman, P.J., Odom, S.L., Sandall, S.R., Schwartz, I.S., *et al.* (2000). Key influences on the initiation and implementation of inclusive preschool programmes. *Exceptional Children*, 67, 83–98.

Lindsay, G. (2007). Educational Psychology and the Effectiveness of Inclusive Education/Mainstreaming. *British Journal of Educational Psychology*, Vol 77, No.1, p. 1-24.

Lingard, T. (1994). The acquisition of literacy in secondary education. *British Journal of Special Education*, 21, 180-191.

Lipsky, D.K., and Gartner A. (1992). Achieving fall inclusion: Placing the student at the centre of education reform. In W. Stainback and S. Stainback (Eds.), *Controversial issues confronting special education* (pp. 3-12). Boston, Allyn and Bacon.

Little, J.W. (1993). Teachers' professional development in a climate of educational reform. *Educational Evaluation and Policy Analysis*, 15, 129–150.

Loeb, R., Sarigiani, P. (1986). The impact of hearing impairment on the self-perceptions of children, *Volta Review*, 88, 89-100.

Lombard, R.C., Miller, R.J., and Hazelkorn, M.N. (1998). School-to-work and technical preparation: Teacher attitudes and practices regarding the inclusion of students with disabilities. *Career Development for Exceptional Individuals*, 21, 161–172.

Loreman, T., Deppeler, J. and Harvey D. (2006). *Inclusive Education: A Practical Guide to Supporting Diversity in the Classroom*. Allen & Unwin.

Losardo, A., and Notari-Sylverson, A. (2001). *Alternative Approaches to Assessing Young Children*. Baltimore: Brookes.

Lynch, J. (2001). *Inclusion in Education: The Participation of Disabled Learners*. Paris: UNESCO.

MacQueen, KM, McLellan, E. Kay, K. and Milstein, B. (1998). Codebook development of team based qualitative research. *Cultural Anthropology Methods Journal*, 10, 31-36.

Madden, N.A. and Slavin, R.F. (1983). Mainstreaming students with mild handicaps: Academic and social outcomes. *Review of Educational Research*, 53, 519-589.

Marsh, H.W., Relich, J.D., and Smith, I.D. (1983). Self-concept: the construct validity of interpretations based upon the SDQ. *Journal of Personality and Social Psychology*, 45, 173–187.

Marston, D. (1996). A comparison of inclusion only, pull-out only and combines services models for students with mild disabilities. *Journal of Special Education*, 30, 121-132.

May, K.M. (1997). Searching for normalcy: mothers caregiving for low birth weight infants. *Pediatric Nursing* 23 (1), 17–20.

McInerney, D.M. and McInerney, V. (2002). *Educational Psychology: Constructing Learning*, Sydney: Prentice Hall.

McKeever, P. and Miller, K. (2004). Mothering children who have disabilities: a Bourdieusian interpretation of maternal practices. *Social Science and Medicine* 59, 1177–1191.

McLeskey, J., and Waldron, N.L. (2002b). Professional development and inclusive schools: Reflections on effective practice. *Teacher Educator*, 37, 159–173.

McNamara, D.R. and Waugh, D.G. (1993). Classroom organisation: A discussion and grouping strategies in the light of the "Three Wise Men's" report in *School Organisation*, 13(1), pp. 41-50.

McWilliam, R.A. (2000). Recommended practices in interdisciplinary models, in S. Sandall, M. McLean, and B. Smith (Eds.), *DEC recommended practices for early intervention/early childhood special education* (pp. 47-54). Soparis West: Longmont, Co.

Mehta, A.C. (2007). *Elementary Education in India: Analytical Report 2005-06*. New Delhi: National University of Educational Planning and Administration and Department of School Education and Literacy, Ministry of Human Resource Development, Government of India.

Meijer, C.J.W. (Ed.) (2003). *Special Education Across Europe in 2003: Trends in provision in 18 European countries*. European Agency for Development in Special Needs Education Available at *www.european-agency.org* (accessed on 14th April 2009).

Merriam, SB. 1988. *Case Study Research in Education: A Qualitative Approach*. San Francisco: Jossey-Bass.

Meyer, L.H., Park, H.S., Grenot-Scheyer, M., Schwartz, I.S., and Harry, B. (Eds.). (1998). *Making friends: The influences of culture and development*. Baltimore: Paul H. Brookes.

MHRD (Ministry of Human Resource Development) (2009). *http://education.nic.in/secedu/Uploading09/IEDSS%20Proforma%2009.pdf* (Accessed 2nd April 2009).

MHRD (2005). *Inclusive education action plan for inclusive education of children and youth with disabilities*, August 20, 2005. Available at *http://www.education.nic.in/INCLUSIVE.asp.*

Minke, K., Bear, G., Deemer, S. and Griffin, S. (1996). Teachers' experience with inclusive classrooms: implications for special education reform, *Journal of Special Education*, 30, 152–186.

Mishna, F (2003). 'Learning disabilities and bullying: Double jeopardy'. *Journal of Learning Disabilities*, 36, 336-347.

Montgomery, M.S. (1994). Self-concept and children with learning disabilities: Observer-child concordance across six context-dependent domains. *Journal of Learning Disabilities*, 27, 254–262.

Morgan, G. (1983). Research as Engagement: a Personal View. In G. Morgan (Ed.), *Beyond Method: Strategies for Social Research*. Newbury Park, Ca.: Sage.

Mrug, S., Wallander, J.L. (2002). Self-concept of Young People with Physical Disabilities: does integration play a role? *International Journal of Disability, Development and Education*, 49, 267-280.

Mukhopadhyay, S., and Mani, M.N.G. (2002). Education of children with special needs. In R. Govinda (Ed.), *India education report: A profile of basic education* (pp. 96–108). New Delhi, India: Oxford University Press.

Mundschenk, N.A., Foley, R.M., and Swedburg, K.A. (2005). Collaboration: Building teams to facilitate inclusive practices. In P. Zionts (Ed.), *Inclusion strategies for students with learning and behaviour problems* (2nd ed., pp. 57–91). Austin, TX: PRO-ED.

Nabuzoka, D and Smith, P.K. (1993). 'Sociometric status and social behaviour of children with and without learning difficulties' *Journal of Child Psychology and Psychiatry,* 34, 8, 1435-1448.

Nagi, Saad Z. (1965). "Some conceptual issues in Disability and Rehabilitation". In M. Sussman (ed.). *Sociology and Rehabilitation. Washington*, DC: American Sociological Association.

Nambissan, G. (2003). *Educational Deprivation and Primary School Provision: A Study of Providers in the City of Calcutta*, IDS Working Paper 187, Social Policy Programme, June 2003, Falmer: Institute of Development Studies.

National Curriculum Council (2002). *Creating Inclusive Schools: Guidelines for the implementation of the national curriculum policy on inclusive education.* Malta: Ministry of Education.

National Report of Pakistan (2008). *Universal Periodic Review.* Available at *www.upr-info.org/IMG/pdf/PAK_PAK_UPR_S2_2008_**PAKISTAN**_uprsubmission.pdf* (Accessed on 12th June 2009).

NCERT (2005). *National Curriculum Framework*, New Delhi, India.

Nordic Disabled Person Organisations (2001). Highlights from the Final Report of the 2000, Nordic Conference on Disability and Development. *Disability World*, Issue No. 7 March-April. Available at *http://www.disabilityworld.org/03-04_01/news/nordicconf.shtml* (Accessed on 11th April 2009)

Oliver, Mike (1983). *Social Work with Disabled People.* Basingstoke: Macmillans.

Oliver, Mike (1990). *The Individual and Social Models of Disability*. Paper presented at Joint Workshop of the Living Options Group and the Research Unit of the Royal College of Physicians on People with Established Locomotor Disabilities in Hospitals Monday 23 July 1990. *http://www.leeds.ac.uk/disabilitystudies/archiveuk/Oliver/in%20soc%20dis.pdf* (Date of Retrieval: 25th September 2006).

Oliver, Mike (1996). Defining Impairment and Disability: Issues at Stake. In Colin Barnes and Geof Mercer (Eds.), *Exploring the Divide. Leeds*: The Disability Press, pp. 29-54.

Opdal, L.R. and Wormnaes, S. (2001). Teachers' opinions about inclusion: a pilot study in a Palestinian context, *International Journal of Disability, Development, and Education*, 48, 143–161.

Opdal, L.R. and Wormnaes, S. (2001). Teachers' opinions about inclusion: a pilot study in a Palestinian context, *International Journal of Disability, Development, and Education*, 48, 143–161.

Osborn, A. (1953). *Applied Imagination: Principles and Procedures of Creative Thinking*. New York: Charles Scribner's Sons.

Osgood, R. (2005). *The History of Inclusion in the United States*. Washington, DC: Gallaudet University Press. 226 pages.

Owens, R. (1998). *Organizational Behaviour in Education* (6 ed.). Needham Height, MA: Allyn and Bacon.

Ozoji, E.D. (1995). Special education perspectives for the future. In E.D. Ozoji and I.A. Nwazuoke (eds), *Professionalism in Special Education in Nigeria* (Jos: National Council for Exceptional Children), pp. 174-180.

Panda, P. (2005). *Responsiveness of Preservice Teacher Education Programme Towards Inclusive Education in India: Appraisal of Curriculum Dimensions and Practices*. Paper presented in ISEC 2005, 1st-4th August 2005. Glasgow, Scotland.

Pandey, Y. (2006). *From Special Education to Inclusive Education: an Analysis* of Indian Policy Paper Presented at Achieving Equality in Education: New Challenges and Strategies for Change, Kuala Lumpur, Malaysia (16-21 July 2006) Available at *http://www.icevi.org/publications/inclusive_educational.html* (Accessed 30th May 2009)

Papalia, D.E. and Olds, S.W. (1992). *Human Development*. New York: McGraw-Hill Inc.

Paranjpe, A.C. (1986). *Theoretical Psychology: Meeting of East and West*. New York: Plenum Press.

Patton, M.Q. (1990). *Qualitative evaluation and research methods.* (2nd ed.). Newbury Park, Ca.: Sage.

Pearl, R., Farmer, T.W., Van Acker, R., Philip, R.C., Bost, K.K., Coe, M., and Henley, W. (1998). The social integration of students with mild disabilities in general education classrooms: Peer group membership and peer-assessed social behaviour. *The Elementary School Journal*, 99(2), 167-185.

Peck, C., Donaldson, J. and Pezzoli, M. (1990). Some Benefits Nonhandicapped Adolescents Perceive For Themselves From Their Social Relationships With Peers Who Have Severe Handicaps. *The Journal of the Association For Persons With Severe Handicaps*, 15, 241–249.

Peck, Charles A., Debbie Staub, Chrysan Gallucci, Ilene Schwartz (2004). Parent Perception of the Impacts of Inclusion on their Nondisabled Child. *Research and Practice for Persons with Severe Disabilities*, Vol. 29, No. 2, 135–143.

Peshawaria, R., Menon, D.K., Ganguly, R. Roy, S., Pillay, R., and Gupta, A. (1995). *Understanding Indian Families: Having Persons with Mental Retardation*. Secunderabad: National Institute for the Mentally Handicapped.

Peters, Susan, C. Johnston and P. Fergusan (2005). A Disability Rights in Education Model for Evaluating Inclusive Education. *International Journal of Inclusive Education* 9(2), pp 139-160.

Pivik, J., Mccomas, J. and Laflamme, M. (2002). Barriers and Facilitators to Inclusive Education. *Council of Exceptional Children*. Vol. 69, No. 1, pp. 97-107.

Plazer, G.L. (1985). *The physical attractiveness phenomenon*, London, Plenum.

Priestley, M., Corker, M., Watson, N. (1999). Unfinished business: disabled children and disability identity, *Disability Studies Quarterly*. 19, 2.

Rainforth, B. and York-Barr, J. (1997). Collaborative Teamwork: Integrated Therapy Services *In Educational Programmes For Students With Severe Disabilities*. Baltimore: Paul H. Brookes.

Rankin, D., Hallick, A., Ban, S., Hartley, P., Bost, C. and Uggla, N. (1994). Who's Dreaming: A General Education Perspective on

Inclusion. *The Journal of the Association for Persons With Severe Handicaps*, 19, 235–237.

Reed, F., and Monda-Amaya, L. (1995). Preparing preservice general educators for inclusion: A survey of teacher education preparation programmes in Illinois. *Teacher Education and Special Education*, 18(4), 262–274.

Reynolds, W.N. (2003). *Reynolds bully victimization scales for schools manual*. San Antonio, TX: The Psychological Corporation.

Richards, G., and Clough, P. (2004). ITE students' attitudes to inclusion. *Research in Education*, 72, 77–86.

Ringlaken, R.P. and Price, J.R. (1981). Regular classroom teachers' perception of mainstreaming effects, *Exceptional Children*, 47, 302–304.

Roberts, C. and Zubrick, S. (1992). Factors influencing the social status of children with mild academic disabilities in regular classroom, *Exceptional Children*, 59(3), 193–202.

Rogers, C.M., Smith, M.D., Coleman, J.M. (1978). Social comparison in the classroom: The relationship between academic achievement and self-concept, *Journal of Educational Psychology*, 70, 50-57

Rogers, J. (1993). The inclusion revolution. *Phi-Delta-Kappa-Research Bulletin*, 11, 1-6.

Rossman, G.B., and Salzman, J. (1995). *Evaluating inclusive education programmes: A survey of current practice: Preliminary analysis and typology*. New York: National Centre on Educational Restructuring and Inclusion.

Rothlisberg, B.A., Hill, R., and D'Amato, C.R. (1994). Social acceptance by their peers of children with mental retardation. *Psychological Reports*, 74, 239-242.

Rouse, Martyn and Lani Florian (2006). Inclusion and achievement: student achievement in secondary schools with higher and lower proportions of pupils designated as having special educational needs. *International Journal of Inclusive Education,* Vol. 10, No. 6, November 2006, pp. 481–493.

Ryndack, D. and Alper, S. (1996). *Curriculum Content for Students with Moderate and Severe Disabilities in Inclusive Settings*, Needham Heights, MA: Allyn and Bacon.

Salisbury, C., Palombaro, M. and Hollowood, T. (1993). On The Nature and Change of An Inclusive Elementary School. *The*

*Journal of the Association for Persons with Severe Handicaps*, 18, 75–84.

Sasso, G.M., Simpson, R.L. and Novak, C.G. (1985). Procedures for facilitating integration of autistic children in public school settings. *Analysis and Intervention in Developmental Disabilities*, 5, 233-246.

Save the Children (2006). *Inclusive Education: A Policy Statement.* Source: *http://www.eenet.org.uk/key_issues/policy/SC%20UK%20IE%20policy%20English.pdf* Date of Retrieval: 20th March 2009.

Save the Children (2008). *Making Schools Inclusive: How change can happen, Save the Children's experience*. London: Author.

Schmidt, M. and Cagran, B. (2008). Self-Concept of Students in Inclusive Settings. *International Journal of Special Education*, Vol. 23, No. 1, pp. 8-17.

Schmidt, M. and Cagran, B. (2009). Self-Concept of Students in Inclusive Settings. Retrieved from *http://www.internationalsped.com/documents/2%20Self%20Concept.doc* 23 January 2009.

Schumm, J.S., and Vaughn, S. (1991). Making adaptations for mainstreamed students: General classroom teachers' perspectives. Remedial and Special Education, 12(4), 18–27.

Schumm, J.S., Vaughn, S., Haager, D., McDowell, J., Rothlein, L., and Saumell, L. (1995). General education teacher planning: What can students with learning disabilities expect? *Exceptional Children*, 61, 335-352.

Seale, C. and Silverman D., (1997). Ensuring rigour in qualitative research, *European Journal of Public Health* 7 (4), pp. 379–384.

Sebba, J. and Ainscow, M. (1996). International developments in inclusive schooling: mapping the issues, *Cambridge Journal of Education*, 26(1), 5–18.

Sebba, J. and Ainscow, M. (1996). International developments in inclusive schooling: Mapping the issues. *Cambridge Journal of Education*, 26(1), 5-18.

Semmel, M.I., Abernathy, T.V., Butera, G., and Lesar, S. (1991). Teacher perceptions of the Regular Education Initiative. *Exceptional Children*, 58, 9–23.

Shakespeare, T. (1996). *Disability, identity and difference*. Leeds, UK: The Disability Press, 94-113. Retrieved May 7, 2005, from *http://www.leeds.ac.uk/disability-studies/archiveuk/Shakespeare/Chap6.pdf*

Sharpe, M., York, J. and Knight, J. (1994). Effects of Inclusion on The Academic Performance of Classmates Without Disabilities: A Preliminary Study. *Remedial and Special Education*, 15, 281–287.

Shepard, Jon; Robert W. Greene (2003). *Sociology and You.* Ohio: Glencoe McGraw-Hill.

Shetty, R. (2006). *Do the disabled get their due*? Available at *http://ibnlive.in.com/news/is-mumbai-giving-disabled-their-due/24766-3.html*

Shimman, P. (1990). The impact of special needs students at a Further Education College: A report on a questionnaire. *Journal of Further and Higher Education*, 14(3), 83-91.

Simpson, R.L., de Boer-Ott, S.R., and Smith-Myles, B. (2003). Inclusion of learners with autism spectrum disorders in general education settings [Electronic version]. *Topics in Language Disorders*, 23, 116–133.

Singal, N. (2006a). An Ecosystemic Approach for Understanding Inclusive Education: An Indian Case Study. *European Journal of Psychology of Education,* Volume XXI, Number 3, pp. 239-252.

Singal, N. (2006b). Inclusive Education in India: International Concept, National Interpretation. *International Journal of Disability, Development and Education*, Vol. 53, No. 3, September 2006, pp. 351–369.

Singal, N. (2008). Working towards inclusion: Reflections from the Classroom. *Teaching and Teacher Education*, 24, 1516–1529.

Singal, N. (2005). Mapping the field of inclusive education: a review of the Indian literature. *International Journal of Inclusive Education,* Vol. 9, No. 4, October–December 2005, pp. 331–350.

Singal, N. (2005a). *Responding to difference: Policies to support 'inclusive education' in India*, paper presented at the Inclusive and Supportive Education Congress 2005, University of Strathclyde, Glasgow.

Singal, N. (2007). Working towards inclusion: Reflections from the classroom. *Teaching and Teacher Education*, 24 (2008) 1516–1529.

Smith, T.E.C., Polloway, E.A., Patton, J.R. and Dowdy, C.A. (1998). Teaching Students with Inclusive Needs in Inclusive Settings. Second Edition. Boston: Allyn and Bacon.

Smith, M. (2000) Secondary teachers perception towards inclusion of students with severe disabilities, *National Association of Secondary School Principals (NASSP) Bulletin*, 84(613), 54–60.

Smith, P.K. and Tippett, N. (2007). *Bullying and Disability*. Briefing for Anti-Bullying Alliance *http://www.antibullyingalliance.org.uk/downloads/pdf/spotlight_brief_issue9.pdf*

Smith, T.E.C., Finn, D.M., and Dowdy, C.A. (1993). *Teaching students with mild disabilities*. Ft. Worth, TX: Harcourt Brace Jovanowich.

Snell, M. and Drake, G.P. (1994). Replacing cascades with supported education. *Journal of Special Education*, 27, pp. 393-409.

Soodak, L.C. (2003). *Classroom Management in Inclusive Settings*. THEORY INTO PRACTICE, Volume 42, Number 4, Autumn 2003.

Spalding K. and McKeever P. (1998). Mothers' experiences caring for children with disabilities who require a gastronomy tube. *Journal of Paediatric Nursing* 13 (4), 234–243.

Sreekumari, A.B. (2003). *Evaluating the Outcomes of Inclusive Education: A Case Study from India*. Paper presented in International Conference on Inclusive Education, 16-19 December 2003. Source: *www.ied.edu.hk/csnsie/resources/proceedings2003/proc17.pdf* Date of Retrieval 20th March 2009.

SSA (2001). *Scheme of Sarva Shiksha Abhiyan*. Ministry of Human Resource Development, Government of India. Available at: *http://india.gov.in/sectors/education/sarva_shiksha.php*

Stainback, W. and Stainback, S. (1989). Practical organisation strategies. In S. Stainback, W. Stainback and M. Forest (Eds.), *Educating all students in the mainstream of regular education* (pp. 71-87). Baltimore: Paul H. Brooks.

Stainback, W. and Stainback, S. (1984). A rationale for merger of special and regular education. *Exceptional Children*, 51, 102-111.

Stancliffe, R.J. (1999). Proxy respondents and the reliability of the Quality of Life Questionnaire Empowerment Factor. *Journal of Intellectual Disability Research*, 43 (3): 185-193.

Stein, R.J. (1996). Physical self-concept. In B.A. Bracken (Ed.), *Handbook of self-concept* (pp. 374–394). New York: Wiley.

Strickland, B. and Turnbull, A. (1990). *Developing and Implementing Individualised Education Programmes*, Ohio: Merrill.

Stubbs, S. (1993). *Integrating Disability into Development Programmes*. EENET. Source: www.eenet.org.uk/theory_practice/integrat.shtml.

Stubbs, S. (1997). *The rights of children with disabilities* (Manchester, Enabling Education Network). Available online at: *www.eenet.org.uk*

Swick, K. and Laura Hooks (2005). Parental Experiences and Beliefs Regarding Inclusive Placements of their Special Needs Children. *Early Childhood Education Journal*, Vol. 32, No. 6, June 2005.

Swick, K. (1993). *Strengthening parents and families during the early childhood years*. Champaign, IL: Stipes Publishing Co.

The Persons with Disabilities (Equal Opportunities, Protection of Rights and Full Participation) Act, 1995. Government of India.

Thomas, G. (1997) Inclusive schools for an inclusive society, *British Journal of Special Education*, 24(3), 103–107.

Thomas, G., Walker, D. and Webb, J. (1997). *The Making of the Inclusive School*. London Routledge Falmer.

Turnbull, A.P., Brotherson, M.J., and Summers, J.A. (1986). Family life cycle: Theoretical and empirical implications and future directions for families with mentally retarded members. In J.J. Gallagher and P.M. Vietze (Eds.), *Families of handicapped persons: Research, programmes, and policy issues* (pp. 45-66). Baltimore: Paul H. Brookes.

Udvari-Solner, A. (1997). Inclusive education. In C.A. Grant and G. Ladson-Billings (Eds.), *Dictionary of multicultural education* (pp. 141-144). Phoenix, AZ: Oryx Press.

UN Convention on the Rights of Persons with Disabilities (2006). Available at *http://www.un.org/disabilities/default.asp?id=259.*

UN Convention on the Rights of the Child (1989). Available at *http://www2.ohchr.org/english/law/crc.htm.*

UN (2003). Biwako Millennium Framework.

UNESCO (1994). Final Report: World conference on special needs education: Access and quality (Paris, UNESCO).

UNESCO (1994). The Salamanca Statement and Framework for Action on Special Needs Education. UNESCO.

UNESCO (2001). Including the excluded: Meeting diversity in education. Example from Uganda. *Combating Exclusion in Education.* Paris: UNESCO.

UNESCO (2004). *Changing Teaching Practices using curriculum differentiation to respond to students' diversity.* France: Author.

UNICEF (2003). *Examples of Inclusive Education: India.* Source: *http://www.unicef.org/rosa/InclusiveInd.pdf* Date of Retrieval: 7th March 2009.

United Nations (1993). *The Standard Rules on the Equalization of Opportunities for Persons with Disabilities.* New York: Author.

UPIAS (1976). *Fundamental Principles of Disability.* London: Union of the Physically Impaired Against Segregation.

Van Gurp, S. (2001) Self-concept of Deaf Secondary School Students in Different Educational Settings, *Journal of Deaf Studies and Deaf Education*, 6, 54-69.

Vehmas, Simo (2004). Ethical Analysis of the Concept of Disability. *Mental Retardation*, Vol. 42, No. 3, pp. 209–222.

Villa, R.A., Thousand, J.S., Meyer, H. and Nevin, A. (1996). Teacher and administrator perceptions of heterogeneous education, *Exceptional Children*, 63, 29–45.

Wall, R. (2002). Teachers' exposure to people with visual impairments and the effect on attitudes toward inclusion, *Review*, 34, 111–119.

Wang, M.C., Rubenstein, J.L., and Reynolds, M.C. (1985). Clearing the road to success for students with special needs. *Educational Leadership*, 43, 62-67.

Webber, J. (2005). Responsible inclusion: Key components for success. In P. Zionts (Ed.), *Inclusion strategies for students with learning and behaviour problems* (2nd ed., pp. 29–55). Austin, TX: PRO-ED.

Welsh, E. 2002. Dealing with Data: Using NVivo in the Qualitative Data Analysis Process. Forum: Qualitative Social Research [On-Line Journal] Available URL: *http://www.qualitative-research.net/fqs/*], 3 (2).

Wenitzky, N., Stoddart, T., and O'Keefe, P. (1992). Great expectations: Emergent professional development schools. *Journal of Teacher Education*, 43(1), 3–18.

Westling Allodi, M. (2000). Self-concept in children receiving special support at school, *European Journal of Special Needs Education*, 15, 69-78.

Wheeler, J.J. (1991). *Educating students with severe disabilities in general education settings: A resource manual*. Pierre, SD: South Dakota State Department of Education, Office of Special Education.

White, B.L. (1988). *Educating the infant and toddler*. Lexington, MA: D.C. Heath (Lexington Books).

Whitworth, J.W. (1999). 'A Model for Inclusive Teacher Preparation', *Electronic Journal of Inclusive Education Fall*, Vol. 1, Ed 2, 1999 Ohio: Wright State University.

WHO (1999). *International Classification of Diseases*, 10th Edition. Geneva: Author.

Wiederholt, J.L., Hammil, D.D. and Brown, V.L. (1983). *The Resource Teacher: A Guide to Effective Practices*. Second Edition. Boston: Allyn and Bacon.

Wikler, L.M. (1986). Periodic stresses of families of older mentally retarded children: An exploratory study. *American Journal of Mental Deficiency*, 90, 703-706.

Wolery, M. (1994a). Assessing children with special needs. In M. Wolery and J.S. Wilbers (Eds.), *Including children with special needs in early childhood programmes* (pp. 71-96). Washington, DC: National Association for the Education of Young Children.

Wolfensberger, W. (1972). *Normalization: The Principle of Normalization in Human Services*. Toronto: National Institute on Mental Retardation.

Woolfolk, A. (2001). *Educational Psychology*. Needham Heights, MA: Allyn & Bacon.

World Bank (2003). Education for All: Including Children with Disabilities, *Education Notes*, August 2003.

World Bank (2007). *People with Disabilities in India: From Commitments to Outcomes*. Human Development Unit, South Asia Region.

World Health Assembly (2001). *International Classification of Functioning*.

World Health Organisation (1980). *International Classification of Impairments, Disabilities, and Handicaps: A Manual of*

*Classification Relating to the Consequences of Disease*. Geneva: Author.

World Health Organisation (1999). *ICIDH-2: International Classification of Functioning and Disability*. Beta-2 draft, full version. Geneva: Author.

Yin, R.K., 1989: *Case Study Research—Design and Methods*, revised edition, Sage Publications, Newbury Park, California.

York, J., Vandercook, T., Macdonald, C., Heise-Neff, C. and Caughey, E. (1992). Feedback About Integrating Middle School Students With Severe Disabilities In General Education Classes. *Exceptional Children*, 58, 260–269.

Zigmond, N., and Baker, J.M. (1996). Full inclusion for students with learning disabilities: Too much of a good thing? *Theory into Practice*, 35, (1), 26-34.

# Index